Financial Stability and Growth in Emerging Economies:
The Role of the Financial Sector

Forum on Debt and Development (FONDAD)

FONDAD is an independent policy research centre and forum for international discussion established in the Netherlands. Supported by a worldwide network of experts, it provides policy-oriented research on a range of North-South problems, with particular emphasis on international financial issues. Through research, seminars and publications, FONDAD aims to provide factual background information and practical strategies for policymakers and other interested groups in industrial, developing and transition countries.

Director: Jan Joost Teunissen

Financial Stability and Growth in Emerging Economies

The Role of the Financial Sector

Edited by
Jan Joost Teunissen and
Mark Teunissen

FONDAD
The Hague

Financial Stability and Growth in Emerging Economies: The Role of the Financial Sector

Proceedings of a Conference on "Financial Stability and Development in Emerging Economies: Steps Forward for Bankers and Financial Authorities", held at De Nederlandsche Bank in Amsterdam on 3-4 June 2002 and organised by the Forum on Debt and Development in the context of the Global Financial Governance Initiative, with the co-sponsorship of the Dutch Ministry of Foreign Affairs, De Nederlandsche Bank, IDRC, ECLAC, the International Monetary Fund, the World Bank, and UNCTAD.

Editors: Jan Joost Teunissen and Mark Teunissen

The views expressed in this book do not necessarily represent those of the Forum on Debt and Development or any of the co-sponsors. The summaries of the floor discussions, following the papers, attempt to convey the sense and substance of what was discussed. They have not been reviewed by all of the participants.

ISBN: 90-74208-21-5

This publication was made possible thanks to the support of the Department for Development Cooperation of the Dutch Ministry of Foreign Affairs, and De Nederlandsche Bank.

Additional copies may be ordered from FONDAD at
Noordeinde 107 A, 2514 GE The Hague, the Netherlands
Tel: 31-70-3653820 Fax: 31-70-3463939 E-Mail: info@fondad.org

Contents

Acknowledgements

This book is yet another result from the Global Financial Governance Initiative (GFGI), which brings together Northern and Southern perspectives on key international financial issues. In this project, Fondad is responsible for the working group Crisis Prevention and Response, jointly chaired by José Antonio Ocampo, executive secretary of the United Nations Economic Commission for Latin America and the Caribbean (ECLAC), and Jan Joost Teunissen, director of Fondad. GFGI's main sponsors are the Canadian International Development Research Centre (IDRC) and the Dutch Ministry of Foreign Affairs. The book has been produced in close cooperation with De Nederlandsche Bank (DNB).

Fondad very much appreciates the continuing support of the Dutch Ministry of Foreign Affairs and the co-sponsoring of this conference by De Nederlandsche Bank, ECLAC, IDRC, UNCTAD the World Bank, and the International Monetary Fund.

A special thanks goes to Age Akkerman, Adriana Bulnes and Julie Raadschelders, who assisted in the publishing of this book.

Notes on the Contributors

Mark Le Gros Allen (1947) is deputy director of the Policy Development and Review Department of the IMF. He joined the IMF in1974 and has successively held the positions of economist in the Exchange and Trade Relations Department, economist in the Geneva Office, advisor, mainly on debt issues, in the Exchange and Trade Relations Department, division chief, West Africa, of the African Department, assistant director, International Capital Markets, of the Exchange and Trade Relations Department, senior resident representative of the IMF in Poland, senior advisor of the Policy Development and Review Department, working mainly on IMF surveillance policy, debt and financial crisis management, senior resident representative of the IMF in Hungary, and finally deputy director of the Policy Development and Review Department.

Age Bakker (1950) is deputy executive director at De Nederlandsche Bank and professor of Money and Banking at the Vrije Universiteit of Amsterdam. Previously he has held various positions at De Nederlandsche Bank and at the IMF (1979-81). He is a member of the Monetary Policy Committee of the European System of Central Banks, and member of a number of policy committees within the framework of the Group of Ten and the OECD. He has been actively engaged in preparing the introduction of the euro in the Dutch financial system. His publications range from European monetary cooperation, the international monetary system to the functioning of financial markets. Recently he has chaired a working group on Causes of Financial Sector Consolidation for the Group of Ten.

Amar Bhattacharya (1952) is senior advisor, Poverty Reduction and Economic Management Network at the World Bank. In this capacity, he is responsible for coordinating the Bank's work on international financial architecture. He was principal author of a World Bank policy research report on "Private Capital Flows to Developing Countries" and has authored several publications relating to the recent financial crisis. Since joining the Bank, he has a long-standing involvement in the East Asia region, including as division chief for

Country Operations, Indonesia, Papua New Guinea and the South Pacific. He was chief officer for Country Creditworthiness. Prior to joining the World Bank, he worked as an international economist at the First National Bank of Chicago.

Henk Brouwer (1946) is executive director and deputy governor of De Nederlandsche Bank since July1997. Previously he held various positions in the ministries of Finance, of the Interior, and of Social Affairs and Employment. Before joining De Nederlandsche Bank, he was treasurer general at the Ministry of Finance. He is member of the Economic and Financial Committee (EFC) of the European Union and chairman of the G-10 Deputies. He served as alternative governor for the Netherlands at the IMF, is a member of Working Party 3 at the OECD, and regularly participates in meetings at the Bank for International Settlements.

Marek Dabrowski (1951) is a professor of economics and one of the founders of the Center for Social and Economic Research (CASE), Warsaw. He has been a policy advisor to governments and central banks in Bulgaria, Georgia, Kyrgyzstan, Kazakhstan, Macedonia, Moldova, Mongolia, Romania, Russia, Ukraine, Uzbekistan, and Yugoslavia. In1989-1990 he was first deputy minister of Finance of Poland. From1991 to 1993 he was a deputy in the Sejm (the lower house of the Polish Parliament). From 1991 to 1996 he was the chairman of the Council of Ownership Changes, an advisory body to the prime minister of Poland. Since 1998 he has been a member of the Monetary Policy Council of the National Bank of Poland. His recent research interests concentrate on macroeconomic policy problems and the political economy of transition.

Heiner Flassbeck (1950) is senior economist at UNCTAD's Division on Globalization and Development Strategies since November 2000. Before joining UNCTAD he was vice minister of Finance in Germany in 1998-1999. From 1990 to 1998 he has been chief economist of the German Institute for Economic Research in Berlin. He has been economic advisor to several governments in developing and transforming countries. His publications cover macroeconomic topics ranging from labour and employment to problems of monetary policy and the exchange rate regime.

Stephany Griffith-Jones (1947) is professorial fellow at the Institute of Development Studies at Sussex University. She started her career in 1970 at the Central Bank of Chile. Before joining the Institute of Development Studies, she worked at Barclays Bank International in the UK. She has led many research projects on debt and private capital flows, and has acted as senior consultant to governments in Eastern Europe and Latin America and to many international agencies, including the World Bank, the IDB, the EU and UNCTAD. She has published widely on international finance and macroeconomic policies, especially in relation to Latin American and East European economies.

Frans van Loon (1942) is managing director and global head, Governments and International Organisations at ING in Amsterdam. In 1967 he joined the World Bank, and was investment officer for Latin America, Africa and Asia at the International Finance Corporation from 1969 to 1974. From 1974 to 1981 he was with the Inter Alpha Group of Banks, first as regional representative for South-East Asia and then as general manager in Singapore. In 1981 he joined ING Barings where he held various positions in the International Division to become in 1990 the managing director and global head of the Emerging Markets Group, before reaching his actual position at the end of 2001. He is chairman of the Advisory Committee on Multilateral Organisations of the IIF in Washington.

Yung Chul Park (1939) is a professor of economics at Korea University. He served as ambassador for International Economy and Trade, Ministry of Foreign Affairs and Trade of Korea, chairman of the Board of Korea Exchange Bank in Seoul Korea and a member of the board of Korea Telecom. He previously served as the chief economic adviser to president Doo Hwan Chun of Korea, as president of the Korea Development Institute, as president of the Korea Institute of Finance, and as a member of the Bank of Korea's Monetary Board. He also was the director of the Institute of Economic Research at Korea University, taught at Harvard University and Boston University as a visiting professor and worked for the IMF. From June to December of 1998, he managed the merger of Korea's two largest commercial banks as chairman of the CBK-Hanil Bank Merger Committee. He has widely published on international finance and monetary economics.

Wouter Raab (1955) is director, Foreign Financial Relations at the Ministry of Finance in the Netherlands since July 2000. His main responsibilities are IMF and World Bank matters, including the reform of the international financial architecture, European integration and EMU and, since May 2002, export credit insurance. He started his career at the Ministry of Social Affairs and Employment in 1982. In 1987 he moved to the Ministry of Finance to work at the General Financial and Economic Policy Directorate. In 1991 he moved to the Foreign Financial Relations Directorate to become head of the Multilateral Banks Division and head of the International Monetary Affairs Division.

Eisuke Sakakibara (1941) is professor of economics at Keio University and Director of the university's Global Security Research Center. He started his career at the Ministry of Finance of Japan, then moved to the IMF before returning in 1975 to the Ministry of Finance. From 1977 to 1981 he was associate professor of economics at the Institute for Policy Science of the Saitama University and visiting associate professor of economics at Harvard University. In 1981 he joined again the Ministry of Finance as director of Planning and Research at the International Finance Bureau. From 1983 to 1985 he was with the Japan Center for International Finance as special advisor to the president, then returned to the Ministry of Finance where he held different positions to become in 1995 director-general. From 1997 to 1999 he was the vice minister of Finance for International Affairs. He has published widely on financial issues.

Barbara Stallings is at present professor at the Watson Institute for International Studies at Brown University. At the time of the conference in Amsterdam, she was director of the Economic Development Division at ECLAC in Santiago de Chile, and visiting professor at Brown University. Before joining ECLAC in 1993, she was professor of political economy at the University of Wisconsin-Madison for 15 years. She was also a visiting professor and researcher at Harvard, Yale and Columbia universities and at several research centres in Latin America and in Japan. She is a specialist in development economics and international finance. Most recently she has been working on topics related to domestic finance in Latin America and East Asia, through projects at ECLAC, WIDER and the University of Tokyo. She was a member of the working group that produced Secretary General Kofi Annan's recent report on financing for development.

Jürgen Stark (1948) is vice president of the Deutsche Bundesbank since September 1998. He started his career in 1978 at the Ministry of Economics, to join the Federal Chancellery in 1988. In 1992 he moved to the Ministry of Finance. From 1995 to 1998 he was involved as state secretary of the Federal Ministry of Finance and as the Personal Representative of the Federal Chancellor in the preparation of World Economic Summits. He has been a member of the EU Monetary Committee and of the Economic and Financial Committee. In 1998 he became a member of the International Relations Committee of the European System of Central Banks. Since 2001, he is a member of the Financial Stability Forum and the Committee on the Global Financial System.

Rogério Studart (1961) is at present working as a Financial Sector Specialist at the Inter-American Development Bank. At the time of the conference in Amsterdam, he was economics affairs officer at the Economic Development Division of ECLAC. Previously, he has been an associate professor at the Instituto de Economia of the Universidade Federal do Rio de Janeiro. He has led research projects on development finance, financial markets and macroeconomics, and has acted as a consultant for state governments in Brazil, private corporations and international agencies, including the World Bank and UNCTAD. He has published widely on monetary issues and development finance.

György Szapáry (1938) is deputy president of the National Bank of Hungary (NBH) since 1993. He has worked at the European Commission and has held several positions at the IMF, including economist at the African Department, resident representative in Mali, senior economist and division chief at both the Asian and European Department, assistant director of the Asian Department and senior resident representative in Hungary. He has been alternate governor for the European Bank for Reconstruction and Development, and president of the Board of Directors of the International Training Centre for Bankers in Budapest. He is the author of several articles on economic and financial issues.

Charles Wyplosz is professor of economics at the Graduate Institute of International Studies, University of Geneva and a research fellow of the Centre for Economic Policy Research (CEPR) in London. He graduated in Engineering from Ecole Centrale (Paris) and in Statistics from the University of Paris, before receiving a PhD in economics from Harvard University. He is managing editor of *Economic Policy*, and serves on the scientific board of several scientific reviews. He has widely published on exchange rates, macroeconomic policy and labour markets. From 1992 to 1998 he has advised the Government of the Russian Federation. He is a consultant to various organisations such as the IMF, the World Bank, the United Nations, the European Parliament, the French Government and the European Commission. His recent research focuses on currency crises and the architecture of the international financial system, European Monetary Union and exchange rates in transition economies.

Abbreviations

ACU	Asian currency unit
ADBI	Asian Development Bank Institute
AFTA	ASEAN Free Trade Area
AMF	Asian Monetary Fund
APEC	Asia Pacific Economic Cooperation
ASEAN	Association of South-East Asian Nations (Brunei, Burma, Cambodia, Indonesia, Laos, Malaysia, the Philippines, Singapore, Thailand, Vietnam).
ASEAN+3	ASEAN and China, Japan, and Korea
BIS	Bank for International Settlements
CCA	common currency area
CEE	Central and Eastern Europe
CEEC	Central and Eastern European countries
CEPAL	see ECLAC
DIT	direct inflation-targeting
DNB	De Nederlandsche Bank
EBRD	European Bank for Reconstruction and Development
ECB	European Central Bank
ECLAC	Economic Commission for Latin America and the Caribbean (of the UN); (in Spanish CEPAL)
ECU	European currency unit
EMS	European Monetary System
EMU	European Economic and Monetary Union
ERM	Exchange Rate Mechanism (European)
ERM-II	Exchange Rate Mechanism II (for EMU)
EU	European Union
FDI	foreign direct investment
FPC	Fiscal Policy Committee
FTAA	Free Trade Area of the Americas
G-7	Group of Seven
GATT	General Agreement on Tariffs and Trade
GDP	gross domestic product
HICP	Harmonised Index of Consumer Prices
HIPC	Heavily Indebted Poor Countries

IMF	International Monetary Fund
IFI	international financial institutions
IIF	Institute for International Finance
Mercosur	Southern Cone Common Market (in Latin America)
MFN	most favoured nation (trade status)
MPC	Monetary Policy Committee
NAFTA	North American Free Trade Agreement
NPL	non-performing loan
OCA	optimum currency area
OECD	Organisation for Economic Cooperation and Development
PPP	purchasing power parity
RER	real exchange rate
SDR	special drawing right
SDRM	Sovereign Debt Restructuring Mechanism
UK	United Kingdom
UN	United Nations
UNCTAD	United Nations Conference on Trade and Development
US	United States
VAR	vector autoregression
WPI	wholesale price index
WTO	World Trade Organization

Preface

Financial crises have occurred for as long as financial markets have existed, but for emerging markets, the past seven years have been extremely turbulent. In December 1994 the 'Tequila' crisis erupted. In 1997 the Asian crisis started in Thailand and spread to South Korea, Malaysia, the Philippines and Indonesia. On top of this came the crises in Russia, Brazil, and more recently in Turkey and Argentina.

But what about the next seven years? Will these be rich years for financial stability in emerging economies, or will these be as meagre as the past seven? The outcome will depend on what policymakers and investors have learned from the events in the last seven years.

Let me summarise a few of the most evident lessons. A first lesson has been that – although much depends on a country's specific circumstances – fixed exchange rate regimes are more demanding and maybe more dangerous than flexible regimes. Mexico, all of the Asian crisis countries, as well as Turkey and Argentina pursued fairly rigid exchange rate regimes in the run up to their crises. In the face of adverse external shocks or unsound domestic budgetary and wage policies, fixed exchange rates can more readily lead to ill-suited monetary policies and to an overvaluation of the exchange rate. The strengthening of the dollar against the yen in 1996, for instance, squeezed the competitiveness of the Asian emerging markets and led to substantial current account imbalances. Argentina's currency board may have helped the anti-inflation programme, but at a very high cost. If such a fixed exchange rate policy is not based on sound macroeconomics, a crisis may become inevitable.

A second lesson has been that sound debt management is crucial. In both Mexico and the Asian crisis countries, short-term foreign borrowing was excessive. The crisis in Argentina shows that the burden of foreign currency debt gives the government an incentive to remain with a regime with an overvaluated exchange rate for too long.

A third lesson has been that investors and policymakers need access to reliable and accurate information on a country's state of play. In South Korea in 1997, for example, international investors had no idea that the central banks' liquid foreign currency reserves were actually depleted. Once the actual figures became available to the markets, the crisis was triggered. This point has been well taken by the international financial community, which has invested vast resources in developing international standards and codes and other transparency initiatives.

A fourth lesson has been the importance of a strong and well-supervised financial sector. In most of the crisis countries, banking supervision was poor, giving banks scope to act irresponsibly, for instance by borrowing heavily from abroad and then speculating on favourable exchange rate developments while profiting from interest rate differentials. We know from the experience in Asia that it takes a lot of time to clean up banks' balance sheets once they have become messy. In my opinion, to enhance the financial system, emerging countries, especially in Asia, should more vigorously stimulate the entry of foreign-owned banks. This can help improve banking practices relatively quickly, while avoiding the dangers of large cross-border borrowing. A significant presence of foreign banks is one of the characteristics of financial markets in European emerging countries.

Will the future be spared of crises? That is idle fantasy. It is my hope, however, that we will see fewer crises and, maybe more importantly, less contagion of crises between emerging markets. The Argentine crisis has not seriously spilled over into other economies, with the exception of Uruguay that has close banking system links through Argentine branches and deposit holders.

This lack of contagion can indeed, at least in part, be attributed to the initiatives by policymakers. First, macroeconomic policies in emerging economies have generally improved since the Asian crisis. Fewer countries pursue fixed exchange rate policies and current account imbalances are smaller, especially in Asia. Debt management has also improved, as indicated by smaller shares of short-term debt in total foreign borrowing. The transparency initiatives, moreover, seem to have given investors a greater ability to discriminate between countries. A positive development is that although capital flows to emerging markets have declined, foreign direct investment, with its potentially larger positive spill-over effects on economic growth, has continued to increase.

Stability in emerging markets is not only important for these countries themselves; it has a global dimension as well. Indeed, economic developments in emerging markets have an increasing impact on developments in the industrialised world as our trade and especially financial flows have grown much faster than our economic production. Multinational investors can make handsome profits by taking appropriate risks in emerging markets and diversifying their portfolios, but can also face large losses if a crisis occurs. The impact on developed countries can be large: wealth, trade, bank lending and even general confidence may be depressed. Nonetheless, at the same time, we need to recall that there is a mutual interest in sustaining this interdependence. Actually, if anything, this interdependence will increase in step with the ageing populations in the developed world. From an economist's viewpoint, there seems to be a certain logic to increasing capital flows toward the younger emerging markets, and repatriating these flows in due course as the share of retired workers in the developed world rises.

Nout Wellink
President
De Nederlandsche Bank

Introduction

Jan Joost Teunissen and Mark Teunissen

Life is full of mistakes, and no domain of human activity escapes this basic rule – including economic activity. As György Szapáry, deputy governor of Hungary's Central Bank, reminds us in a discussion in this book about the recurrence of financial crises over the last ten years: "Bernard Shaw once said, that experience is that wonderful thing that allows us to recognise a mistake when we make it again. All the crises seem to have the same causes."

But let's remain optimistic. Experience may help us not only reduce the frequency of financial crises, but also their extensiveness, depth and duration. Moreover, experience may offer clues as to how financial stability and development could be promoted, nationally, regionally, and internationally. That is precisely what this book aims to do.

The book discusses four specific, yet broad, issues of financial stability and development. The first is the lessons that can be drawn from the recent experience in Latin America with financial liberalisation, privatisation, and volatile international capital flows. The second is the convergence challenges faced by transition countries in Central and Eastern Europe in the run-up to accession to the European Union and eventually the Economic and Monetary Union (EMU). The third is the prospects of regional financial cooperation in Asia. The fourth is the role that market participants and financial authorities can play in promoting financial stability and development.

The Global and Regional Level: Views From Asia

Often, the global dimension is lacking in the analysis of financial crisis and stability in emerging developing economies. Implicitly (or even explicitly), it is taken for granted that, *alas*, international economic relations are as they are, and nothing can be done to change them. However, former deputy minister of Finance of Japan, Eisuke Sakakibara, takes a different stance. In his chapter, he strongly advocates a change in the current global governance system, predicting the end of Pax Americana, that is: global capitalism under American hegemony.

In support of such a bold prediction, Sakakibara reminds us of the history of the world economic system in the last 1200 years. For more than ten centuries, it was dominated neither by the Americans nor the Europeans, but by the Asian and Islamic empires. "Except for the last 150 years," he says, "(these empires) were the centre of the world economy."

Not only is China now becoming a key player in the Asian and world economy, observes Sakakibara, but Asia as a whole is increasing its role. He believes that Asia is likely to regain its position as "hub" of the global economy, reorienting the centre of gravitation from West to East. Asians may help to speed this process a bit by getting their acts together and increasing the intensity of regional economic cooperation. In doing so, they would be paving the way for financial stability and growth in their own region, as well as in the world economy as a whole. In addition, they would provide the much needed countervailing power to western dominated international organisations, and thus contribute to a healthy competition among global and regional institutions and improve their performance.

Discussing the prospects of financial cooperation in Asia, Sakakibara suggests that the Asian countries should take three subsequent steps. First, they should coordinate their foreign exchange policies to achieve the stability of their currencies. Second, they should form an Asian currency unit (ACU) with a flexible snake around the central value, just like Europe did many years ago when it established the European currency unit (ECU) and the snake. Finally, when the need emerges to jointly defend the ACU, the logical next step would be to create the more ambitious Asian Monetary Fund, or whatever name one wishes to give to an Asian organisation that caters to regional financial coordination, surveillance and intervention.

In his comment on Sakakibara, Amar Bhattacharya of the World Bank argues that Asia should follow a two-fold track. It should ask for and play a major role in the global governance system and, at the same time, strengthen its own regional arrangements. He stresses Asia's interest in a well functioning global financial system, "given the inherent fact that financial markets are global".

In her comment on Sakakibara, Barbara Stallings, professor of economics at Brown University in the United States, compares Sakakibara's proposals on financial cooperation in the Asian region with those of other experts. She argues that Sakakibara's proposals "are more optimistic, but less clear, than most others", and that they focus exclusively on government-to-government relations, while others also look at the involvement of private sector institutions.

Yung Chul Park and Kee Hong Bea, economics professors from Korea University, analyse the more specific issue of whether financial liberalisation in East Asian countries has led to stronger financial ties with financial markets in the United States and Europe, or with one another. They conclude that the former is the case. They find that western financial institutions have now penetrated the East Asian capital markets to such an extent that they dominate them in two major services: underwriting in the primary market and trading and consulting in the secondary market.

To western market participants, this may seem a positive development, since it can be seen as a contribution to the creation of a global market for goods and services, but to Park and Bea it is not all that positive. They point to serious concerns among East Asian policymakers. One is that the gap in financial technology and expertise between East Asian countries and the advanced industrial countries will remain so large that East Asia may never be able to catch up with its western competitors. Another is that the advanced countries dominating the global financial system do not seem to be interested in reducing the incidence of financial crisis in emerging economies; so far they have failed to strengthen the supervision of cross-border financial flows and regulate large foreign financial institutions.

Finally and most important of all, say Park and Bea, it is hard for East Asian policymakers to predict how the branches and subsidiaries of foreign financial institutions will behave in times of crisis. Will they panic again and move out at the first sign of crisis as they did in 1997? Since most of the East Asian countries have not been able to borrow from international capital markets in their own currencies, "they will be continuously exposed to the currency and term mismatch problems that triggered the crisis in 1997," observe Park and Bea.

In his comment on Park and Bea, Heiner Flassbeck of UNCTAD agrees that regional monetary cooperation can be a proper answer to the challenges from globalisation and liberalisation. However, he warns that regional monetary systems do not prevent financial crisis and turmoil.

The National Level: Views From Latin America and Central and Eastern Europe

Brazilian economist Rogério Studart moves to the national level of the financial stability issue by looking at recent developments in the financial sector in Latin America. More specifically, he analyses the strength and fragility of the banking sector in Argentina, Brazil, Chile and Mexico. He describes the main changes in the macroeconomic environment and microeconomic regulation of Latin American banks and analyses the ways in which these changes are linked to bank performance and financial crises. He finds that the financial crises in the 1990s in Latin America led to improvements in the regulation and supervision of the financial sector and particularly of the banking sector. Such regulation and supervision in Argentina, Brazil, Chile and Mexico became even stricter than in the United States. Also, domestic financial systems were privatised and opened up to foreign banks. But despite these changes, the Latin American banking sector remained fragile. According to Studart, this unfortunate state of affairs can only be explained by linking macroeconomic and microeconomic aspects of the banking business and analysing how they interacted to generate bank crises and the boom-bust performance of credit in the region in the 1990s.

Studart concludes that banking activity is highly pro-cyclical. Capital account liberalisation and liberalisation of the domestic financial sector facilitated the surge of capital inflows from abroad. This surge of capital flows led to economic growth and successful price stabilisation, which stimulated banks in Latin America to expand their credit extension. When crises hit the region and capital flows stopped pouring in, the banks assumed defensive strategies. Credit stagnation resulted in lower growth, thus feeding into negative expectations. So while the regulation and supervision of banks in Latin America have improved substantially, "it has become evident that additional measures are required to achieve growth and stability of the banking sector in the region – so that the sector can make a significant contribution to the long-term development of the region," says Studart.

In his comment on Studart, Jürgen Stark, deputy governor of Germany's Central Bank, stresses the crucial role of sound macroeconomic policy resulting in stability. Given the current high mobility of capital, "the effects of bad economic policy ... can be much more serious now than was the case a decade ago," says Stark.

Taking the debate on the lack of "fiscal discipline" (in Latin America and elsewhere) as his point of departure, Charles Wyplosz, professor of economics in Geneva, proposes that the responsibility for setting the budget balance and ensuring debt sustainability should be delegated to independent (national) Fiscal Policy Committees. He argues that this solution is likely to enhance attempts at regional cooperation in the realm of exchange rate policy. In his view, Latin America will be a prime beneficiary of such an approach, since "the politicisation of fiscal policy has been excessive and has resulted in deep and repeated economic instability".

In his comment on Wyplosz, Mark Allen of the IMF stresses that, in a mature political system, discussions on the stance of fiscal policy are *political* decisions, not purely *technocratic* ones. "But perhaps Wyplosz' proposal is part of the spadework for creating such mature political systems," Allen recognises.

Turning to the financial stability challenges for Central and Eastern European (CEE) countries entering the European Union (EU), Henk Brouwer, deputy governor of the Central Bank of the Netherlands, and his colleagues Ralph de Haas and Bas Kiviet assess the potential risks of the banking sector. This sector is by far the most important part of the financial systems in the CEE countries and, as such, is the main source of risk for financial stability in this region.

They identify specific potential risks or challenges. First of all, there is the risk of large capital inflows. Such inflows have already increased substantially, and are likely to increase further in the run-up to actual EU (and subsequently EMU) accession. Although capital inflows as such are conducive to economic growth, they could contribute to real exchange rate appreciation, which might in turn erode competitiveness. Also, they could contribute to riskier lending practices and unwarranted currency mismatches in the financial sector. Second, there is the risk of excessive government involvement in banks' credit decisions as well as connected and imprudent lending to bank insiders, such as management or shareholders. Third, many accession countries still need to improve substantially their legal framework, in particular the enforcement of creditor and shareholder rights. Fourth, the low level of financial intermediation by banks is a potential source of risk, in the case that banks try to expand their client base by operating in new and riskier markets, such as those for company start-ups. Finally, the limited development of the non-bank financial sector in accession countries is another potential risk. In absence of well-developed capital markets (or in other words, if the private sector fully depends on banks for their funding), a banking crisis could have severe consequences for the real economy. Vice versa, this dependence of the corporate sector on the banking system also implies that the financial consequences of corporate failures would to their full extent be borne by their creditor banks.

In a postscript to the chapter by Brouwer *et al.*, Mark Teunissen reviews the recent EU decision to let the ten candidate countries enter the union in 2004. He observes that this decision has intensified the debate on how quickly these countries should join EMU. Most accession countries are in favour of entering EMU as fast as possible. However, overly quick compliance with *nominal* convergence criteria would force the candidate countries to undertake very tight budgetary and monetary policies, thus slowing down their already limited progress in *real* convergence towards the euro area, says Teunissen.

In his comment on Brouwer *et al.*, György Szapáry, deputy president of Hungary's Central Bank, discusses three characteristics of the financial sector in CEE countries: the low degree of financial intermediation, the dominance of the banking sector over the capital markets, and the high degree of foreign ownership. Marek Dabrowski, a former deputy minister of Finance from Poland, elaborates on the possible sources of financial fragility in the CEE countries, arguing that the biggest danger lies in the continuation of substantial fiscal deficits.

The Role for Market Participants and Financial Authorities

Age Bakker, of De Nederlandsche Bank, discusses the role of central banks in promoting financial stability. He observes that the link between price stability and financial stability is a complex one, and reminds us that in the run up to the Asian crisis, large imbalances were built up in the real estate and other asset markets while inflation was low. He therefore raises the question: Can central banks deliver both stable prices and financial stability simultaneously?

Bakker's answer is, that there are three ways in which the central bank should be involved in financial stability. The first is the identification of vulnerabilities in the financial system (by monitoring risks). The second is the analysis of the transmission of shocks in the financial system (analysing transmission channels and financial market behaviour). The third is, the implementation of policies to make the financial system shock resistant.

Other ways in which central banks can promote financial stability include: performing the role of lender of last resort, (partially) guaranteeing bank accounts through a deposit insurance system, overseeing payment and settlement systems, supervising both on individual firms (bottom-up) as well as on systemic risks of failing firms and the macroeconomic consequences (top-down).

Stephany Griffith-Jones, of the Institute of Development Studies in Sussex, stresses the importance of considering the global level in fostering financial stability (in addition to the regional and national levels), and the importance of simultaneously achieving economic growth. "I think it is often forgotten that the ultimate aim is growth and employment," she says.

Going to the issue of global financial regulation, Griffith-Jones defines two aims for international financial development. The first is the pursuit of financial stability, that is the whole agenda of crisis prevention and crisis management. The second is the provision of sufficient capital flows, both private and public, to developing countries to help sustain growth. She observes that progress on achieving the first aim has been insufficient and asymmetrical and that there have been important reversals. In her view, we are still missing a global financial regulator. Considering that the lack of accountability of financial markets is one of the deepest flaws in democracy, Griffith-Jones says that "the only, very technocratic, way of doing it is actually through regulation".

Progress on achieving the second aim has also been problematic, says Griffith-Jones. Most developing countries are receiving insufficient capital flows. She believes that this is not just a temporary phenomenon, but a more permanent structural feature of the global financial system. Global fund managers seem to have less appetite for emerging markets. And when they invest a little bit of their money there, they pull out quickly when they see problems. Griffith-Jones sees coming up with ways to encourage sufficient stable flows to developing countries as a new challenge for the international community.

Frans van Loon, of ING, presents some views from the private sector. He recognises the "deep unease" with financial globalisation, which is "so broadly felt", but argues that over the last ten years, the attention of both the financial community and civil society has focused too much on cross-border flows. As a result, domestic financial sector development has been neglected. So the new emphasis is on strengthening domestic financial systems, "because weak financial systems have too often been at the centre of broader economic crises in emerging markets".

Van Loon reports on three lines of action that bankers all over the world (as members of the Institute of International Finance) have agreed on. The first line of action deals with ways to promote domestic financial sector development, the second with the need to improve arrangements for reducing risk (which includes improving investor relations and improving macroeconomic and financial data collection and dissemination), and the third with implementing an orderly sovereign debt restructuring process (which includes the application of collective actions clauses).

Wouter Raab, of the Dutch Ministry of Finance, addresses the question of what ministries of Finance of the developed world can do to foster global financial stability. He sees four levels of action. The first is active participation in multilateral fora such as the IMF, the World Bank and the Financial Stability Forum. "We believe in a strong rules-based international system where there is equal treatment and in which every country has a voice," he says. The second level of action is that countries keep their own house in order. International savings should not be used to finance public deficits in the developed world, but rather investment in developing countries, says Raab. The third, more indirect, level of action for ministries of Finance is to advocate trade liberalisation, in particular the reduction of agricultural subsidies in developed countries since they prevent developing countries from exploiting their comparative advantages. Fourth, the ministries of Finance should oversee adequate regulation, supervision and – in Europe – the integration of national financial markets. "A deeper and more liquid EU-wide capital market will be able to provide participants from inside or outside Europe with more tailor-made financial instruments, will facilitate access to credits at lower costs and will be better able to absorb shocks," argues Raab.

Part I

Latin America: How to Achieve Stability and Growth?

1

Changing Expectations, Capital Surges and the Banking Sector: Argentina, Brazil, Chile and Mexico in the 1990s

Rogério Studart

The financial crises in 1994-95 and 1997-98 in developing economies led to an overall cry for improvements in regulation and supervision of the financial sector, in particularly of the banking sector. In addition, further privatisation and opening of domestic financial markets to foreign banks was recommended as a way to increase both stability and efficiency of credit provision by domestic banks (e.g. Burki and Perry, 1998). In Latin America, several countries followed such recommendations and their financial regulation and supervision have improved significantly.

Despite these changes, the crisis of 2001-02 in Argentina (where after 1994 the strictest bank regulation was introduced) indicates that the Latin American banking sector remains fragile. In addition, the problem of credit stagnation became more acute after 1997-98 (Barajas and Steiner, 2002). Thus it has become evident that additional measures are required to achieve growth and stability of the banking sector in the region – so that the sector can make a significant contribution to the long-term development of the region.

Explaining the fragility of the Latin American banking sector requires an integrated macro- and microeconomic analysis. In the 1990s, the interaction of macro- and microeconomic imperfections generated bank crises and resulted in the boom-bust character of credit provisioning in the region. We must consider that financial activity is almost by definition forward-looking, and highly influenced by changes in expectations. Banks tend to be highly pro-cyclical (see e.g. Borio and Lowe, 2000; BIS, 2000), whereas their risk-taking is limited by regulation.[1] Bearing that in mind, the 1990s seem to be a particularly interesting period to examine how the banking sector behaves (and how that behaviour affects macroeconomic performance), because it is a period of profound changes in regulation and in macroeconomic expectations.

This chapter explores in a preliminary manner these issues (with special emphasis on the period after the Tequila crisis). It builds on research currently undertaken in ECLAC and in particular develops some of the issues raised in a recent paper (Stallings and Studart, 2002). Section 1 briefly describes the main changes in the macroeconomic environment and in regulation of the Latin American banks between the end of the 1980s and the beginning of 1990s (particularly in Argentina, Brazil, Chile and Mexico) and their relations with bank performance and crises in the period. Section 2 deals with the regulatory and microeconomic changes after the Tequila crisis. Section 3 shows how banks reacted to the new regulatory and macroeconomic environments. Section 4 summarises our findings and presents our conclusions.

1 Exuberant Expectations, Surges of Capital Flows, Policy Regimes and the Banking Sector in the 1990s

In the first half of the 1990s, there was a spectacular expansion of financial markets in the developed economies.[2] A significant surge of

---

1 This problem goes beyond the usual asymmetric information problem and has to do with at least two processes: Waves of optimism in the banking sector lead to credit expansion, which increases aggregate demand and affects income and cash flow of consumers and the productive sector. In times of expansion, real and financial asset prices increase, and so does the value of collateral. Through these self-fulfilling processes, banks tend to increase their leverage and thus their vulnerability to changes in the variables that affect their risks: economic activity and level of employment (credit risk), borrowing interest rates (liquidity risk), and asset prices (market risk).

2 For an analysis of the causes and the consequences of the expansion of financial markets in developed economies, see e.g. Fornari and Levy (1999).

Figure 1 Latin America: Net Capital Transfers and GDP Growth
(percentage of GDP)

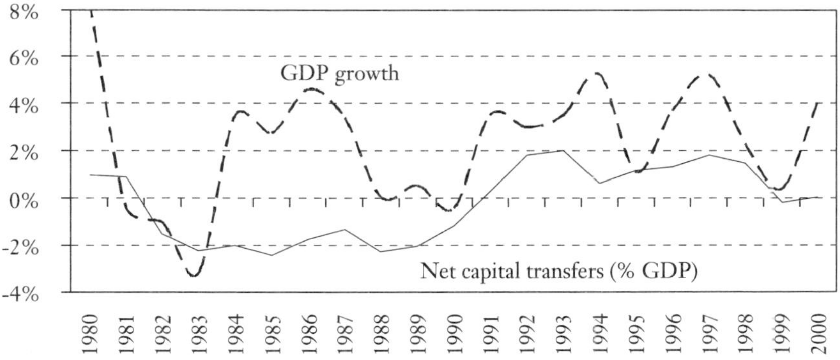

Source: Elaborated by the author based on data from ECLAC.

capital flows to developing countries followed; capital flows more than tripled from 1991 to 1995.[3] These flows have only been a fraction of those between mature economies, but are large compared to the size of developing economies and their domestic financial markets.

The buoyancy in the international markets certainly influenced economic policy and economic performance in Latin America in the late 1980s and the early 1990s. Almost a decade of balance-of-payments constraints and net negative resource transfers (see Figure 1) had led to very poor macroeconomic performance and high inflation in Latin America. Now, the surge of capital inflows significantly surpassed the needs to finance both the current and the capital account, generating systematic accumulation of reserves, and removing the external constraint for the expansion of domestic demand and imports. Using these exceptional external conditions, many countries in the region adopted some type of exchange-based price stabilisation programmes, including fixed or pegged exchange rates and trade liberalisation – that were effective in reducing inflation (Table 1). Generally, the higher the inflation and the worse

[3] Even though country-specific features did affect the distribution of such flows between developing economies, the push factors, related to the changes in financial markets in developed economies, seem to be the most important factor in explaining such growth (Studart, 2001a).

Table 1 Selected Macroeconomic Indicators

	Argentina	Brazil	Chile	Mexico	Latin America
Growth (% GDP)					
1980s	-1.1	1.7	2.9	1.9	
1990s	4.1	3.1	6.6	3.5	
Inflation (%)					
1980s	451	348	20	65	
1990s	9	181	8	18	
Fiscal surplus or deficit (% GDP)					
1980s	-3.4	-8.4	0.3	-8.1	
1990s	-1.1	n.a.	1.4	0.1	
Current account (% GDP)					
1980s	-1.8	-2.0	-6.5	-1.2	-2.0
1990s	-2.6	-2.0	-2.9	-3.6	-2.8
External debt (% GDP)					
1980s	46	37	82	52	50
1990s	40	31	45	38	41
Implicit income elasticity of imports					
1980s	10.5	-0.1	0.5	1.7	0.0
1990s	4.7	5.3	1.6	2.6	3.4

Source: Elaborated by the author based on data from ECLAC.

the economic performance in the 1980s, the more rigid were the exchange rate regimes adopted.

Argentina, for instance, had hyperinflation and negative average GDP growth in the 1980s, and adopted a currency board system. It was effective in breaking down the inflation dynamics mainly by dollarising a significant part of spot transactions and forward contracts. Brazil – with a long history of indexation, high inflation but positive economic growth in the 1980s – adopted a pegged system and an ingenious monetary reform in 1994 (required to break up with the inflation dynamics by dismantling the main mechanisms of indexation of the economy). From 1988 to 1994, Mexico, with much lower inflation rates and slightly higher average growth rates in the 1980s, adopted a managed exchange rate regime, with devaluations that were subsequently much lower than the inflation rate. Chile had already reduced its inflation to reasonable levels in the 1980s, but it still pursued a gradualist anti-inflation programme that relied strongly on overvalued exchange rates.

Exchange rate based stabilisation programmes (if associated with trade opening and significant capital inflows) often produce rapid results in reducing inflation, and also lead to positive growth rates – usually associated with rapid expansion of consumers' demand. In Argentina, Chile and Mexico, rapid reduction of inflation and positive economic growth characterised at least the first four years of such stabilisation programmes. The negative facet of exchange rate based stabilisation programmes is usually the deterioration of current account balances and accumulation of external debt, increasing external vulnerability and loss of growth dynamics after the initial years. Thus, reversals of capital flows tend to deeply affect domestic production, as domestic policymakers must respond to such reversals by increasing interest rates or adopting deflationary measures – usually through further fiscal retrenchment.

The fact that macroeconomic recovery in Latin America in the early 1990s was associated with a financial boom in developed economies is, in our viewpoint, crucial for understanding the performance of the banking sector in the 1990s. The international setting of the early 1990s was marked by rising liquidity, declining international interest rates, and increased access to the financial markets of industrial countries. This led to a surge of optimism in Latin American financial markets, and banks in particular. Given that the financial business is forward-looking by nature, changes in expectations can have profound effects on the decisions to expand credit and assume risks. The more unregulated the market, the more pronounced is this pro-cyclical bias. Therefore, in order to have the whole picture of the relation between the surges in capital flows to Latin America in the 1990s, we need to discuss the changes in regulation.

Financial Liberalisation, Credit Booms and Crises Before 1995

Figure 2 presents the financial and capital account liberalisation indexes, constructed using the methodology developed in Morley, Machado and Pettinato (1999) and regularly published in ECLAC's annual *Economic Survey*. Except for Chile, most Latin American economies went through a process of financial liberalisation at some

Figure 2 Financial and Capital Account Liberalisation Index

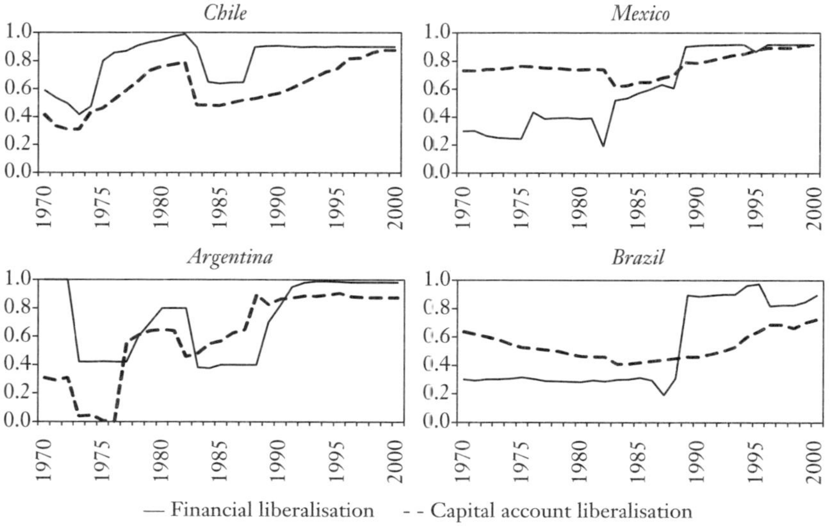

Note: The reform indexes are calculated by ECLAC using the methodology developed in Morley, Machado and Pettinato (1999).
Source: ECLAC.

point in the end of the 1980s and beginning of the 1990s. The authorities no longer set interest rates, directed credit, and captured a large share of bank deposits as required reserves, and commercial banks became free to make their own decisions on borrowers, loan volume, and prices.

Around the same time, capital account liberalisation enabled local corporations and banks to issue securities in international markets and engage in transactions in foreign currencies. In addition, in the 1990s, barriers for foreign institutions to local markets were levied. These processes of financial liberalisation *cum* capital account opening led to rapid expansion of bank credit, followed by bank and often exchange rate crisis.

We will use Figure 2 as a background for a brief description of these reforms in each of the four economies under analysis.

Chile

Chile was the first to embark on a liberalisation process, beginning shortly after the military coup in 1973. Changes included freeing of interest rates, eliminating directed credit, reducing reserve requirements, and relaxing regulation and supervision more generally. As in the other three countries, a rapid increase in lending followed the liberalisation process, ending with a banking crisis in 1981-84. The crisis forced the authorities to take immediate action, restructuring the banking sector through the intervention in 21 private financial institutions, including the two largest banks in the country. Later, 14 of these institutions were liquidated while the rest was rehabilitated and privatised again.

Soon after the crisis, policymakers introduced changes in regulation and supervision, built on the lessons drawn. The crisis thus led to a modern system of prudential regulation and increased supervisory capacity by the state. A new banking law was promulgated in 1986, encompassing a lower debt-to-capital ratio, reserve requirements according to banks' leverage position, mandatory information disclosure to the public, a partial public guarantee of deposits, restrictions on loans to "related" clients, and a strict separation between the core business of banks and their subsidiaries. After introducing restrictions, external financial liberalisation was implemented gradually, as firms were initially allowed to issue bonds and shares in external markets; later, institutional investors (banks, pension fund managers, and insurance companies) were permitted to hold external assets, while capital controls were gradually eased. In 1997, further changes included adoption of the Basel Committee's 8 percent rule.[4]

Mexico

After a long period of recovering from the 1982 banking crisis, Mexico embarked on an ambitious new process of financial liberalisation in 1988: interest rates were freed, liquidity requirements were eliminated, credit allocation directives were abolished, and the previously nationalised banks were privatised again. The response of the banking system was almost immediate. Lending expanded rapidly (around 30 percent per year in real terms from 1989 to 1994), and the share of loans to the private sector rose from 10 percent to 40 percent of GDP (Yacamán, 2001).

---

[4] For more details, see Budnevich (2000) and Held and Jimenez (2001).

Default rates also increased rapidly in the period – indicating reckless lending practices.[5] Bad lending and unhealthy macro-economic policies contributed to the build-up of the financial crisis that followed. The use of an exchange rate anchor to control inflation led to overvaluation of the Mexican peso, large current account deficits, and strong capital inflows. A significant part of these flows was intermediated by just deregulated domestic banks. These banks profited from the big differentials between domestic and international interest rates – which in turn stimulated credit growth. But when the capital flows were reversed, the stage for a twin crisis (in the sense of Kaminsky and Reinhart, 1999) was set – and it actually happened in 1994. From 1994 onwards past-due loans ratios soared with the fall of economic activity.

Argentina

The Argentine financial liberalisation began at the end of the 1980s[6] and shared some characteristics with Mexico. Liberalisation took place in the context of an exchange rate based stabilisation programme (Plan de Convertibilidad). It lifted most of the controls on domestic and foreign operations of the domestic financial system that had been imposed during the period of high inflation and external constraints. The international financial buoyancy of the early 1990s led to a surge of optimism in the Argentine markets. Simultaneously, price stability and a fixed exchange rate regime abruptly reduced both inflation and exchange rate risk. These factors created a fertile environment for the rapid growth of financial activity, but also for increasing maturity and exchange rate mismatches.

---

[5] As pointed out by EIU (2001) p. 7, the first years of Mexican bank privatisation were characterised by "reckless – sometimes fraudulent – lending as a result of poor supervision and underdeveloped regulations. Poor credit-analysis procedures and few internal controls characterised the sector during this time. Banks put themselves in a precarious position as their lending outpaced their deposits, and they funded the shortfall through inter-bank borrowing – mainly from foreign banks". As a consequence, non-performing loans increased from around 2% of total loans in 1990 to 9% in 1994, prior to the peso crisis (McQuerry, 1999).

[6] Argentina had an aborted attempt at financial liberalisation in the late 1970s, but it was reversed as part of the overall abandonment of reforms at that time. For an analysis of the earlier attempt, see Studart and Hermann (2001, pp. 34-38).

Until 1994, recovery of the Argentine banking sector was impressive. Deposits and loans grew rapidly, while peso and dollar lending rates fell significantly, although they remained very high in comparison to those found in most developed economies and a significant number of developing economies. These results were a mix of several important features: (i) a process of monetisation, which normally follows price stability, led to a rapid growth of deposits in the banking sector; (ii) an increase of foreign capital inflows, which improved the confidence in the Convertibility Plan, raised banks' propensity to make dollar-denominated loans and borrowers' willingness to borrow in dollars, thus leading to a rapid process of dollarisation of both liabilities and assets of the banking sector. (iii) the increase of competition among banks and the improvement of overall confidence reduced banks' liquidity preference, resulting in a rapid expansion of credit. In the case of domestic banks, this increased liquidity pushed them into being less careful in their lending strategies and thus deteriorated portfolio quality.

Brazil

Brazil also went through financial liberalisation before 1994, but started from a stronger initial position than the other countries. In Brazil, the initial liberalisation preceded price stabilisation. As universal banking became legal since the 1988 reform, a very rapid process of consolidation took place in Brazil's banking sector. From 1989, there was a sharp reduction in the number of commercial banks, investment banks, and finance companies, most of which became universal banks.

Following the successful 1994 price stabilisation programme, the abrupt decline of inflationary gains led banks to search new sources of income, which initially generated a rapid expansion of credit – basically through consumer and business loans. This rapid and sometimes careless expansion, the high interest rate policy, and the rising unemployment provoked a rise of non-performing loans and repayment arrears. The monetary authorities failed to restrict this credit expansion, in spite of setting very high reserve requirements. Credit expansion with interest rates that remained very high became an increasingly dangerous mix.

The Tequila Crisis and the Stability of the Banking System

The devaluation of the Mexican peso in December 1994 set off a crisis that severely damaged the country's banking system and had ramifications elsewhere in the region and in the world. The effects were quite different in each of the four economies we are analysing.

The direct problems in Mexico created by the devaluation were less significant than in the other three countries, because Mexican regulations limited banks' foreign exchange exposure (although loopholes enabled banks to get around some of the restrictions; see O'Dogherty and Schwartz, 2001). There were several serious indirect problems, including a sharp drop in economic activity, a hike in interest rates, and an increase in demand for dollars. The consequence was a growing inability of debtors to service their obligations, leading to a further rise in the already high level of non-performing loans. Initially, however, the authorities thought the banking crisis would be limited in scope, because of the restrictions on foreign exchange exposure. In addition, the lack of an established regulatory authority meant that information was scarce. Thus, the approach was incremental, with solutions adopted as new problems appeared (McQuerry, 1999).

Argentina was the country in the region that was particularly affected by the Tequila crisis, and the Argentine banking system was hit hard. The currency board system in Argentina meant that domestic monetary authorities had no other instrument to face the potential capital outflows but to allow domestic rates to rise in 1995. This rise in interest rates provoked an increase of arrears and defaults, and reduced confidence of depositors, leading to significant withdrawals of deposits. Even though the Convertibility Plan had been successful for almost five years, depositors expressed their fears of devaluation by withdrawing dollar deposits. Thus, in addition to a liquidity problem, banks had to face increased exchange rate mismatching. The combination of deteriorating quality of assets and loss of deposits pointed to the vulnerable side of the seemingly solid Argentinean system. In order to avoid an open banking crisis, the Argentine Central Bank began injecting liquidity through its discount window, backed by the sale of dollar-denominated bonds – which in turn led to an increasing exchange rate exposure of the government – and by reducing reserve requirements for banks. Despite these steps, the accumulated losses of deposits were huge, corresponding to 12 percent of the banking sector's net worth by the first semester of 1995.

The Brazilian banking crisis of 1995 stems from developments in Brazil that happened before the Tequila crisis, but this crisis clearly deepened the problems. The fundamental reasons were associated with the abrupt adjustment that the banks had to undertake due to the success of the 1994 stabilisation programme (Plano Real). During the 1980s, banks earned substantial profits from inflationary gains associated with the peculiar role of double intermediary of the public debt that the Brazilian banks enjoyed during the long period of high inflation and indexation. The abrupt decline of these gains and the high fixed costs in Brazil's banking sector initially led private banks to expand credit, which allowed the boom in consumer demand following the 1994 stabilisation programme. The number of non-performing loans and repayment arrears increased, due to rapid and sometimes careless expansion of credit, high interest rate policy, and rising unemployment. The monetary authorities failed to restrict this expansion, in spite of setting very high levels of reserve requirements. Interest rates were maintained at high levels, which made credit expansion even more dangerous. The public banks faced additional problems due to their limited capacity to restructure their portfolios (dominated by state government debt) and their high operational costs (in view of the job stability of many of their employees). The Tequila crisis was "the last straw" in a process of increasing bank problems.

Chile was much less vulnerable than the other countries for two reasons. First, its macroeconomic performance was barely affected by the Tequila crisis, due to its lower levels of external debt, strong trade balance, and sound domestic fundamentals (e.g. high growth and fiscal balance). Second, as explained above, the Chilean banking system had already gone through major changes in supervision, regulation, and structure. In fact, from 1991 onwards, bank activity started expanding at a rate that was slightly higher than that of GDP, such that the relation between loans and GDP expanded from 45 percent in 1990 to 66 percent in 1999 – much higher than the peak achieved in 1984. Other indicators also point to an improvement in the efficiency and further consolidation of the banking sector (Ahumada and Marshall, 2001: 46-47).

Table 2 Bank Regulation and Supervision - Selected Indicators

	Argentina	Brazil	Bolivia	Chile	Mexico	Peru	Venezuela	US
Regulation								
Minimum capital-asset ratio requirement (%)	11.5	11	10	8	8	9.1	10	8
Actual risk-adjusted capital ratio (%)	16.4	15.8	11.4	12.3	13	12.7	14	12
Capital stringency index	6	3	5	3	4	5	2	4
Capital regulation index	8	6	8	5	7	6	2	6
Overall bank activities and ownership restrictiveness index	1.8	2.5	3	2.8	3	2	2.5	3
Supervision								
Supervisors per institution	2.4	4	6	3	11.5	3.6	1	0.1
Official supervisory index	12	15	11	13	10	14	14	14
% top ten banks rated by international agencies	100	100	20	50	n.a.	50	40	100
Private monitoring index	8	8	7	8	6	8	6	8

2 Regulatory Changes and Bank Performance after the Tequila Crisis

The Tequila crisis set the course for profound changes of regulation and supervision in Latin America – changes which were perceived as a *necessary* condition[7] to avoid future similar bank difficulties (Livacic and Sáez, 2000). The speed and depth of the changes in regulation

[7] We emphasised "necessary" because we want to make the point until the end of this chapter that such improvements in regulation and supervision were necessary, but not sufficient to mitigate the instability problem. In addition, we will argue that in some cases the more stringent regulation made the problem of credit rationing more acute in those economies.

and supervision varied with the information available to authorities, their perception of the severity of the problems confronting them, and the instruments they had at hand. Table 2 provides some indicators, using a database built in 1999 by the World Bank (see Studart and Stallings (2002) for a detailed analysis).

Chile stands out as completely different from the other three countries, because the Tequila crisis had almost no impact on the banking sector. It shows the importance of Chile's earlier steps in cleaning up the banking sector, establishing a modern regulatory and supervisory system, and maintaining comprehensive real macroeconomic balances.

In Argentina, after 1995, it became clear that, given its monetary and exchange rate regime, (i) its banking sector was highly vulnerable to changes in domestic interest rates, exchange rates, and depositor confidence; (ii) domestic banks were more vulnerable than the foreign-owned ones; (iii) since the capacity of the monetary authorities to intervene in periods of crisis was very limited under the Convertibility Plan, some additional mechanisms were needed to increase systemic liquidity (especially for dollar deposits). In order to overcome these weaknesses, an initial set of measures was introduced to restructure the sector by injecting more capital, promoting mergers and acquisitions, and creating incentives to the expansion of foreign banks. By 1997, Argentina had one of the strictest regulations in the region.

Brazil also took important steps to strengthen its banking system, but, as mentioned above, these measures were not prompted by the Tequila crisis itself. During the first three years of the successful stabilisation programme, the government promoted an in-depth restructuring of the private sector. Forty banks (of the 271 that existed in July 1994) were intervened by the Central Bank and a further 32 went through restructuring that resulted in mergers and acquisitions. In the process of restructuring, foreign banks were allowed to enter the economy. The number and participation of foreign banks increased significantly after 1995, representing a competitive challenge to Brazilian banks.

In addition to the restructuring of the banking sector, a series of complementary regulatory measures was also decreed in 1995. A deposit insurance fund was established, and capital requirements for establishing new banks were increased. Separately, new Central Bank regulations were adopted to promote accountability and avoid bailouts, by insuring that the shareholders of institutions sold or transferred were liable for any previous wrongdoing. Perhaps the most significant of these additional measures was the law giving the Central Bank authorisation to preventatively restructure financial institutions that were not meeting system requirements or were demonstrating financial problems. As a result, 205 financial institutions have been taken over or intervened by the Central Bank since the start of the Real Plan; some 25 percent of those institutions were banks. Overall, 92 percent of these financial institutions were closed, and 65 percent of the intervened banks were closed since mid-1994. An indicator of the effectiveness of the changes was the lack of a serious banking crisis in the face of the devaluation of 1999.

By 1997, Brazil already possessed one of the strictest regulations in the region (see Table 2). An additional effort has been made to comply with the recommendations implicit in the 1988 Basel Accord and its 1995 revisions. By the end of 1994, the Central Bank of Brazil introduced minimum capital requirements along the lines of the Basel Agreement. This led to an increase in the minimum capital requirements, narrower operational limits, and the introduction of the concept of comprehensive consolidated supervision of financial conglomerates, including branches and subsidiaries abroad and non-financial firms linked to bank conglomerates as well.

Mexico moved more slowly than Argentina and Brazil in dealing with its financial crisis. Indeed, Mexico has remained in constant banking difficulties since 1995 and is still involved in a costly process of restructuring its banking system. The government set up several programmes to help recapitalise and strengthen the banks, which involved the purchase of the banks' non-performing loans to clean up their balance sheets. In addition, a number of banks were intervened and later re-sold, leading to a dramatic increase of foreign participation in the banking sector (Graf, 1999). In December 1998, new financial legislation was approved by the Congress and then implemented. Chief among the changes were: (i) a new deposit insurance system, which ended the *de facto* unlimited deposit insurance that existed previously and increased the oversight of the deposit-insurance agency; (ii) stricter accounting standards, which increased the transparency of credit operations both for supervisors and the public, imposed stricter standards for handling past-due loans, and substantially increased loan-loss provisions; (iii) a series of measures to improve lending practices and new laws on credit transactions, aimed to speed up the process of foreclosing on assets and allow for a wider range of property to be used as collateral, and (iv) stricter rules on capital quality (EIU, 2001).

In addition, to reduce possible future exchange rate mismatching, the Bank of Mexico established stricter ceilings on foreign currency liabilities (according to banks' capital) and imposed compulsory liquidity coefficients in foreign currency according to both the size and the maturity of these liabilities (Yacamán, 2001). Banking activity declined from 1994 to 1996 (as a percentage of GDP); only in 1996 overall lending started growing again, whereas lending to the private sector only began to rise in 2000.

3 Macroeconomic Adjustment, Changes in Expectations and the Banking Sector in the Second Half of the 1990s

By 1997-98, all four economies had made profound changes towards stricter regulation and supervision. Indeed, as Studart and Stallings (2002) indicate, by 1997, regulation and supervision in the four Latin American economies were significantly stricter than that of the United States (see Table 2). The processes of restructuring and privatisation of the banking sector also led to a much more internationalised and a slightly more concentrated banking sector (see appendix Table A1 and A2).

For many (e.g. World Bank, 2002), these new characteristics of the banking sector in Latin America were indications of greater competition and efficiency – which could lead to a higher supply of credit at lower spreads – and stability. This view proved over-optimistic.

Increasing External Financial Dependencies and Changes in Expectations in the Banking Sector

While regulation became stricter, optimism about Latin America of the early 1990s declined – as is reflected in both key financial flows and prices of Latin American assets (see appendix Figure A1). The changes in expectations were highly influenced by the deterioration of economic fundamentals in the region – deeply associated with inconsistencies created by the policy regimes adopted in the early 1990s. Indeed, using excessive capital inflows and trade opening as tools for growth and stabilisation of prices had important costs, as is well known by now.

Long-term expectations, and thus investment, tended to be highly depressed in the second half of the 1990s, as a result of the macroeconomic uncertainties and competitive pressure put on investors. In addition, consumer credit in the region is highly rationed, due to the characteristics of the domestic financial structure mentioned below. In contrast with investment, consumption responds rapidly to changes in the supply of credit.

Not surprisingly, thus, in most of the economies in the region, the growth dynamics in the 1990s were highly associated with consumption expansion (Chile again being one of the very few exceptions) and with deterioration of the current account – despite the growth of exports.[8] External imbalances increased, resulting in greater external financial dependency. Output and exports were growing at a pace that was lower than needed to solve the created macroeconomic imbalances.

As external dependency grew, so did the constraints on domestic policy. First, to maintain the attractiveness for international investors and domestic borrowers, monetary policy in many countries aimed to keep interest differentials high, whereas fiscal discipline was used as a tool for adding credibility to the stability of exchange rate regimes.[9] Thus, attracting capital flows became a crusade of the policy package, and not only of exchange rate policy.

Second, high levels of interest rates made the process of fiscal adjustment difficult and led to loss of international competitiveness of domestic corporations. It also led to volatile, low levels of economic activity (appendix Figure A2), and volatile changes in unemployment, that had an upward trend in Brazil and Chile. Given the loan structure in most Latin American banking systems, changes in unemployment are likely to affect the levels of past due loans. The level of unemployment is likely to directly affect banks' default rates, but the mere volatility of unemployment rates tends to increase the "perceived default risk" (defined as the expected variance of the levels

---

[8] The problem lies in the rapid increase of the income elasticity of imports (Table 1, last column) caused by abrupt trade liberalisation and exchange rate misalignments.

[9] Of course, fiscal discipline was also required for assuring sustainable growth of aggregate demand and supply in a context of low inflation.

of past due loans), leading to a more conservative approach of the banking sector.

Third, with increased international integration of domestic financial markets and the widening of dollar-denominated liabilities and assets in a significant numbers of countries, the process of policy-induced dollarisation was a fact. The case of Argentina was perhaps the most dramatic, as the currency board significantly reduced banks' perceived exchange rate risks and stimulated them to expand their dollar-denominated loans (more on this below).

Thus, as mentioned above, stricter regulation and supervision, in the context of deteriorating macroeconomic fundamentals and expectations, directly affected the expectations and the behaviour of the banking sector – and therefore its performance in the second half of the 1990s.

Argentina

In Argentina total lending and lending to the private sector had increased in dollar terms until 1998, but this trend has reversed from 1999 onwards (Figure 3a). Figure 3b indicates an even more worrisome aspect of the performance of the banking sector: total lending to the private sector as a percentage of GDP stagnated at around 20 percent, which is very low. In addition, even though the intermediation spreads were relatively low, lending interest rates remained very high (between 5 and 12 percent) (Figure 3c) – despite the increase in competition, due to the entry of foreign banks and the openness of the banking sector, and the decline of past due loans from 1995 onwards (Figure 3d).

The currency mismatches of the Argentine banking sector, which were already high in 1994-95, continued to rise (Figure 3d).[10] The high exchange rate exposure was at the heart of the bank crisis that happened after the 2002 devaluation of the Argentine peso. It is directly related to the initial success of the currency board and reflects the confidence of both public and bankers in the currency board. It also seems to be related to the increasing share of foreign banks in total assets of the sector. After the Brazilian real devaluation

---

[10] As measured by the relation between deposits plus other liabilities in US dollars and total assets, the level of foreign currency exposure has been increasing since the early 1990s, culminating in ratios that are over 50% in 2001 (Figure 3d).

Figure 3 Financial Indicators for Argentina

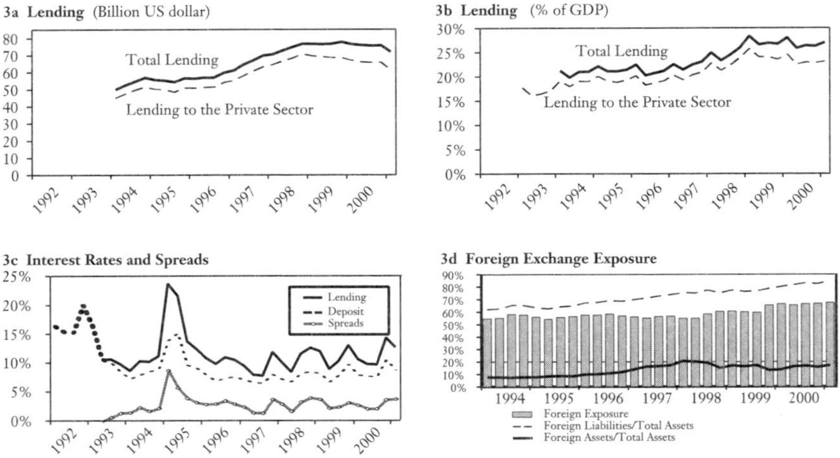

Source: IMF CD-ROM (September 2001).

in January 1999, depositors increasingly turned this confidence into fear of possible devaluations and a search for "exchange rate hedging". As dollar-denominated deposits increased, domestic banks increasingly preferred to lend in dollar in order to maintain exchange rate mismatches under control.

In sum, regulation and supervision in Argentina should have improved the banking sector stability, and the sector has definitively become more efficient after 1994-95. However, the macroeconomic environment has delayed the recovery of banking activity and led to building exchange rate risks and default risks. In this context, the bank crisis that followed the devaluation of the peso was thus highly predictable (see Studart, 2002).

Brazil

The performance of the banking sector of Brazil deteriorated after the Asian crisis. First of all, after the rapid growth of lending in the first half of the 1990s, lending to the private sector almost stagnated from 1997 onwards, and began to shrink in 2000 (see Figures 4a and 4b).

As regards the costs of borrowing, the picture is even more worrisome. Spreads in the Brazilian banking sector were outrageously large before 1994. From 1999 onwards, the Brazilian

Central Bank introduced several measures to reduce these spreads, including a significant decline in reserve requirements, reduction of taxation on bank operations and an increase of the disclosure of interest rates charged by different banks.

In addition to these measures, the Central Bank of Brazil expected that increased participation of foreign banks and stronger competition would further reduce the interest rates.[11] From 1995 onwards, spreads have been reduced significantly (Figure 4c). However, they seem to have stagnated at very high levels (around 30 percent) and recent Central Bank of Brazil reports indicate that they are rising slightly again.

The reasons behind these high spreads are interrelated: the remaining macroeconomic uncertainty and the high levels of past due loans. Indeed, past due loans remained more than 10 percent of total loans of the banking sector, despite the decline of past due loans since 1999 (mainly due to the brief recovery of the economy in the end of 1999 and 2000).

Figure 4 Financial Indicators for Brazil

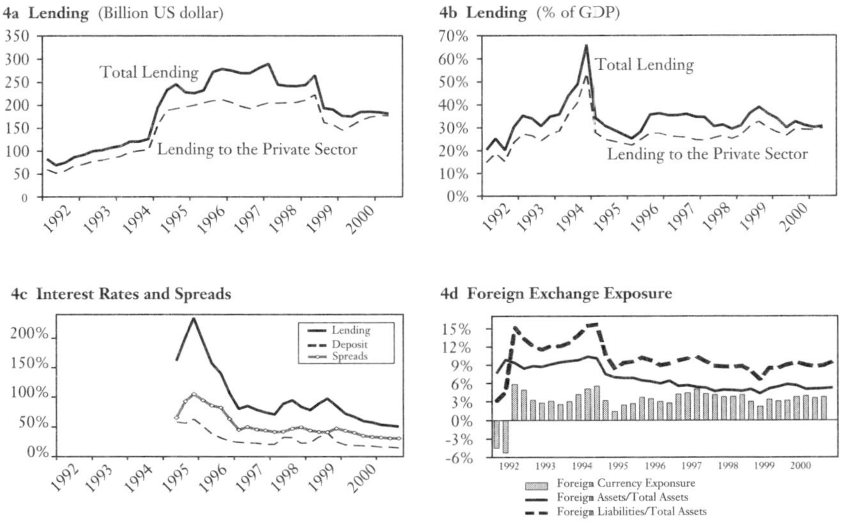

Source: IMF CD-ROM (September 2001).

[11] For a thorough analysis of the main determinants of spreads in Brazil and the policies introduced to reduce them, see BCB (2000).

Figure 5 Financial Indicators for Mexico

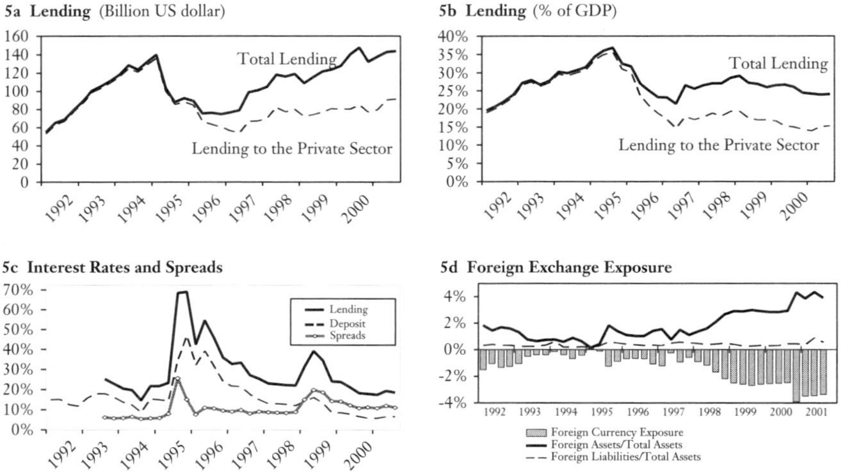

Source: IMF CD-ROM (September 2001).

Mexico

The case of Mexico is, in some aspects, similar to that of Brazil. As mentioned before, after the Tequila crisis, the domestic banking sector has been involved in a costly process of restructuring. Despite the good growth performance from 1996 onwards, lending to the private sector in US dollars declined significantly from 1994 to 1997 (Figure 5a). In addition, from 1994 onwards, there was not only a substantial decline in lending to the private sector as percentage of GDP, but also this percentage stagnated at very low levels (less than 20 percent) until recently (Figure 5b).

As regards the cost of borrowing (Figure 5c), even though the spreads are still very high (around 12 percent) they have declined substantially from 1995 onwards. But the fact is that, despite all the restructuring and increased competition (coming especially from the entry of new foreign banks), spreads remain high and show no clear tendency to decrease since 1999.

At first sight, this seems paradoxical given the rapid decline of past due loans from 1998 onwards. But this paradox vanishes once one takes into consideration that the Mexican economy is again facing a deterioration of its growth performance.

Chile: An Exception?

Out of the four cases, Chile seems to have performed best in the 1990s. As explained above, this had to do with the fact that its macroeconomic performance was barely affected by the Tequila crisis, and that the Chilean banking system had already gone through major changes in supervision, regulation, and structure.

Total lending and lending to the private sector have increased almost steadily from 1991 onwards, both in dollar terms and as a percentage of GDP. Private lending almost equals total lending and increased from US$15 billion in 1993 to around US$40 billion in 2000 (Figure 6a). Figure 6c shows a significant reduction of lending rates, while the spreads remain impressively stableuntil the end of 1998, increasing slightly after 2000.

Despite this good performance in the 1990s, Chile is also suffering from credit stagnation from 1999 onwards (Figure 6a). Furthermore, even though the default rates are still remarkably low, they are rising as a result of increasing unemployment.

Figure 6 Financial Indicators for Chile

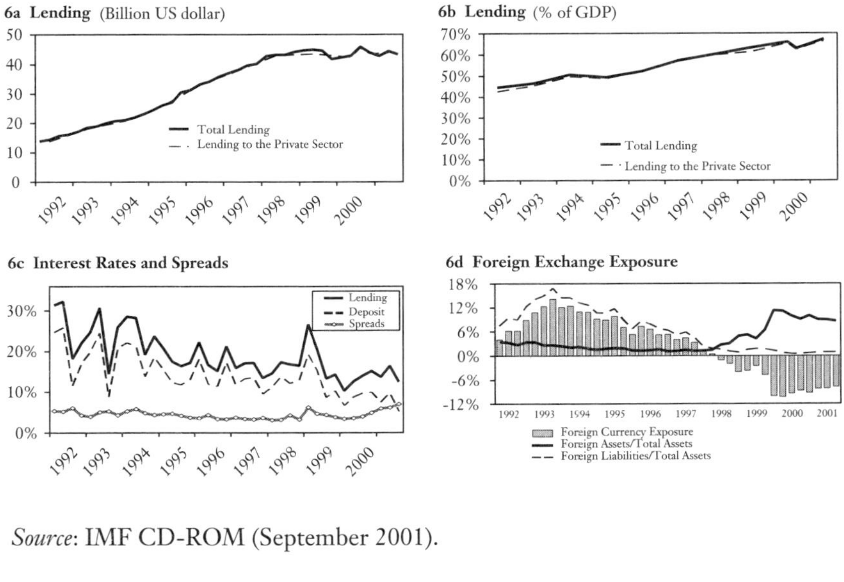

Source: IMF CD-ROM (September 2001).

4 Concluding Remarks

Banks are in the business of intermediating deposits and other types of liabilities to fund their assets – which in the case of most Latin American economies are composed of loans to the private sector, very few private bonds and government bonds. As intermediaries, they manage the risks related to the potential changes in the quality of their assets and the maturity and currency mismatches implicit in the process of intermediation.

Changes in bankers' expectations and in the structure of their liabilities tend to change their preferences in terms of the maturities and composition of their assets – and there is a good deal of evidence that banking activity is highly pro-cyclical. Changes in the macroeconomic environment affect both potential access to liquidity and the structure of bank liabilities. Finally, financial regulation sets the limits of banks' risk-taking behaviour – which is directly related to the maturity and exchange rate mismatches between their assets and liabilities.

The story of the Latin American banking sector in the 1990s can certainly be explained by the set of variables described above. The significant surge of capital flows to developing countries in the first half of the 1990s was facilitated by capital account liberalisation and domestic financial liberalisation. This surge of capital flows reduced the external constraints to macroeconomic expansion and permitted the adoption of different types of successful price stabilisation programmes, often anchored on more-or-less rigid exchange rate regimes and trade opening. The improvement of growth performance and the achievement of price stability created a self-fulfilling process of rising expectations.

This rise of expectations, stimulated by optimism of international markets and by economic recovery (and often the loss of inflationary gains), also affected the behaviour of domestic banks. In the four economies under analysis, similar processes of credit expansion took place. Credit expansion combined with high lending interest rates, poor macroeconomic performance (particularly if associated with high and increasing unemployment rates) and poor regulation and supervision are a recipe for bank crises – Argentina, Brazil and Mexico demonstrated the recipe works well.

The Tequila crisis exacerbated the problems that were present previously in the banking sectors of Argentina, Brazil and Mexico, and led to deep economic contraction, and thus higher unemployment and higher levels of past due loans in Mexico, forced abrupt rises in interest rates in Argentina, Brazil and Mexico and caused significant devaluations in Mexico. The crisis was the last straw in a process of mounting financial instability leading to a banking crisis.

The changes in regulation and supervision that followed the Tequila crisis were a response to the problems of stability faced by the bank sector in Latin America after 1994-95. They increased the "potential stability", but to be effective these changes also required a certain stability of macroeconomic variables that directly affect intermediation risks: exchange rate, interest rates and economic growth. The stricter regulatory setting was implemented in a context of a deteriorating macroeconomic environment, which was deeply associated with the volatility of capital flows in 1997-98. As a consequence, domestic banks increasingly assumed defensive strategies as their capacity and willingness to expand credit were significantly reduced. This seems to explain partly the expansion of treasury activities (acquisition of short-term highly paid government bonds), and the credit stagnation that is plaguing these economies – including Chile.

In addition, the stricter regulation and supervision simply could not avoid the bank crisis in Argentina. This has to do again with the fact that financial regulation and supervision often serve as mechanisms to reduce excessive risk-taking by banks – in a context where the variables that determined such risks fluctuate within a narrow band. In the Argentinean case, whereas the economic recession and the high interest rates led to a rise in past-due loans (the default risk) the mere possibility of collapse of its exchange rate regime led to a simultaneous rapid increase of the liquidity risk (dollar deposit drain) and the market risk. When the convertibility collapsed, the process of financial instability that was mounting turned into a bank (solvency) crisis.

Like the Tequila crisis, the Argentinean crisis has once again sounded wake-up calls to Latin America. But this time it indicates the limits of regulation and supervision to prevent crises in a context of highly unstable macroeconomic settings and expectations.

References

Ahumada, A. and J. Marshall (2001), "The Banking Industry in Chile: Competition, Consolidation and Systemic Stability", BIS Papers No. 4, Basel.

Barajas Estrada, Adolfo and Roberto Steiner (2002), "Credit Stagnation in Latin America", IMF Working Paper No. 02/53, Washington D.C.

Barth, J. R., G. Caprio Jr., and R. Levine (2001a), "The Regulation and Supervision of Banks around the World: A New Data Base", Policy Research Working Paper Series, No. 2588, World Bank, Washington D.C.

—— (2001b), "Bank Regulation and Supervision: What Works Best", Policy Research Working Paper Series, No. 2725, World Bank, Washington D.C.

Banco Central do Brasil (BCB) (2000). "Juros e Spreads: avaliação de um ano do programa", Brasilia.

Bank of International Settlements (BIS) (2000), *Cycles and the Financial System*, Annual Report, Basel.

—— (2001),"The Banking Industry in the Emerging Market Economies: Competition, Consolidation and Systemic Stability", BIS Papers No. 4, Basel.

Budnevich, C. (2000), "El sistema financiero chileno y su institucionalidad regulatoria: las políticas bancarias en los noventa", In: O. Muñoz (ed.), *El estado y el sector privado: construyendo una nueva economía en los años 90*, FLACSO/Dolmen, Santiago de Chile.

Burki, S.J. and G. Perry (1998), *Beyond the Washington Consensus: Institutions Matter*, World Bank, Washington D.C.

Economist Intelligence Unit (EIU) (2001), *Country Finance: Mexico*, April.

Fornari, F. and A. Levy (1999), "Global Liquidity in the 1990s: Geographical and Long Run Determinants", BIS Conference Papers No. 8, Basel.

Graf, P. (1999), "Policy Responses to the Banking Crisis in Mexico", BIS Policy Papers No. 6, Basel.

Held, G. and L.F. Jiménez (2001), "Liberalización financiera, crisis y reforma del sistema bancario chileno: 1974-1999", In: R.Ffrench-Davis and B. Stallings (eds.), *Reformas, crecimiento y políticas sociales en Chile desde 1973*, CEPAL/LOM, Santiago de Chile.

Kaminsky, G. and C. Reinhart (1999), "The Twin Crises: The Causes of Banking and Balance of Payments Problems", In: *American Economic Review*, Vol. 89, No. 3.

Litan, R., P. Masson and M. Pomerleano (eds.) (2001), *Open Doors: Foreign Participation in Financial Systems in Developing Countries*, Brookings Institution, Washington D.C.

Livacic, E. and S. Sáez (2000), *La supervisión Bancaria en América Latina en los Noventa*, Serie Temas de Coyuntura No. 10, ECLAC, Santiago de Chile.

McQuerry, E. (1999), "The Banking Sector Rescue in Mexico", In: *Federal Reserve Bank of Atlanta Economic Review*, Atlanta, Third Quarter.

Morley, S., R. Machado and S. Pettinato (1999). *Indexes of structural reforms in Latin America*, Serie Reformas Economicas No. 12, ECLAC, Santiago de Chile.

O'Dogherty, P. and M. Schwartz (2001), "Prudential Regulation of Foreign Exchange: The Mexican Experience", BIS Papers No. 1, Basel.

Stallings, B. and W. Peres (2000), *Growth, Employment, and Equity: The Impact of the Economic Reforms in Latin America and the Caribbean*, Brookings Institution, Washington D.C.

Stallings, B. and R. Studart (2002), *Financial Regulation and Supervision in Emerging Markets: The Experience of Latin America since the Tequila Crisis*, Series Desarrollo Económico, ECLAC, Santiago de Chile.

Studart, R. (2001a). "The Banking System and Credit in Argentina, Brazil, Chile and Mexico: the Challenges of Stability and Growth", Paper presented at the conference on "Domestic Finance and Global Capital in Latin America" organised by the Latin America Research Group Research Department, Federal Reserve Bank of Atlanta, Miami, Florida, November 1 and 2.

—— (2001b). "Dollarization: An Intellectual Fad or a Deep Insight?", In: *Journal of Post Keynesian Economics*, Vol. 23, No.4, pp. 639-662.

Studart, R. and J. Hermann (2001), "Sistemas financeiros no Mercosul: perspectivas a partir das reformas dos anos 1990", Texto para Discussão No. 799, IPEA, Brasilia.

Yacamán, J.M. (2001), "Competition and Consolidation in the Mexican Banking Industry after the 1995 Crisis", BIS Papers No. 4, Basel.

World Bank (2002), *World Development Report 2002*, World Bank, Washington D.C.

Appendix

Table A1 Indicators of Concentration in the Banking Sector
(share in total deposits)

	1994				2000			
	Number of Banks	Largest 3 Banks	Largest 10 Banks	HH Index	Number of Banks	Largest 3 Banks	Largest 10 Banks	HH Index
Latin America								
Argentina	206	39.1	73.1	756.9	113	39.8	80.7	865.7
Brazil	245	49.9	78.8	1220.9	193	55.2	85.6	1278.6
Chile	37	39.5	79.1	830.4	29	39.5	82.0	857.9
México	36	48.3	80.8	1005.4	23	56.3	94.5	1360.5
Venezuela	43	43.9	78.6	979.2	42	46.7	75.7	923.1
Asia								
Republic of Korea	30	52.8	86.9	1263.6	13	43.5	77.7	899.7
Malaysia	25	44.7	78.3	918.9	10	43.4	82.2	1005.1
Philippines	41	39.0	80.3	819.7	27	39.6	73.3	789.9
Thailand	15	47.5	83.5	1031.7	13	41.7	79.4	854.4
Central Europe								
Czech Republic	55	72.0	97.0	2101.5	42	69.7	90.3	1757.8
Hungary	40	57.9	84.7	1578.8	39	51.5	80.7	1241.8
Poland	82	52.8	86.7	1263.6	77	43.5	77.7	899.7
Turkey	72	40.7	79.1	957.2	79	35.9	72.0	710.2

Source: IMF (2001:11).

Table A2 Foreign Bank Assets as Share of Total Bank Assets
(percentages)

	1994	1999	2000
Latin America			
Argentina	17.9	48.6	49
Brazil	8.4	16.8	23
Chile	16.3	53.6	54
Colombia	6.2	17.8	26
Mexico	1.0	18.8	24
Peru	6.7	33.4	40
Venezuela	0.3	41.9	42
Central Europe			
Czech Republic	5.8	49.3	66
Hungary	19.8	56.6	62
Poland	2.1	52.8	70
Turkey	2.7	1.7	n.a.
Asia			
Korea	0.8	4.3	3
Malaysia	6.8	11.5	18
Thailand	0.5	5.6	12

Source: IMF (2000: 153) for 1994 and 1999; BIS (2001: 25) for 2000.

Figure A1 Some Indicators of Changes in Expectations Towards Latin America in the 1990s

Latin America: Issues of Bonds in the International Markets
(US$ billion; polynomial trend line)

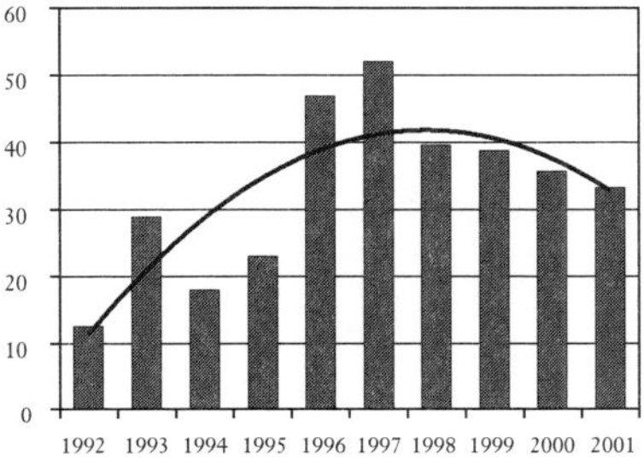

Source: Elaborated by the author based on data from International Financial Statistics (IMF).

Latin America: Issues of ADRs
(US$ billion, trend line)

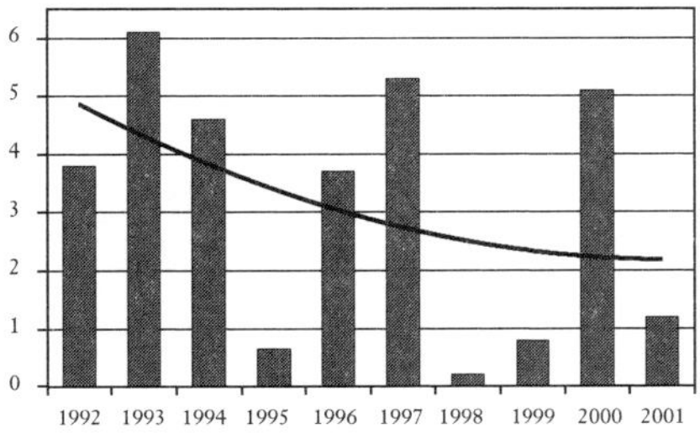

Source: Elaborated by the author based on data from International Financial Statistics (IMF).

Latin America: Stock Exchange Index (31/1/92=100; trend line)

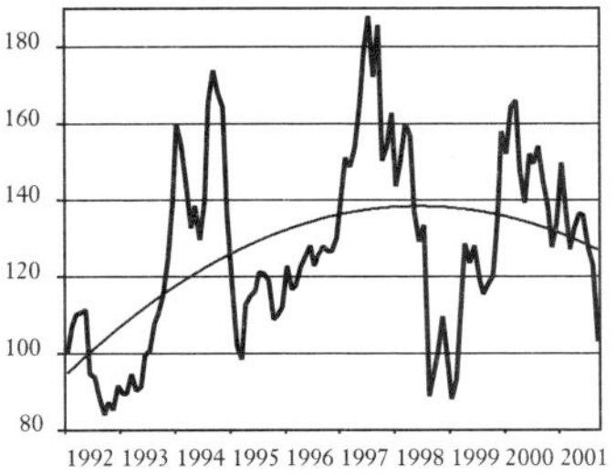

Source: Elaborated by the author based on data from IMF, Emerging Markets Division.

Latin America: Euro-bond Spreads
(90 days average; Basis points over US Treasury bond rates; linear trend line)

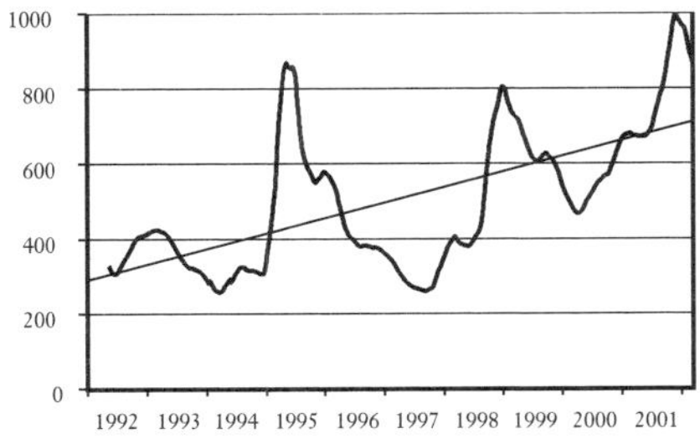

Source: Elaborated by the author based on data from JP Morgan.

Figure A2 Growth Volatility after the Tequila Crisis
(GDP growth rates)

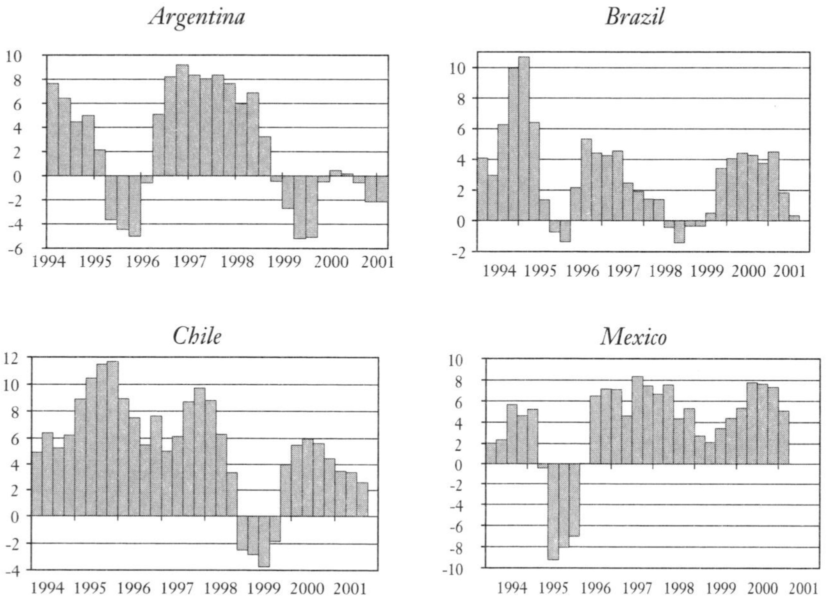

Source: ECLAC.

2

Comment on Rogério Studart

Jürgen Stark

The chapter by Rogério Studart focuses on the crucial issue of how to achieve stability and growth. To put it differently: what are the preconditions for sustainable non-inflationary growth? In this regard, let me quote a famous saying of a former German economics and finance minister, who once said: "Stability is not everything, but without stability everything is nothing". This saying was originally about price stability. However, it also applies to financial stability and macroeconomic stability and in particular to developments in Latin American countries over the past few years.

By financial stability I mean sound financial institutions and the ability of markets to function well. Rogério Studart makes an important contribution to the issue of financial stability. His analysis of the banking sector of four Latin American countries sheds light on crucial topics. He thoroughly scrutinises the close links between regulation and supervision of the banking sector, changing expectations and financial cycles and macroeconomic performance. To a large degree, I share his conclusions. In particular, I agree that "the Argentine crisis ... indicates the limits of regulation and supervision to prevent crises in a context of highly unstable macroeconomic settings and expectations".

Rogério Studart focuses on banking regulation and supervision, and in this area he has done an excellent job. However, something important is missing: the crucial role of macroeconomic stability and the related policies. Moreover, understanding the links between financial stability and macroeconomic stability is imperative for understanding developments in Latin America. In this regard – and that is my first comment – it is important to avoid any misunderstanding. Rogério Studart talks about a trade-off with respect to stability and growth. However, one should be clear on that point. According to the "orthodox" view, financial stability and price stability are the platforms to maximise economic growth. Policies directed at exploiting short-term trade-offs between price stability and economic activity and growth, risk contributing to instability – or unsustainable inflationary growth – over longer horizons.

My second comment will be on macroeconomic policy and particularly on exchange rate policy and the liberalisation of capital movements. Argentina is a striking example in this respect. In just over a decade the country has managed to lurch from one disaster to the next. Now the economic and social situation is most precarious.

Because Argentina had one of the most strictly regulated financial sectors in the region since 1997 – as Rogério Studart correctly mentions – other policy areas are responsible for the mess, primarily exchange rate policy. The decision in 1991 to peg the peso to the US dollar was correct at that time. After years of hyperinflation, the introduction of the currency board – accompanied by an IMF-supported programme – was a successful and decisive element in the Argentinean disinflation strategy. However, while the US dollar-based currency board maximised the credibility of the commitment to price stability in the short run, it also was responsible for Argentina's competitiveness problem. While economic and political developments worsened, Argentina was increasingly caught in a vicious circle that became inconsistent with the currency board. Following the rise of the dollar since 1997-98 and the devaluation of the Brazilian real in 1999, the peso became overvalued, resulting in protracted high current account deficits, substantial external borrowing needs and downward pressure on growth. At the same time, the priority of monetary policy to defend the exchange rate also hampered domestic growth. Briefly said, the currency board played a central role in both the initial success and ultimate collapse of Argentina's stabilisation and reform efforts. In the end, Argentina became a textbook case for problematic exchange rate fixing.

Another – related – problem is that Argentina followed an unsustainable fiscal policy in the context of a currency board system. A "hard peg" solution requires a sound fiscal policy and a high degree of flexibility of the economy and particularly in the labour market. Although fiscal policy had started off in the right direction, the programme was far from being successful. The fiscal regime tying the federal government and the provincial governments together remained full of loopholes. The lack of a sound fiscal framework hindered credibility and contributed to the build-up of an unsustainable foreign debt burden. Finally, a policy based on illusions ended up by defaulting against creditors.

Only in a very narrow view can the crisis in Argentina be regarded as a special case, because Argentina was the first country with a "hard peg" exchange rate system to abolish this regime under market pressure, in particular stemming from inside the country. From a broader standpoint, however, Argentina is only another example of an emerging market economy formerly adhering to a pegged exchange rate system that eventually became embroiled in a currency, debt and banking crisis. Experience has shown that fixed exchange rates may render economies whose capital markets are opening up more crisis-prone. Pegged exchange rates increase the risk of the national currency being overvalued. Moreover, fixed rates entail the risk of excessive foreign-currency debt, since under such conditions cheaper foreign loans are often not hedged against exchange rate losses. That, however, ultimately heightens the risk of a crisis. As a consequence of the most recent crises, there has been a growing trend towards choosing flexible exchange rate regimes.

Of course, financial crises are not unique to current financial systems; history is replete with banking and currency crises. The increasing integration of global financial markets in the past two decades, however, appears to have introduced some new elements and concerns. Under conditions of unrestricted capital flows, pegged exchange rate systems became increasingly crisis-prone. Admittedly, fixed exchange rate systems are viable when certain demanding requirements are met. But in the real world of policy slippages and protracted structural problems, we have to accept that these requirements will not be met in the long run. Sooner or later, therefore, the sustainability of a pegged exchange rate system will be undermined. The lesson to be learned from exchange rate regimes is that a country that has given priority to pegged rates must figure out whether or not it can keep its internal flexibility sufficiently high to enable it to make all the necessary adjustments. In particular, with priority given to fixed rates, monetary policy has to be completely subordinated to the exchange rate target. Moreover, there is not much room for fiscal policy. It has to be conducted in a stabilityoriented manner in order to maintain domestic and external confidence. Thus, a stable exchange rate is only sustainable if the corresponding fundamentals are adequately streamlined. A pegged currency alone cannot guarantee lasting market confidence.

Mexico was the first emerging market economy to go through this experience, followed by East Asian economies, Brazil, Argentina and other countries. This raises the question of why Chile, the fourth country Rogério Studart mentions, was different. This brings me to my third comment. For over a decade, this country also had a fixed exchange rate system – or to be more precise: an exchange rate band – and was successful in resisting contagion from the Mexican and East Asian crises. Of course, as we all know, capital controls constitute the difference. Because Chilean policymakers were wary of allowing large capital inflows that could eventually reverse themselves violently, they imposed capital controls on these inflows. By limiting in part the openness of the capital account, some degree of control on the exchange rate front was possible while at the same time monetary policy could be conducted with some independence. Evidence of their effectiveness is mixed. Total capital inflows were not substantially abated. Also, it was not possible to prevent a trend appreciation of over 30 percent between 1990 and 1997. More important, there has not been an appraisal of the opportunity cost of these controls given by lost investment.

The example of Chile should not give rise to misinterpretations. On the road towards capital account liberalisation, capital controls may at best act as a "temporary substitute" for still-underdeveloped supervisory and risk management systems. However, it still does not make sense to call for a reversal of the liberalisation of capital transactions. In principle, the fact that the free movement of capital contributes to the optimum allocation of resources is not open to question. But that must not imply liberalisation at all costs. More importantly, there is a clear need for an orderly process of liberalisation. Greater emphasis should be put on appropriately sequencing the process of liberalisation. Priority should be given to establishing a domestic financial market and the commensurate institutions and supervisory bodies. In the case of long-term capital flows, and especially direct investment, there is less danger of them being withdrawn in the event of economic difficulties. Therefore, liberalisation should start in this area. Opening up the market to short-term capital flows is something which should be handled with care. This should be done more towards the end of the liberalisation process.

Recent financial crises prove that, where capital is highly mobile, the effects of bad economic policy and an insufficient framework can be much more serious now than was the case a decade ago. Therefore, crisis prevention through intensified bilateral and multilateral IMF surveillance is of prime importance. In particular, deficiencies in member countries' economic policies must be identified at an early stage. However, further-reaching IMF financial support for the process of liberalisation is neither justifiable nor necessary. In particular, the IMF should not unduly give incentives for the rash liberalisation of capital movements and later on take action to "bail out" those countries. It appears that in some cases the IMF pushed countries to speed up the process of capital account liberalisation and stood ready to bail out the country in the case of a crisis, thereby creating moral hazard. The IMF has drawn conclusions from recent crises and now requires an adequate financial supervisory structure before promoting the liberalisation of capital flows.

The crises in Argentina, Mexico and other emerging market economies are examples of the disastrous consequences the instability of macroeconomic policy has had for financial stability. Conversely, banking crises have often preceded currency crises, for instance in the Scandinavian countries or recently in Turkey. In effect, crises of all types have often had common origins: the build-up of unsustainable economic imbalances and misalignments in asset prices or exchange rates, often in a context of financial sector distortions and structural rigidities. Of course, not all corrections of imbalances involve a crisis. Whether they do or not depends, apart from the magnitude of the imbalances themselves, on the credibility of policy to correct the imbalances and on the robustness of the country's financial system.

In my fourth and last comment, I will argue that, as recent financial crises demonstrate, it is all about policy. This is particularly true in the case of Argentina, where the lack of political leadership and of a broad consensus regarding stability and sound public finances is the fundamental obstacle to reform. In a broader context, however, this is true of all emerging market economies, which urgently need strong domestic institutions. Strong domestic institutions are of utmost importance for financial stability and development. This includes, above all, an independent central bank committed to price stability, an independent judiciary and the rule of law, a government sector that – apart from following a truly sound fiscal policy – is accountable and transparent, and last but not least efficient banking supervision. Admittedly, external surveillance by the IMF plays an important role in crisis prevention and resolution. However, the basic principle that "stability begins at home" should be taken to heart by emerging market economies (and the IMF). In this respect, Martin Feldstein was right when he recently wrote that "Argentina doesn't need the IMF".[1]

Financial stability is an important precondition for a sound economy. The significance of financial stability could particularly be demonstrated against examples of financial instability, as the social and economic tragedy in Argentina proves. However, a lesson to be learnt from developments in Argentina includes that – to end with a statement by Rogério Studart with which I fully agree – "improvements in regulation and supervision were necessary, but not sufficient to mitigate the instability problem".

---

1 Feldstein, M., "Breaking the Habit: Argentina Doesn't Need the IMF", In: *Wall Street Journal Europe*, May 29th, 2002.

3

Fiscal Discipline in Emerging Market Countries: How to Go About It?

Charles Wyplosz

The collapse of Argentina's currency board has been largely blamed on fiscal indiscipline at the federal and mostly provincial levels. For example, while the crisis was gathering strength in the Spring of 2001, the IMF Managing Director stated unambiguously that the problem's origin was to be found in the fiscal deficit, not the currency overvaluation:

> "Argentina's programme aims at strengthening confidence through fiscal consolidation to achieve the programme's targets for 2001 and fiscal balance by 2005, while promoting the recovery of investment and output through fiscal incentives and regulatory changes. Firm implementation of the programme is needed to initiate a virtuous circle of stronger public finances, lower interest rates, and a recovery of economic activity. In this regard, it is essential that tax compliance be improved and that expenditures be contained, in accordance with the commitments under the federal pact of December 2000.
>
> "Argentina's convertibility regime, the independence of the central bank, and the high capital and liquidity defenses of the banking system are important pillars of the country's economic strategy and have been vital in helping withstand turbulent international financial conditions in recent years. The IMF therefore welcomes the authorities' reaffirmation of their commitment to these policies."
>
> Horst Köhler, *IMF News Brief*, No. 01/44, May 21, 2001.

At the same time, Dornbusch articulated a similar view:

> "A devaluation strategy must be considered perilous; a government that goes that way is likely to take Argentina back to 1990 but with this extra; the country will also be totally bankrupt. Not a good policy idea! [The] central issue of Argentina is the bankruptcy of the government."
>
> Rudi Dornbusch, *World Economic Trends*, No. 2, April, 2001.

However, his interpretation is not fully shared. Stiglitz (2002), for instance, writes:

> "Did those large deficits, corruption and public mismanagement cause the Argentine crisis? Many American economists suggest that the crisis would have been averted had Argentina followed the advice of the International Monetary Fund (IMF) religiously, especially by cutting back on expenditures (including at the provincial level) more ruthlessly. Many Latin Americans, however, think that the full IMF plan would have led to an even worse crisis – sooner. I think it is the Latins who are right."
>
> Joseph Stiglitz, "Argentina, Shortchanged: Why the Nation That Followed the Rules Fell to Pieces," In: *The Washington Post*, May 12, 2002.

Why do these distinguished observers, like much of the profession, disagree so sharply on such a basic question? The general public would be shocked to find out that the famously-dissenting profession of economists cannot decide whether the peso was overvalued or not, and whether Argentina's public finances were lethally off-balance. More shocking even is the apparent inconsistency of as clear-headed a macroeconomist as Stanley Fischer, who states two views in the same text, first:

> "The growth performance was based too much on large fiscal deficits, especially as the decade progressed. The deficit of the federal government averaged 1 percent of GDP in the first half of the 1990s and 3 percent in the second half."

and then:

"The question that has to be asked at this time of recession is whether Argentina really needs fiscal adjustment. The obvious concern is that such an adjustment would only impede the recovery of the economy. After all, neither public debt (at around 50 percent of GDP) nor the fiscal deficit (at around 2.5 percent of GDP) are particularly high by international standards – indeed both would satisfy the Maastricht criteria, as would its inflation performance. The problem is that with the current level of spreads on Argentine bonds, the debt dynamics are on an escalating path."

Remarks by Stanley Fischer at the Argentine Bankers Association Meeting, Buenos Aires, June 25, 2001.

Fischer would not use technical jargon, but he is describing a self-fulfilling crisis. The fiscal position was perfectly sound and would have remained perfectly safe if markets had not started to expect a crisis. The peso overvaluation prompted fears of a devaluation, which led to high interest rates. The combination of currency overvaluation and high interest rates, the classic hallmark of an excessively tight monetary policy, provoked a deepening recession. The recession resulted in declining tax revenues and a budget deficit, especially in the provinces, as Figure 1 illustrates. The rational perception that the fiscal situation was unsustainable led to increasing concerns about the currency board survival, hence higher interest rates and a worsening vicious circle that could only break out in a full-blown crisis.

Figure 1 Budget Balance and GDP Growth: Argentina 1993-2001

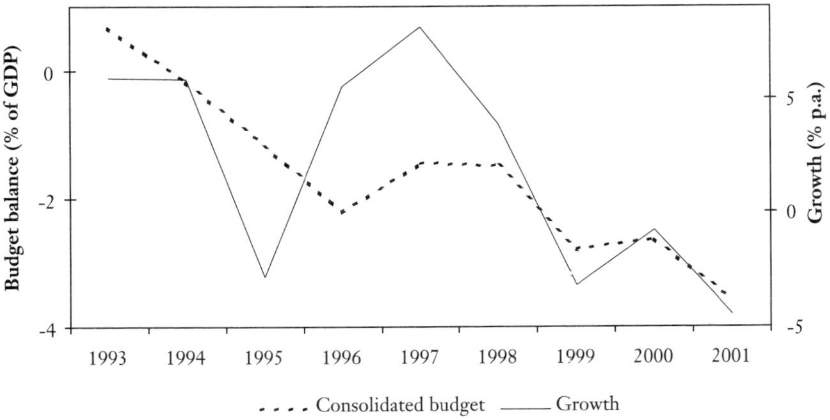

Source: Ministry of Economy, Argentina.

This description seems to vindicate both opposite views, but with the subtle nuance inherent to self-fulfilling processes. Had Argentina been growing, the budget would not have been in deficit, or the deficit would have been small enough to be accompanied by a declining debt-to-GDP ratio. The slowdown was partly due to worsening international conditions, partly to an overvalued peso. The refusal of the Argentine authorities to prepare an exit from the straitjacket of the currency board – while the economic situation was good – is the fundamental source of the crisis. It left the Argentine economy vulnerable to adverse national or international conditions. While a crisis was therefore unavoidable, its timing remained to be determined by some event dramatic enough to unleash a pressure commensurate with the hardness of the exchange rate regime. It turned out that the (mild) deterioration of public finances played this role.

Thus the real puzzle is why the budget deficit, well below levels which are considered lenient elsewhere, unleashed one of the worst crises of the past several decades. Three reasons come to mind.

First, without any monetary policy left, fiscal policy had to take up all of the burden of dealing with shocks. Worse, with monetary policy structurally excessively tight – due to peso overvaluation – fiscal policy became structurally lax. The deficit, which has been widening, would have had to widen further, with uncertain results.

Second, the fiscal record of the Argentine authorities is chequered with spectacular failures. A lack of discipline had long characterised monetary policy too. This is the reason why adopting the straitjacket of a currency board had been hailed as a positive step. Over the 1990s, the deficit has been trending downward, confirming fears that fiscal policy had become Argentina's Achilles heal.

Third, while the federal government had displayed some willingness and ability to avoid fiscal indiscipline, its ability to rein in provincial governments was increasingly in doubt. As the recession continued, the federal structure encouraged a classic free-rider problem: each provincial government had an interest in collective discipline but a strong incentive to depart from rigour. Coupled with political gaming, there was no reason to expect that the federal government would be successful in negotiating fiscal discipline with the provinces.

This interpretation of the Argentine crisis leads to a number of conclusions. The first one concerns the appropriateness of the currency board arrangement; it will not be pursued further in this chapter. The second one concerns the dual challenge faced by fiscal policy: in the short run, fiscal policy must be available as an instrument to deal with large macroeconomic shocks while being subject in the long run to an overriding discipline constraint. This is another instance of the debate between rules and discretion. The third conclusion is that discretion in fiscal policy is more desirable the tighter is monetary policy. Countries which adopt extreme exchange rate fixity regimes (currency boards, dollarisation, monetary union membership) face a steeper trade-off between fiscal policy rules and discretion. Finally, in "federal" arrangements, such as federal states or monetary unions, the overall budget deficit becomes a matter of common concern for all "sub-federal" entities, which requires adequate safeguards, possibly in the form of legally binding arrangements or institutions.

These are the issues explored in this chapter. The debate on rules and discretions has been mainly applied to monetary policy. The result has been significant progress all over the world. From New Zealand to Sweden, and from Mexico to Poland, an increasing number of countries have made their central banks independent and entrusted the conduct of monetary policy to Monetary Policy Committees. The same principles can be applied to fiscal policy as well. I suggest that the budget deficit – not the size and structure of public spending and taxes – should be delegated to independent Fiscal Policy Committees for precisely the same reasons. I further argue that this solution is likely to enhance attempts at regional cooperation in the realm of exchange rate policy.

The next section examines the common logic of monetary and fiscal policies.[1] Section 2 draws some important lessons from the experience with monetary policy, recognising a number of differences between monetary and fiscal instruments. A workable definition of debt sustainability is proposed in Section 3. How to achieve debt sustainability while allowing the counter-cyclical use of fiscal policy? Section 4 presents a proposal inspired by monetary policy institutions. The link between debt sustainability and exchange rate cooperation, including the institutional aspects, is analysed in Section 5. Section 6 concludes.

---

1 The case for regional exchange rate cooperation is developed in Wyplosz (2002).

1 The Common Logic of Monetary and Fiscal Policies

Faith in the ability of macroeconomic policies to effectively erase business cycles and foster growth has long been oscillating, and it is now at a low point. During the last decade, policy activism has been rejected, increasingly replaced by rules of various kinds.[2] Most central banks now accept responsibility only for price stability and most governments put budget balance at the forefront of their concerns.

The sharp change from the trigger-happy 1970s can be traced back to both facts and academic research. Double-digit inflation and record levels of public debts in peace time have exposed the excesses of unconstrained policymaking. Academic research has analysed the limits of discretion.

In the field of monetary policy, the first shot has been fired by Friedman's celebrated defense of a monetary rule. Subsequent work by Lucas (1972) and Sargent and Wallace (1975) have developed the view that monetary policy is only effective if it is unanticipated. The obvious implication was that there should not be any systematic attempt at using monetary policy to support growth. Combined with Friedman's and others analyses on the cost of inflation, the conclusion has been that central banks ought to restrict themselves to delivering low inflation. More recent work, e.g. Blinder (1998), expresses doubts about the "only unanticipated money matters" view, but recognises the view that monetary policy must concentrate on inflation in the long run. Current conventional wisdom follows the view set forth *inter alia* by Svensson (1999) that central banks ought to be mainly driven by a medium-run inflation target, while carrying out counter-cyclical actions in the short run, in the spirit of Taylor (1993).

In the field of fiscal policy, a similar evolution is under way. The principle of Ricardian equivalence, put forward by Barro (1974), carries implications for fiscal policy similar to the results obtained by Lucas (1972) and Sargent and Wallace (1975) for monetary policy: Ricardian equivalence implies that fiscal policy is not an effective counter-cyclical instrument. The next step is the view that governments tend to misuse fiscal policy for short-term political

---

[2] See "Symposium on Keynesian Economics Today", In: *Journal of Economic Perspectives*, Winter 1993 issue.

advantage (Drazen, 2000; Persson and Tabellini, 2000). The natural conclusion is that fiscal policy should not be used as a macroeconomic policy tool and should focus instead on aiming at a low and sustainable public debt. This view is now enshrined in the Stability and Growth Pact adopted by the European Monetary Union and in fiscal codes in place in various countries, in the form of multi-annual limits on spending (the Netherlands, New Zealand, Sweden, the UK and the US) or on public debts (New Zealand, Poland and Switzerland).

Much as strict monetary rules have been abandoned for being too rigid and arbitrary, fiscal rules are unlikely to be the final word. The next stage is to recognise the deep similarity between monetary and fiscal policies. Both have a short-run counter-cyclical role to play (the Ricardian equivalence is not found to be a robust description of how fiscal policy operates, see e.g. Bernheim, 1987, Gruen, 1991). When left in the hands of undisciplined political authorities, both produce adverse long-run effects: inflation for monetary policy, public debts for fiscal policy.

The Latin American experience is a case in point. Figure 2 shows the evolution of the overall public debt in the region. Over the 1970s, and even more spectacularly over the early 1980s, fiscal indiscipline has been the rule and public debts have exploded. Public debts have fragilised these economies, often resulting in crises and defaults. Consequently, over the subsequent decade, most countries have concentrated on bringing their debt levels down, with many successes.

Thus both macroeconomic policy instruments can be useful in the short run and dangerous in the long run. The challenge, therefore, is to combine short-run flexibility with long-run discipline. This may look like squaring the circle but considerable progress has been achieved in the realm of monetary policy. The recipe is now well-known and reasonably uncontroversial. Central banks have been made independent and given a very precise long-run mandate: price stability. Decisions are typically made by formally independent Monetary Policy Committees (MPC) who can exercise judgment but not for political expediency.

Can fiscal policy also be used as a macroeconomic instrument without necessarily bringing about deficits and a growing debt? In theory, the answer is obviously positive: deficits can be balanced over the cycle while being as strongly counter-cyclical as appropriate. The

Figure 2 Public and Publicly Guaranteed Debt of Latin America, 1970-1999
(percentage of GDP)

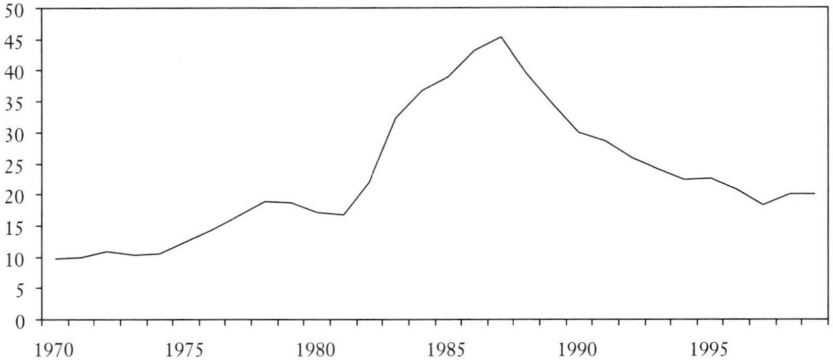

Note:
The countries are: Argentina, Barbados, Belize, Bolivia, Brazil, Chile, Colombia, Costa Rica, Dominican Republic, Salvador, Ecuador, Grenada, Guatemala, Guyana, Haiti, Honduras, Jamaica, Mexico, Nicaragua, Panama, Paraguay, Peru, Vincent and the Grenadines, Trinidad and Tobago, Uruguay, Venezuela.
Source: World Development Indicators, World Bank

challenge for fiscal policy, therefore, is to credibly combine long-term commitments with short-term flexibility.

2 Lessons From Monetary Policy

In comparison with monetary policy, fiscal policy is relatively ineffective. Its impact is rather slow, (too) long lasting, and uncertain (Blanchard and Perotti, 2000). The debate on Ricardian equivalence underlines that much depends on how economic agents perceive fiscal policy actions. Temporary tax measures are understood to be largely ineffective, for agents adjust their saving behaviour. "Permanent" tax measures are of limited credibility. Spending actions raise the question of how they are to be financed, which may elicit partially off-setting private reactions. In the extreme case where the debt path is seen as unsustainable, restrictive fiscal policies have been observed to exert an expansionary effect if they are seen as stabilising an otherwise explosive public debt (Giavazzi, Jappelli and Pagano, 2000).

A complicating factor for fiscal policy is that assessing the budget constraint is not easy. Governments are held accountable to deliver both explicit and implicit entitlements such as welfare payments and the retirement of future generations. This complexity cannot be fully eliminated, but the effectiveness of fiscal policy can be enhanced by improving the visibility of implicit commitments and by eliminating off-budget items.

A further complicating factor is that fiscal policy is subject to democratic oversight. Every action has to be approved by the parliament. The result is a high degree of politicisation which naturally involves differences of opinion but also open the door to lobbying by a myriad of interest groups that care little for the common public good.[3]

Having recognised these differences, five main lessons can be drawn:

Lesson 1: Less activism.

Fiscal policy is a less good instrument than monetary policy. Whenever monetary policy alone can deal with the situation, fiscal policy should remain inactive, relying only on the automatic stabilisers, certainly avoiding to become pro-cyclical.

Lesson 2: Long-term debt sustainability ought to be a binding constraint.

Most modern central banks are given a clear, explicit mandate to aim at price stability. The equivalent long-term concern for fiscal policy is debt sustainability, and it ought to be made explicit.

Lesson 3: Qualified freedom over the business cycle.

Like monetary policy, once its long-term constraint is set and serves as an anchor, fiscal policy can be used as a counter-cyclical tool whenever it can make a contribution to economic (price and output) stability.

Lesson 4: An ability to respond in real time.

Part of the advantage of monetary over fiscal policy is its speed of reaction. The counter-cyclical use of fiscal policy requires that the automatic stabilisers be powerful enough and, for discretionary actions, that the decision and implementation lags be sharply reduced.

---

3 See von Hagen and Harden (1994).

Lesson 5: Long-term commitments must be backed up by specific legal and/or operational arrangements.
Monetary policy is now typically subject to a clear long-term mandate via legal arrangements. The debt sustainability imperative of fiscal sustainability is rarely backed by a similar legal mandate. Europe's Stability and Growth Pact is quite unique in this respect.

3 Defining Debt Sustainability

Long-term debt sustainability requires that the debt level does not increase as a percent of GDP. Where it is high, the objective ought to be more demanding, calling for a decline in the debt-to-GDP ratio.

Alternative definitions have been proposed. The Maastricht Treaty, and the Stability and Growth Pact adopted by the European Monetary Union, have made popular a budget deficit target set at 3 percent of GDP. The target is highly arbitrary, the result of heavy bargaining when the Treaty was being negotiated.[4] The arbitrariness by itself would be of little concern if it did not make the threshold difficult to grasp by public opinions. Two recent incidents (Germany and France, the largest economies in the euro zone) well illustrate the political sensitivities at stake. More importantly, a small deficit is neither necessary nor sufficient for debt stability. The debt, as a ratio to GDP, can grow even if the budget is balanced, as it can decline even if the budget is in deficit.[5] Countries can default on their debts even if they have small deficits, as was the case in Mexico in 1995 and in Argentina in 2002.

Another definition of debt sustainability is that the debt should be "low". This is the definition adopted by New Zealand, for instance. But, of course, what does "low" mean? Truth is that there is no clear

---

[4] As is well-known, the idea comes from Germany which operates a "golden rule" stating that the deficit should not exceed public investment, which presumably pays for itself. Germany has estimated that public investment averages 3% of GDP, an estimate hard to check given the imprecision of what constitutes public investment.

[5] If b is the debt-to-GDP ratio, d the deficit-to-GDP ratio, the evolution of the debt is given by the following formula: $b = d + (i - n)\, b$, where i is the nominal interest rate and n is the growth rate of nominal GDP.

definition of what is a reasonable public debt level.[6] The 60 percent Maastricht convergence criterion, for example, is an accident of history, the average debt level in Europe on the day the Maastricht Treaty was finalised. Is zero debt desirable? In principle, because taxes are distortionary, the lowest possible debt level would be desirable under the assumption that the tax burden is lower where the debt is smaller. However, there is no indication that this assumption holds in practice. In the OECD area, for instance, the partial correlation coefficient is negative (-0.03) and non-significant (*t*-statistics = 0.42).[7] Figure 3 shows nine Latin American countries for which data is available. The partial correlation coefficient is 0.08 and non-significant (*t*-statistics = 0.50). Another view is that the government borrows on behalf of credit-constrained citizens, which implies that some positive debt level is welfare-enhancing. Similarly, with standards of living likely to continue to rise over the foreseeable future, intergenerational equity calls for some negative transfers to richer future generations.

The only reasonable conclusion is that a moderate debt level is desirable, but "moderate" cannot, and should not be precisely pinned down. We simply have to rely on good judgment as to what is a desirable debt level for a country at a moment of its history. "Judgment" is the crucial word here. It means that human thinking, guided by clear principles, is a superior alternative to binding rules built around unavoidably arbitrary numbers. It requires that such judgment be made by reasonable people, free from political or other pressure.

---

6 See Perotti *et al.* (1998) for a discussion of sustainability as well as for useful references. They consider fiscal policy to be sustainable when there is no need for sharp adjustments. These authors conclude that, because sustainability cannot be appropriately defined and measured, attention should shift to controllability. In a sense, this is the view adopted here too, as the focus shifts to institutions which are likely to deliver a debt that remains under control, independently of its size.

7 It can be objected that the three Scandinavian countries and Japan are outliers. Without these four countries, the partial correlation coefficient is positive (0.13) and significant (*t*-statistics = 2.27), but it is not clear why these countries should be excluded. The Scandinavian countries illustrate the main point that a low debt level may be intentionally accompanied by a large tax burden, while Japan shows that small governments can run unsustainable fiscal policies.

Figure 3 Public Debts and the Tax Burden in 1999
(percentage of GDP)

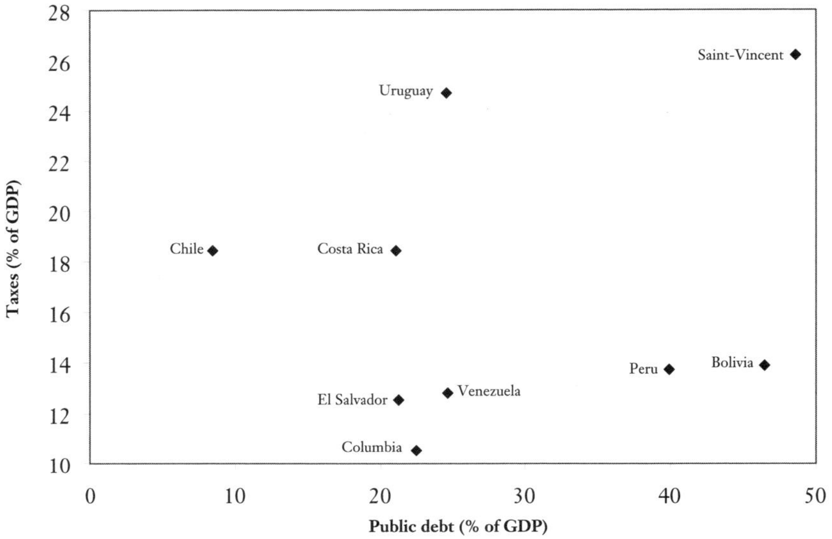

Source: World Development Indicators, The World Bank.

4 Institutions for Debt Sustainability

Summarising so far, two central arguments have been developed. First, fiscal policy ought to combine short-run flexibility with long-run discipline. The aim is to allow for the counter-cyclical use of fiscal policy when monetary policy alone is not enough, while ensuring that the public debt remains sustainable at all times. Second, debt sustainability cannot be defined in a precise way. In general terms, it means that the debt-to-GDP ratio is not allowed to drift upward endlessly and, where the debt is high, that it is on a declining trend. This section develops a proposal which matches these requirements.

The proposal starts from two premises. First, fiscal discipline cannot be entrusted to rigid, arbitrary rules. It requires qualified human judgment. Second, the same challenge, combining short-run flexibility with long-run discipline, has been met in the area of monetary policy by setting up adequate institutions. Accordingly, the section describes similar institutions for fiscal policy.

Rationale

Long-run constraints are notoriously hard to enforce because of the time inconsistency problem: there will always exist circumstances where giving up a commitment is actually welfare improving, although as seen from the current perspective it is highly undesirable. The challenge, therefore, is to provide incentives for the authorities to abide by past commitments. The proposed solution is to rely on the delegation mechanism: a principal entrusts an agent to deliver a particular task. The question is which agent, which task, and which control.

The experience of central banks points to the answers. For both monetary and fiscal policies, the principal is the same – the people. But monetary policy is vastly simpler than fiscal policy. Monetary policy deals mainly with macroeconomic issues, inflation, growth, employment, the exchange rate. Fiscal policy includes deeply redistributive functions that cannot be delegated to a single agent: all democratic countries delegate such choices to their parliamentary institutions which, by construction, embody the diverging interests.

It is essential to realise that fiscal policy fulfils two very different tasks. The first task is structural and redistributive: the size and aims of various spending items and the structure of the tax system. Redistributive decisions cannot be delegated to an agent. The second task is macroeconomic and is largely subsumed by the budget balance.[8] That task does not fundamentally differ from monetary policy and, to a first order of approximation, it can be designed independently from the first one. As such it can be delegated to an agent.

The key aspect of monetary policy is that the agent, the central bank, is given a clear constitutional mandate, and is made independent. These combined attributes sharply reduce the probability that the central bank will renege on its commitments. At the same time, the agent can exercise judgment (this is one reason why monetary rules have been discarded) and today's independent central bankers deliver both long-run price stability and short-run stabilisation. This feature lies at the roots of other cases of

---

8 The macroeconomic effects of spending items and taxes differ, but these differences can be safely taken as second order of magnitude.

delegation, such as anti-trust or financial regulation. There is no reason why it would not work for the macroeconomic aspect of fiscal policy making as well.

Fiscal Policy Committees

In each country, responsibility for setting the budget balance would be delegated to a new institution, the Fiscal Policy Committee (FPC). Like the central banks' Monetary Policy Committees (MPC), the FPC would include a small number of qualified persons appointed for long, non-renewable terms of office. FPC members could not be removed from office unless they violate their mandates and they would not be allowed to seek or receive instructions from governments, members of parliaments or any outside person or group. The FPC would be supported by a staff that would produce its own forecasts of economic conditions and budgetary figures.

The FPC would be given the explicit mandate of ensuring *debt sustainability* over the appropriate horizon. Over the short run this would leave the FPC free to choose deficits and surpluses, as justified by its analysis of current and future conditions.

The power of the FPC would be limited to set annual deficit figures (say, in percent of planned GDP) ahead of the government budgetary cycle. Its decision would have the force of law, and impose itself on both the government and the parliament.[9] The FPC would have no authority regarding the size of the budget, the tax structure and the allocation of public spending. All these matters would remain as in the currently existing political process.

The budget bill, including spending and revenue projections, would require FPC approval before it becoming law. Any budget that does not comply with the FPC's balance decision would either be

---

9 A step in this direction has been adopted in Italy in the early 1990s. The deficit is decided by the government in the summer, and it takes the form of a law. When the rest of the budget (size, spending, taxation) is set by the government and discussed by the parliament in the fall, the budget law cannot be modified anymore. Von Hagen and Harden (1994) convincingly argue that this step has been crucial in Italy's successful efforts at stabilising and reducing its public debt. Another related development is the increased power of the Belgian High Council for Finances which can issue recommendations regarding the size of deficits at the federal and sub-federal levels, see Von Hagen *et al.* (2001).

void – and would have to be redrawn – or, alternatively, would activate an automatic procedure to bring the budget in line. As an example of the latter, spending and/or tax revenues would be adjusted pro-rata.

In the event of abrupt change in economic conditions during the period of budget execution, the FPC would mandate a change in the budget law. This could take the form of a new deficit figure, leaving again the government and the parliament with the task on adjusting spending and/or revenues. Eichengreen, Hausmann and von Hagen (1999) provide an excellent discussion of the relative merits of fixed review dates *vs.* discretionary interventions.

Finally, exceptional circumstances – unforecastable, by definition – may warrant a suspension of the debt sustainability obligation. This is what lies behind the override provision discussed in the case of monetary policy (see e.g. Roll *et al.*, 1993). Such a procedure must be exceptional: for instance, it could require a parliamentary vote with a super-majority.

The Debt Sustainability Mandate

The debt sustainability mandate can be formulated as the obligation to stabilise the debt-to-GDP ratio over the long run, i.e. cycle after cycle. Countries which start with a high debt, or which face large future commitments (due to an ageing population, for example) could aim at a given reduction of the debt-to-GDP ratio over a given horizon tailored to the length of the business cycles.

Such an arrangement sets the incentives right. The authorities know *ex ante* that any budget relaxation will have to be clawed back in the not-too-distant future. As a result, they are likely to adopt a debt-increasing stance only if they think that it will be efficient, not only in the short run but inter-temporally, i.e. if today's gains outweigh tomorrow's costs. Similarly, they will take advantage from favourable conditions to garner room for manoeuvre in anticipation of future adverse shocks.

An important aspect of these principles is that they eschew any numerical target for the debt level. As noted above, there is no optimal target level for public debts. Setting quantified targets inevitably elicits criticism, to which the response is to create an artificial "holly cow" which may be difficult to change later on. In addition, as made abundantly clear by the Maastricht convergence process, artificial targets can be easily flouted precisely because they lack a solid enough basis to be adhered to.[10]

Democratic Accountability

The present proposal may be seen as a technocratic encroachment on a fundamental aspect of democracy. This is not the case, for the following reasons.

Macro vs. Microeconomics

The reason why fiscal policy is everywhere under direct parliamentary control is that it powerfully redistributes income. This aspect almost entirely originates in choices regarding the size of government, public spending programmes and the structure of taxation. In contrast, budget deficits have a limited intra-temporal reallocation effect. They mostly redistribute income across generations, most of which are not yet in existence and play no part in democratic control.[11] Democratic control is essential for deciding the size of government, the distribution of spending and the structure of taxation, but it has proven inefficient to set the size of the budget deficit. Taking the deficit and the debt out of the standard democratic process does not imply any loss of democratic control where it is fully justified. The macroeconomic aspect of fiscal policy is not different from that of monetary policy. In fact, the similarity between monetary policy and setting the budget deficit can serve as a guide to the procedure of democratic accountability to be applied to a FPC.[12]

---

[10] A common problem with quantified constraints, which also applies to balanced-budget laws, is that they can be escaped through creative accounting, including off-budget spending or the creation of separate government agencies exempt from the constraints, see von Hagen (1992).

[11] It could even be argued that the current generation is ill-suited to provide a fair treatment of future generations.

[12] As I was formulating the present proposal I came upon a nearly identical one by Eichengreen, Hausmann and von Hagen (1999). They go in considerably more details regarding the design and functioning of their proposed National Fiscal Councils.

Parliamentary Oversight

The FPC would be accountable to a national elected body. The FPC will not be goal independent, it will be instrument-independent, since the goal will be set either in its mandate (balanced budget over completed cycles) or by the government (debt target for the length of the legislature). Accountability requires both *ex ante* and *ex post* oversight.

Ex ante oversight takes the form of regular testimony by the FPC president and the timely publications of the minutes of the FPC's policy setting meetings, including the votes of individual committee members, who could also be called to testify to the parliament. The FPC would be bound to publish its analysis, backed by all the technical material and data that may be used.

Ex post, the FPC would be held accountable of its record. In the event that the goal is not achieved, the parliament could take a number of actions: a reprimand to the committee, or to some of its members on the basis of published minutes and votes; the disappointment of the FPC, or some of its members, in case of serious failure.

5 Fiscal Discipline and Exchange Rate Coordination

Principles

When a number of countries decide to coordinate their exchange rate policies, they accept to go a long way towards sharing their monetary policies. The European Monetary System has become increasingly tight in this respect, to the point where full currency unification barely represented an institutional shift, not an economic one any more.[13] No matter how deep is the commitment – from agreeing to bilateral margins of fluctuations to joint pegging to a third currency or basket and to a monetary union – it carries important implications for fiscal policy as well.

First, with monetary policy partly or fully dedicated to the exchange rate commitment, the fiscal policy instrument assumes an increasing role in macroeconomic stabilisation.

[13] This point is elaborated in Wyplosz (1997)

Second, fiscal policy indiscipline represents a direct threat for monetary policy and undermines the exchange rate commitment. Run-away debt must be ultimately monetised, which means that the exchange rate must be devalued. The expectation of such an outcome never fails to trigger speculative attacks, Argentine being a recent example, as noted above.

Third, the exchange rate is partly determined by the policy mix. While we currently do not know precisely how the mix operates, this link is not disputed. When a number of countries undertake to jointly manage their exchange rates, one country's fiscal stance becomes a common concern because it creates an externality that goes beyond the income flow spill-overs.

For these reasons, any exchange rate agreement cannot operate satisfactorily unless it is underpinned by some agreement on national fiscal policies. In Europe, this has taken the form of peer pressure, eventually formalised by the Broad Economic Policy Guidelines as a tool to enforce the Growth and Stability Pact. In federal states – a form of monetary union – local governments typically face restrictions on their budget deficits. When they don't, as is the case in Argentina, the result can be catastrophic.

At the same time, the increased reliance on fiscal policy as a counter-cyclical instrument sharpens the trade-off between short-run flexibility and long-run discipline. Each country needs to use fiscal policy reasonably actively in the short run while committing itself to deliver strict discipline in the long run.

FPCs provide the right answer. Countries that contemplate to coordinate their exchange rates need to be reassured that all members will not rock the boat by running up their debts. At the same time, each country will want to retain national control on both aspects, microeconomic and macroeconomic, of their budgets. The natural solution is to agree to set identical national-level FPCs. By providing the same incentives to deliver fiscal discipline, such an agreement would go a long way towards assuaging fears that one country's indiscipline would wreck the exchange rate agreement. At the same time, national FPCs would guarantee that fiscal policy will be available as a stabilisation instrument.

The Case of Latin America

Latin America exhibits a number of unfavourable economic features.

It has been rocketed by a large number of financial crises. Several countries of the continent have achieved some of the worst inflation performances. Default on public debts have been rather frequent and widespread. Lack of macroeconomic discipline is therefore widespread. A number of countries have taken steps to remedy the situation. One of them, Chile, recently adopted a wisemen arrangement that shares many characteristics with the proposed FPC.

Equally disappointing is the low level of trade integration. Table 1 presents the openness index for those Latin American countries for which comparable data is available. By international standards, given how small their economies are, these countries are not very open. Comparing how trade splits internally (among the 11 countries reported) and externally, trade among Latin American countries is remarkably lower than among EU countries.

Table 1 Trade Openness Index[a] in 2000
(percentage of GDP)

	Total	Internal
Argentina	9.0	
Brazil	9.3	
Chile	25.7	
Mexico	29.7	
Venezuela	19.3	
Colombia	15.1	
Peru	13.4	
Uruguay	14.4	
Ecuador	31.8	
Costa Rica	38.5	
Guatemala	18.6	
Latin America[b]	17.8	2.2
European Union	*27.9*	*16.4*
US	*10.3*	
Japan	*9.0*	

Notes:
[a] The index is the average of exports and imports as a percentage of GDP.
[b] Latin America as consisting of the 11 countries reported above.

Source: IMF.

Figure 4 Trade Openness and Inflation in Latin America

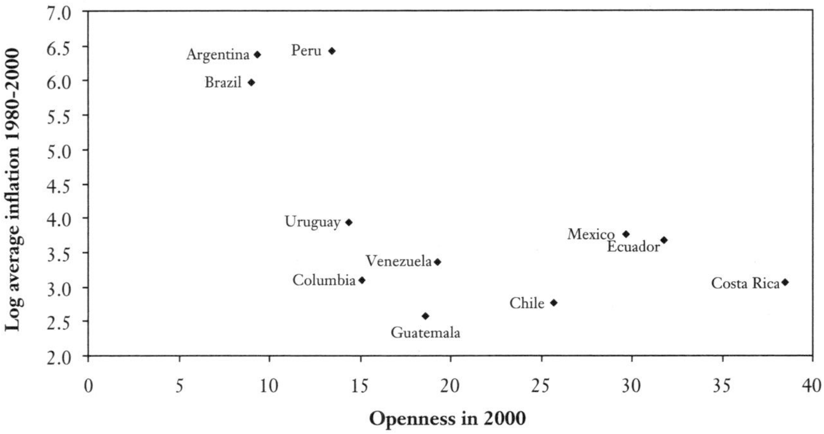

Source: IMF.

The limited extent of intra-Latin America trade is a well-known feature. One of the many reasons is economic instability. For example, Figure 4 displays for the countries shown in Table 1 the apparent association between trade openness in 2000 and inflation over the previous decade. This negative link is well-documented in empirical trade studies. One key channel is exchange rate volatility, as shown in Rose (1999).

An immediate implication is that Latin America would greatly benefit from the gains provided by deeper regional trade. To achieve progress in this direction, it would need to sharply cut exchange rate volatility, which requires enhanced macroeconomic discipline.

So far, Latin American countries have sought greater discipline through purely domestic means. Success has occurred, but occasionally and, sometimes sporadically. The recent tendency has been to seek deeper ties with the US dollar, either through a currency board or through outright dollarisation. The fiscal component of macroeconomic instability seems to remain largely neglected, though. Unless this component is firmly secured, it is to be feared that the successes achieved so far will be short-lived.

Dollar links may have serious advantages, but they fail to bring home the point that fiscal discipline is as essential to macroeconomic stability as tying the exchange rate. Chile, the first country to adopt a sound, largely depoliticised fiscal institution, has done so a decade after stabilising its exchange rate, in fact after it had abandoned a reasonably fixed parity. The failure to ensure simultaneously monetary and fiscal discipline is characteristic of the Latin American experience and lies at the roots of repeated mishaps.

A different route is possible. Jointly undertaking to stabilise their bilateral exchange rates will not only promote regional trade and overall economic efficiency, it will also encourage the Latin American countries to focus on fiscal discipline. Concern over each other's fiscal actions – and their deep politicisation – may have played an important role in discouraging regional exchange rate cooperation. Such concern is understandable and in fact desirable. But it can be turned around from a hindrance to an incentive.

The novelty of FPCs is obviously a barrier. It shakes much conventional wisdom, especially politically. The joint adoption of identical FPC institutions would help break through such barriers. It could make the arrangement more legitimate and it would go a long way towards assuaging suspicions of poor commitment to fiscal discipline. It would open the way to exchange rate cooperation, itself a step towards monetary discipline. Peer pressure could operate in the two spheres of macroeconomic policy: through joint management of bilateral exchange rates and through formal exchanges among the national FPCs.

6 Conclusion

The institutions of fiscal policy discipline have been lagging behind those of monetary discipline. Yet, the challenges are almost identical. While monetary policy has moved away from rules – often adopted two decades ago – the trend now is to introduce fiscal rules. Adopting FPCs would save time and disappointments.

FPCs are the fiscal policy equivalent of MPCs. They superficially clash with the notion that fiscal policy is a purely political function, which must remain fully subject to the usual process of parliamentary oversight. This view misses the crucial distinction between the deficit, which is essentially a macroeconomic choice, and the budget structure (size, allocation of expenditures and taxes) which falls indeed in the domain where democratic oversight is essential. Budget deficits, like interest rates, are best left to non-political bodies which operate in full light and are subject to democratic accountability.

Latin America stands to be a prime beneficiary of such an approach. The politicisation of fiscal policy has been excessive and has resulted in deep and repeated economic instability. That would be a good enough reason to adopt FPCs. There is an additional reason to do it jointly: it would break the barrier of mutual suspicions and open the way, at great last, to more regional exchange rate stability, a key pre-requirement for deeper trade integration.

References

Barro, Robert (1974), "Are Government Bonds Net Wealth?", In: *Journal of Political Economy*, Vol. 82, pp. 1095-1117.

Bernheim, B. Douglas (1987), "Ricardian Equivalence: An Evaluation of Theory and Evidence", In: S. Fischer (ed.) *NBER Macroeconomics Annual 1987*, MIT Press, Cambridge MA, pp. 263-304.

Blanchard, Olivier and Roberto Perotti (1999), "An Empirical Characterization of the Dynamic Effects of Changes in Government Spending and Taxes on Output", NBER Working Paper No. 7269, Cambridge MA.

Blinder, Alan (1998), *Central Banking in Theory and Practice*, MIT Press, Cambridge MA.

Drazen, Allan (2000), *Political Economy in Macroeconomics*, Princeton University Press, Princeton NJ.

Eichengreen, Barry and Charles Wyplosz (1993), "The Stability Pact: More than a Minor Nuisance?", In: *Economic Policy* 26, pp. 65-104.

Eichengreen, Barry, Ricardo Hausmann and Jürgen von Hagen (1999), "Reforming Budgetary Institutions in Latin America: The Case for a National Fiscal Council", In: *Open Economies Review*, Vol. 10, No 4, pp. 415-42.

Friedman, Milton (1968), "The Role of Monetary Policy", In: *American Economic Review*, Vol. 58, pp. 1-27.

Giavazzi, Francesco, Tullio Jappelli and Marco Pagano (2000), "Searching for Nonlinear Effects of Fiscal Policy: Evidence from Industrial and Developing Countries", In: *European Economic Review*, Vol. 44, No. 7, pp. 1259-89.

Gruen, David W. R. (1991), "What People Know and What Economists Think They Know: Surveys on Ricardian

Equivalence", In: *Australian Economic Papers*, Vol. 30, No. 56, pp. 1-9.

Hagen, Jürgen von (1992), "Fiscal Arrangements in a Monetary Union: Evidence from the US", In: Donald E. Fair and Christian de Boissieu (eds.), *Fiscal Policy, Taxation and the Financial System in an Increasingly Integrated Europe*, Kluwer, Dordrecht.

Hagen, Jürgen von and Ian J. Harden (1994), "National Budget Processes and Fiscal Performance", In: *European Economy Reports and Studies*, Vol. 3, pp. 311-408.

Hagen, Jürgen von, Andrew Hughes-Hallett and Rolf Strauch (2001), "Budgetary Consolidation in EMU", In: European Commission, Economic Papers No. 148.

Lucas, Robert Jr. (1972), "Expectations and the Neutrality of Money", In: *Journal of Economic Theory*, Vol. 1, pp. 103-24.

Perotti, Roberto, Rolf Strauch and Jürgen von Hagen (1998), *Sustainability of Public Finances*, CEPR, London.

Persson, Torsten and Guido Tabellini (2000), *Political Economics*, MIT Press, Cambridge MA.

Roll, Eric *et al.* (1993), "Independent and Accountable: A New Mandate for the Bank of England", A Report of An Independent Panel Chaired by Eric Roll, CEPR, London.

Rose, Andrew (2000), "One Money, One Market: Estimating the Effect of Common Currencies on Trade", In: *Economic Policy*, Vol. 30, pp. 7-46.

Sargent, Thomas and Neil Wallace (1975), "'Rational Expectations', the Optimal Monetary Instrument and the Optimal Money Supply Rule", In: *Journal of Political Economy*, Vol. 83, pp. 241-54.

Svensson, Lars E.O. (1999), "Inflation Targeting as a Monetary Policy Rule", In: *Journal of Monetary Economics*, Vol. 43, No. 3, pp. 607-654.

Taylor, John (1993), "Discretion versus Policy Rules in Practice", In: *Carnegie-Rochester Conference Series on Public Policy*, Vol. 39, pp. 195-214.

Wyplosz, Charles (1997), "EMU: Why and How It Might Happen", In: *Journal of Economic Perspectives*, Vol. 11, No. 4, pp. 3-22.

Wyplosz, Charles (2002), "Regional Exchange Rate Arrangements: Some Lessons From Europe", In: J.J. Teunissen, *A Regional Approach to Financial Crisis Prevention: Lessons from Europe and Initiatives in Asia, Latin America and Africa*", FONDAD, The Hague, pp. 23-49.

4

Comment on Charles Wyplosz and José María Fanelli[1]

Mark Allen

One of the first lessons that was drawn from the Mexican crisis and re-confirmed in the subsequent crises has been that an open capital account imposes severe constraints on macroeconomic policy. Countries that want to get full benefit from the access to external capital, especially emerging market developing countries, have to run macroeconomic policies that can meet the demands of international capital markets.

José María Fanelli refers in his paper to the Fund's agreeing on targets with Argentina that were very hard for Argentina to achieve. I think that is true, but this reflects the understanding of the authorities that those were the targets that the markets required, and if there is an error to be attributed to the Fund, it is that it went along with the authorities in their belief that they could implement those policies. It is not clear to me that there was a less demanding set of policies that could have achieved the objective of satisfying the international capital markets. But given the difficulties that countries have had in running policies that meet the demands of the markets, especially in the area of fiscal policy, it is understandable that Charles Wyplosz looks for better mechanisms for delivering the sort of fiscal policy the markets need.

---

1 The paper by José Maria Fanelli has been included in a separate volume, Jan Joost Teunissen and Age Akkerman (eds.), *The Crisis That Was Not Prevented: Lessons for Argentina, the IMF, and Globalisation*, FONDAD, The Hague, 2003, pp. 32-67.

Given the relative success of a technocratic approach to monetary policy in recent years, Wyplosz suggests that fiscal policy can be run along the same sort of lines. Clearly the approach is intriguing, but there are a number of problems which, at the very least, need further analysis. But, as Charles said at the end of his presentation, perhaps this is no more outrageous a proposal than the proposal to have monetary policy run by a Monetary Policy Committee seemed to be when it was initially suggested.

I want to address some of the issues I see with putting fiscal policy in the hands of a Fiscal Policy Committee. I will complement this with some discussion of the work the Fund is doing on debt sustainability, which is very relevant here, since the target of Wyplosz' proposed Fiscal Policy Committee would be ensuring debt sustainability for the country and running fiscal policy in line with that main objective.

Fiscal Policy is a Political Issue

The essence of Wyplosz' proposal is that a Fiscal Policy Committee (FPC) set an obligatory fiscal deficit target aimed at achieving and maintaining debt sustainability. The first problem with the proposal is that, while the Fiscal Policy Committee can set the target for the fiscal deficit, it doesn't control the instruments that will achieve that target. The target is achieved through the sum of the taxing and spending decisions of the government as approved by parliament. This is in contrast with the position of a monetary policy committee, which actually wields the instruments that are applied to meet its targets. In order to deal with this problem, Wyplosz proposes that the Fiscal Policy Committee be backed up by legal restraints on what the government and the legislature can do. The government would be compelled to deliver a budget in which it can spend what it likes and can tax as much as it wants, as long as it comes up with the deficit that was proposed by the Fiscal Policy Committee.

However, these decisions to tax and to spend are the most hotly contested areas of politics – they are what politics is all about. It is very hard to see how the struggles on the trade-offs between spending and taxing decisions will not rebound on the Fiscal Policy Committee itself. When things get tough, the pressures on a Monetary Policy Committee can be very severe, as they are in Poland at the moment. I would see the pressure on a Fiscal Policy Committee being even more severe when the economic conditions were difficult or when the political struggle was intense.

Wyplosz' proposal also assumes that an effective legislative straitjacket can be devised to constrain this mechanism. We have seen fiscal responsibility legislation in a number of countries. Wyplosz mentioned a few examples like the Stability and Growth Pact in Europe, some of the longer-term fiscal legislation in the United Kingdom and the United States. There is also a lot of recent experience in Latin America with fiscal responsibility legislation which is actually not very encouraging. The problem is obviously that, when you pass a law, you can unpass the same law very easily – the time-inconsistency problem. To remedy this, you can make it an organic law, as Ecuador is trying to do at the moment, which will be much more difficult to overturn. But these legislative straitjackets are very hard to implement. It is possible that as popular acceptance of the proposal increased, the legitimacy of such constraints would become stronger, but I do see considerable difficulties for this approach in Latin America, given the current problems with fiscal responsibility legislation.

More generally, I wonder whether these proposals are based on a 'technocratic fallacy'. Just leave economic policy to the economists and let the politicians squabble about something else. While this has become conventional wisdom for monetary policy, I am not convinced that in the longer run it will remain so. More fundamentally, the problem of governance in large parts of the world is to produce a mature political system that internalises the need to make trade-offs and social choices within a given envelope. But I doubt that establishing a Fiscal Policy Committee will help in producing a mature political system in which there is a general understanding of the need to make societal choices within a resource envelope. Discussions on the stance of fiscal policy are political decisions, not purely technocratic ones. But perhaps the Wyplosz proposal is part of the spadework for creating such mature political systems.

Debt Sustainability and Fiscal Policy

This brings me to the work we have been doing in the Fund on sustainability. We have realised the importance of getting a better handle on this concept. The Fund should not lend to a country whose debt is unsustainable, without action being taken to make it sustainable. The discussion of sovereign bankruptcy presumes that a judgment can be made as to what debt structure is sustainable and what unsustainable. A paper on this was discussed recently by the Executive Board and is available on the web.[2] In this paper we look at two aspects of sustainability: the external sustainability of a country's debt, and fiscal sustainability. I shall concentrate on the latter since it fits well with Wyplosz' chapter.

A government's debt is sustainable if the debt dynamics are expected to remain under control, without the need for a major adjustment in policies at some point in the future. The chances of the debt dynamics staying under control are the result of factors both under the control of the authorities and any Fiscal Policy Committee and those beyond their control. They will depend on the stance of fiscal policy, growth and interest rate expectations, shocks hitting the economy, developments in world and partner country goods and financial markets, etc. There is uncertainty about many of these factors. Thus a country's debt and fiscal policy may be sustainable in some states of the world and not in others. At any time one could in principle make the judgment that there is such-and-such a probability of the debt being sustainable. In the Fund, we are planning to be much more explicit about the elements that enter into a judgment on sustainability and the chances of worse outcomes than the baseline projection. But ultimately all we can do at the technical, staff level is to put the elements forward on which the difficult – political – decisions have to be made.

The Fiscal Policy Committee will also have to make these judgments – but the scope for disagreement is going to be large. Not only on the probabilities of distant events, but also on how risky a policy to run, or how fast to converge on a given target. Should the country run a fiscal policy where the chance of a crisis is 1 in 5, or should policy be directed to reducing the chance of a crisis to 1 in 20 or 1 in 100? These are political, not technical, decisions.

One possibility might be to put these elements into the contract of the Fiscal Policy Committee, in the same way that the inflation target

---

2 International Monetary Fund, *Assessing Sustainability*, May 29, 2002. http://www.imf.org/external/np/pdr/sus/2002/eng/052802.pdf

is put into the contract of the governor of the Bank of New Zealand or the Monetary Policy Committee of the Bank of England. But it is quite different to set as a target 'keep inflation below 2 percent', which is clearly defined and manageable than a target in the form, 'keep the risk of the debt becoming unsustainable to 1 in 5'. The next year, if there is a crisis, the Committee could argue that it did a fine job, but this one was just the one year in five. It is hard to specify without a lot more further thought what the precise targets of the Fiscal Policy Committee would be.

There is some discussion of what is a safe debt stock in José María Fanelli's paper. At the Fund we have been looking to see whether there are key thresholds for determining sustainable debt, for example, as used in the HIPC Initiative. And, quite frankly, we have not got very far. We did discover that the probability of a default in an emerging market rose quite sharply when the fiscal debt to GDP ratio went above 40 percent. Below 40 percent, *grosso modo*, the chance of a crisis in the following year is 2 or 3 percent; above 40 percent debt ratio, the chance of a crisis rises to about 20 percent.

Even so, it is not clear what the operational conclusion is. If the Fund were to be very strict with a country whose debt ratio went beyond 40 percent, refusing to lend unless it restructured, in four out of five cases, the country would actually have been sustainable at that level and the restructuring would have been unnecessary. So, these debt sustainability concepts are quite hard to apply to fiscal policy.

The one clear message I got out of the papers by Fanelli and Wyplosz is the importance of low debt ratios well below 40 percent. Only such low ratios give the country room for counter-cyclical fiscal policy, as well as a margin to cope with shocks.

5

Floor Discussion of "Latin America: How to Achieve Stability and Growth?"

The Studart Paper

György Szapáry, deputy governor of Hungary's Central Bank, did not share governor Nout Wellink's optimism in his opening remarks that we will hopefully learn from experience and have both fewer and shorter crises. "This reminds me," Szapáry said, "of what Bernard Shaw once said, that experience is that wonderful thing that allows us to recognise a mistake when we make it again. All the crises seem to have the same causes."

Szapáry stressed that supervision could not play any positive role once a crisis emerged. "Supervision concentrates on avoiding banking crises and allowing banks to function well in a normal situation. In a crisis, supervision cannot really help, because banks will not be able to function well. Banks are as good as their clients are, while clients are as good as the macroeconomic situation is."

Turning to what central banks can do to prevent crises from happening, Szapáry pointed to three lines of action. "First, it is important to control open positions. Many banks get into trouble when they have excessive open positions. Second, one has to find ways of controlling, or at least monitoring, borrowing by clients from abroad. In fact, you are looking at the open positions of the clients, for which of course you do not have a specific institution set up to control, but you can monitor them and try to impress banks by moral suasion when you see that there is over-borrowing by the companies.

Third, one increasingly notices that the internal audits of the banks are often not done correctly, but on top of it, the audit companies are not always doing a good job either. We have seen that in the case of Enron, but we also see it in the case of banks. Sometimes banks are hiding problems and the international audit companies do not bring that to the fore. Perhaps a supervisory agency of audit companies could tackle this increasing problem."

Ariel Buira, a former deputy governor of the Mexican Central Bank, confirmed Szapáry's suspicion that banks may be hiding problems. In the early 1990s, Buira had experienced that Mexican bankers did not reveal non-performing loans in the balance sheets. "They just renewed the credit so that it appeared as current and the indicators of performance remained fine. However, this was only possible with a very poor legal and supervisory framework. If you lent to a company that went broke, it was a very long-winded process to recover your loan. If somebody stopped paying a mortgage, it was virtually impossible to recover the loan. But all these issues of the legal framework have been solved. Supervision has been restrained and greatly improved."

With regard to the issue of capital account liberalisation, Buira recalled Mexico's experience in the 1990s. "Mexico always had a fairly open capital account, but when it joined the OECD there was a strong pressure to lift the one or two remaining restrictions. The main one was allowing foreign investors to buy Treasury bills. This made a huge difference in the size of the problem that came later. If the foreign investors had not been allowed to hold Treasury bills, you would not have had the huge build-up in dollar-denominated debt which later became such a crucial element in the emergence of the 1994-95 crisis."

Buira shared Szapáry's scepticism about the role of supervision in a crisis situation. "Once you have a macroeconomic crisis, a banking crisis is inescapable and inevitable. It does not matter how well capitalised and regulated you are, if mortgages are a fourth of your portfolio, it takes all of the banks capital. If the firms you have lent to cannot pay you, again you are wiped out as a bank."

Aert Houben, of the Dutch Central Bank, endorsed Buira's last view pointing to the case of Argentina. "In Argentina you had a very solid banking system, lots of capital, foreign owned banks with state-of-the-art risk management techniques and so on. Clearly it was the macroeconomic regime and the macroeconomic environment that were driving the crisis."

Houben suggested including another macroeconomic variable in the analysis, the domestic savings ratio. "A low domestic savings rate is a dominant macroeconomic variable in many Latin American countries. That implies that they are dependent on international financial inflows, and therefore are vulnerable to shocks in the international financial sentiment. At the same time, domestic financial markets are not very deep, because they are not generating and intermediating these savings. A complication is, that domestic savings are not easy to steer; it is very difficult to generate more domestic savings. Maybe fiscal policy can play a role here, in pension policies for example, to try and deepen domestic savings and domestic financial markets."

Roy Culpeper, of the Canadian North-South Institute, noticed a clear difference of opinion about the role of foreign banks in developing countries. "Fist, I take it from Rogério's analysis that the presence of foreign owned banks could lead to destabilising competition rather than stabilising competition. This is at odds with what Mr. Wellink was saying in his introductory remarks, that competition from foreign owned banks was much to be encouraged. And Yung Chul Park is making the same point, that the increasing encroachment of foreign owned banks in East Asian economies has played a rather destabilising role. In Canada we always have been rather strict with foreign owned banks. They have never been given much leeway, for precisely the reason that it was thought, and is still thought, that foreign owned banks would undermine the stability of the domestic financial system. There is some real debating material here. It reminds me of Keynes' dictum that 'let's engage in trade and commerce, but ultimately let finance be domestic'."

Culpeper thought that Rogério Studart's reference to unemployment as an indicator of economic performance was an interesting and innovating broadening of traditional indicators. "This is something new, because – as Jürgen Stark commented – financial and price stability are the key objectives. I found it very interesting that Rogério looks at the correspondence between unemployment and non-performance in the banking portfolio. This is encouraging, because the financial sector should worry about the real sector and how it is performing."

Frans van Loon, from the banking and insurance company ING, stressed that the discussion of the financial system needs broadening beyond that of the banks. "It should include savings in whatever form and domestic capital formation in its broadest definition. Specifically, it should include all contractual savings as an increasing important element for domestic stability: contractual savings from insurance, from pensions systems, from social security, the run-over between public and private savings. In this context, I was struck by Jürgen Stark's emphasis on the two points of sequencing and the need to strengthen domestic institutions. Jürgen Stark mentioned as domestic institutions the central bank, the judiciary, the courts and all that. Again, one should add contractual savings mechanisms and pension insurance systems."

Van Loon pointed to the strong interaction in the world of banking between regulation and business, and the impact this has had on banking in Latin America. "In the 1990s, all over the financial world there has been a trend to develop new systems of risk management. They have led to drastic changes in the way we look at risk taking and our daily practice of approving credits. Its influence goes beyond the domestic arrangements in the countries of the advanced banks. The strong foreign dominance of banking in Latin America was also steered from abroad, from Amsterdam, from London, from Frankfurt, based on the new, much more technocratic and very high-quality risk management systems that we have these days. That is somewhat risky, I would dare to say, and may act as a source of instability in financial systems in Latin America."

Another important new element of the 1990s that should be included in the analysis, suggested Van Loon, is the increasing importance of the so-called stockholder value system. "It is a short-term evaluation, where you are looking at the price of your stock, and the effects of that on stockholder behaviour. Both together are leading to a tendency of risk aversion, which has influenced the willingness to take on credit. This may be another source of instability."

Amar Bhattacharya, of the World Bank, stressed that if one wanted to draw lessons from the past crises, one should not forget about the role that weaknesses in the international financial system have played in the build-up of vulnerabilities in Latin America. But since Studart's paper focuses on the domestic aspects, Bhattacharya left that important international dimension aside and dwelled upon the four aspects of domestic financial systems discussed by Studart. "The first is the pace and sequencing of capital and financial liberalisation. The second is the soundness and consistency of macro policy, in particular that of fiscal policy with exchange rate regimes in an open capital account setting. The third is weaknesses in the financial system, and the fourth is weaknesses in the corporate sector including corporate governance and all the institutional fundamentals mentioned by Jürgen. What I found interesting about the paper is that it shows that the weaknesses in the financial system led to a build-up of vulnerability *before* the Tequila crisis, especially in Mexico and in Brazil, but that it did not do so *after* the Tequila crisis. Indeed, the financial system in Latin America does not contribute to the build-up of vulnerability, neither by a credit boom nor by mismatches in the financial system, whether it be in unhedged open position or in maturity mismatches. That is in striking contrast to what happened in East Asia. So, as other people have argued, it was macroeconomic weaknesses impacting on the banking sector, rather than the other way around. That is a very important point that comes through in the paper and is worth stressing."

Stephany Griffith-Jones, of the Institute of Development Studies, stressed the importance of simultaneously improving the *domestic* and the *international* financial system, and she observed that the progress has been very asymmetric. "There has been important progress domestically, but there has not been sufficient progress internationally. Because things are so integrated, as for instance Frans van Loon just said, this asymmetric progress will continue to be problematic and will make countries vulnerable to crises. This is not to say that the domestic system is unimportant, it is important, but it is only one of the conditions."

Jürgen Stark, deputy governor of the German Central Bank, said that although much progress has been made in crisis prevention, this does not hold true for crisis resolution. "We are far away from consensus on private sector involvement in the resolution of financial crises, as well as on access to IMF funds. I agree that we need symmetric progress both at the domestic and international level. At the national level, strong institutions should be in place. The international institutions only exist to deal with deficiencies at the national level. Therefore, there should be a focus on domestic reforms."

Griffith-Jones said that Jürgen Stark had made a very important point in his comment on Wyplosz' paper when he recognised that capital account liberalisation had been carried out too quickly. She wondered: "What do we do about it, now that we know we have liberalised capital accounts too quickly? Can we go back? Or do we just make recommendations for the few countries that have not yet liberalised?"

Following up on these questions, Charles Wyplosz, of the Graduate Institute of International Studies in Geneva, said that, like Griffith-Jones, he was struck by Stark's recognition that official views have changed on the point of capital account liberalisation. "This is something which has been discussed in previous Fondad conferences, where some of us were complaining about the push towards liberalisation and we always identified the villains in this push as the Americans, the British and the Germans. This is what seems to be transparent from these G-7 meetings. It is important to realise that of the views that are strongly held today, some will be thrown away tomorrow as wrong. It always baffles me that policymakers give the impression that they have no doubt that what they say today is right. I want to make it very clear. For example, today Stephany asked 'should we go back now on capital liberalisation?' And we are talking in this conference about South-East Europe while right now the EU is putting tremendous pressure on the accessing countries to remove capital restrictions. So this whole process of capital account liberalisation is not going back. However, in my opinion, EU authorities should recommend capital account restrictions for the accession countries."

Stark replied, "Germany has always emphasised the importance of appropriate sequencing of capital account liberalisation. Practically speaking, for the EU accession countries this means that long transition periods should be implemented."

Griffith-Jones agreed with Rogério Studart that there is a trade-off between financial stability and growth, leading to the question of how tight regulation should be. She added another question: "Should there be more counter-cyclicality in regulation given that financial institutions, and banks in particular, are so pro-cyclical? They may become even more pro-cyclical, because they are using these very sensitive risk models which tend to vary strongly with the cycle, and which the new Basel Capital Accord wants to give a prominent role in determining the capital adequacy ratio."

Charles Wyplosz was sceptical about the usefulness of capital ratios. "It is not sufficiently realised that all capital ratios – no matter how good they are – are based on assets, which go wrong during crises or shake-ups. You can have the best asset ratios possible, but when you need them they will be gone. It is sort of the opposite of what György Szapáry said; you do not need to have regulation in normal times – you need regulation for the worst cases. Therefore, it is almost a hopeless strategy to try to have the good capital ratios. The whole Basel Agreement misses this view completely. If you have an Argentine bank or are holding Argentine assets, the day Argentina is shaking, all of these asset ratios are gone. What you need is Argentine banks holding Dutch or Korean assets and Korean banks holding the others. That is the way to diversify. The first thing you teach students is to diversify, but it is not done and it is not at all creeping into discussions on regulation."

Replying to some of the questions, Rogério Studart said he did not think that the savings rate in Latin America was the problem. "The savings rates in Latin America were not that low, as some speakers suggested. Not the savings rate itself, but rather the allocation of savings to the most productive investment is the problem."

Studart agreed that after the Tequila crisis banking problems did not lead to macroeconomic problems, but rather the other way around. But he warned, "we are getting into a situation of a very stable financial or banking sector, but we are also getting credit stagnation, and that is a problem. We need a system that is both stable and able to provide the credit required for economic development."

With regard to the development of the financial sector in developing countries, Studart believed that progress still has to be made in terms of institutions and institution-building. "If you look at institutions as rules of the games, there have been a lot of improvements. But if you look at institutions as physical institutions, much needs still to be done. Financial institutions and financial markets are required for the system to work well, and that kind of institution-building has not yet progressed enough in Latin America because of a lack of long-term policies. Institution-building is a long-term process, which requires time and stability, especially price stability and macroeconomic stability in the way we thought about it back in the sixties."

The Wyplosz Paper

José Antonio Ocampo, executive secretary of ECLAC, agreed with the two basic ideas in Charles Wyplosz' paper, that there should be short-run fiscal flexibility with long-run fiscal discipline and that good judgement is better than rules. But he had "significant differences" in the diagnosis and in the recommendation. "In the diagnosis, a problem arises, for instance, by looking at Charles' figure on the debt ratios in Latin America. It is not really fiscal deficits but rather currency crises that drive the debt-to-GDP ratios in Latin America. Latin America had a history of fiscal indiscipline, but that is no longer true. If you look at time series of fiscal deficits for the 1990s, you would see that the deficits have actually been kept at very low levels, except in a few countries. Figure 2 in shows that the debt-to-GDP ratio in Latin America exploded once the debt crisis broke, and not before the crisis broke. And the same thing is true of Argentina. Their debt-to-GDP ratio increased sharply once the crisis broke, not before the crisis broke. So the problem with debt sustainability levels in Latin America is no different from how to avoid a currency crisis. The debt dynamics of Latin America are only secondarily determined by fiscal irresponsibility. Public debt dynamics are not determined by too loose fiscal policy, but rather by exogenous shocks, such as currency crises."

Ocampo observed that the reform policies in Latin America have increased the pro-cyclical bias of both monetary and fiscal policy. "We had sharper business cycles in large part because the reforms have enhanced the pro-cyclical bias of macroeconomic policies. I would be a bit careful about saying that the monetary institutions have been so excellent. If you go around Latin America, you will hear that autonomous central banks have certainly increased long-run flexibility, but probably have also increased the pro-cyclical bias of monetary policies."

Ocampo doubted whether a new institution like the proposed Fiscal Committee was really needed. "We have already achieved a lot more fiscal discipline in Latin America through existing institutions: first, through strong ministries of finance and second, through independent central banks. I was a finance minister in Colombia; I talked with the independent central bank about fiscal policy all the time. In our countries, independent central banks necessarily get all the time involved in fiscal policy and are a countervailing power in the fiscal area. Third, we have a lot of international pressure. Unfortunately, that international pressure is a bit pro-cyclical, including the pressure of the IMF. There is not enough pressure during booms, and there is too much pressure during crises. Maybe changing the international pressure will actually help to reduce the pro-cyclicality. There may be one institution that is missing in the institutions, which is a strong advisory board to Congress. Think for instance of the role in the US of the Congress Committee on the budget, that is a very important institution that we are missing. The discussion in our congresses is very poor. So we may be missing some institutions, but a fiscal committee is probably not the sort of institution that we are missing."

Ocampo emphasised the importance of democratic discussions about the budget. "I would say that the increasing democratic discussion is better rather than worse. Technocracy is very good when it is part of a democratic discussion process; it is not good when it is free from democratic discussion. Actually one of the good things we have in Latin America today is that we have many technocrats in the public discussion presenting their views on what a correct fiscal policy is. That discussion should be a part of the process."

Yung Chul Park, of Korea University, wondered whether the proposed Fiscal Policy Committee would be involved in decisions on military spending. "Who is going to decide how much military spending there will be and on what hardware? (Not this Fiscal Policy Committee, oh I see, they will only deal with macroeconomics, right.) But there is the problem of income distribution and other targets related to expenditure, which has macroeconomic implications, and so does macroeconomic fiscal policy has microeconomic implications. Also, the politicians will come in and then they may find out that some of these committee members took bribes... So where do we stand on this?"

Park also had a question for Mark Allen, of the IMF. "I am increasingly disturbed by the IMF asking countries to do certain things, because that is what the markets ask for. What is the market, what are market participants? They are my neighbours, they are my brokers and they are my friends doing all kinds of research at the Deutsche Bank, or Citibank and all these banks. You don't think that the IMF has any influence on these market participants' behaviour? If it does not, well, you are in trouble!"

Zdeněk Drábek, of the WTO, fully agreed with Yung Chul Park's last remark, "because often the conclusion of an IMF programme is a precondition for any orderly lending by the private sector". He also agreed with Park's remark about the link between macro and micro issues. "First of all it is not clear to me how it would be defined, but even if it is, we run into the kind of problems that Yung Chul has just mentioned. Take the example of the Czech Republic, which as of this year is trying to buy fighter planes amounting to 80 billion Czech Crowns. It is bigger than probably the total budget of federal and local authorities together. So obviously they have to go through the parliament. The parliament will be deciding on the purchase of fighter planes, and that is going to generate a debt of enormous proportions for the country. Now I just can't see how this would fit into the scheme of the fiscal policy committee."

Drábek also wondered what the link would be between the Fiscal Policy Committee and the Monetary Policy Committee. "Which of the two decides that their tool should be used as a counter-cyclical instrument, the Monetary or the Fiscal Committee? What incentives would you give to each one of them to operate? How do you ensure that they work consistently? That is another type of question that you will need to answer. It seems to me that it is not only a problem of not having control over fiscal instruments, that Mark Allen has mentioned, but also a problem of how to make these institutions to really operate. I am afraid you will run into very difficult issues."

Brian Kahn, of the Central Bank of South Africa, endorsed Drábek's question about the relationship between the Fiscal Policy Committee (FPC) and the Monetary Policy Committee (MPC). To explain the difficulties that are likely to arise, he mentioned South Africa's recent experience with a sudden change in the exchange rate. "I want to emphasise the issue of exchange rate shocks for emerging markets. Inflation targeting may work well in many countries, but the big test is whether it is sustainable in the presence of exchange rate shocks – which have an impact on the debt-to-GDP ratio. In South Africa in 2001, we had a shock of 40 percent depreciation of the rand against the dollar in a period of three months. You can imagine what that has done to our inflation target. This raises the issue of debt sustainability once you take the real exchange rate as part of the sustainability criteria. That leads to the problem of how do you relate to the two institutions together? What is the relation between the FPC and the MPC? These institutions work at different time horizons."

With regard to military spending, Kahn mentioned that South Africa recently had a similar situation as the Czechs. "There was an arms deal over 20 years, a contractual arrangement of around

25 billion dollars. It was very much a political decision that went through parliament. Obviously, it is denominated in dollars, which means that an exchange rate change would have major implications for the future financing of this transaction. How would the FPC deal with such a situation?"

Wouter Raab, of the Dutch Ministry of Finance, agreed on the importance that Wyplosz attaches to sustainable debt, but disagreed with the need for fiscal discretion. "Fiscal discretion leads to a debt bias in the long run since it is not applied symmetrically during the business cycle. Counter-cyclical policy is only applied in a downturn, not in an upturn. A more pragmatic reason why I am against fiscal discretion is that it is likely to have a pro-cyclical effect. For instance, it is important to realise that a recession usually only lasts some three quarters. We often need one or two quarters to identify a recession, then one quarter to decide on appropriate policy, and at least one quarter to implement this policy. This is why the average stimulus comes into force when the recession is already over. These lags make fiscal policy pro-cyclical, as the US witnessed in 2001. The most we can ask of fiscal policy is to let the automatic stabilisers do their work. The degree of stabilisation these offer depends on the economic structure of a country. I would expect that automatic stabilisers work a bit less in emerging markets than in the EU. Nonetheless, we should look for mechanisms to improve the workings of the automatic stabilisers instead of relying on fiscal discretion."

Raab missed the need for market flexibility in the economy in Wyplosz' paper. "One of the most efficient ways of dealing with cyclical shocks is increasing the flexibility of markets to adapt to changing circumstances. In Argentina, people were applauding Argentina's achievements, but I was struck by the inability to address the unemployment situation. Every macroeconomic system with an exchange rate that is delivering over 10 percent of unemployment with no perspectives of getting it down, is bound to come under serious constraints and pressure when exogenous shocks occur – because of the level of unemployment and constraint on the monetary policy authorities to raise interest rates etc. The credibility of a system that is not able to deliver full employment is at stake. It is more efficient, particularly in Europe, to try and make markets more flexible than work in the direction of fiscal discretion."

Raab wondered whether a panel of independent experts of the proposed FPC would be strong enough to apply strict symmetrical fiscal policy around the cycle. "In Wyplosz' proposal, the FPC is fully transparent and democratically accountable to parliament. That could lead to a situation where the parliament does not agree with the proposition. If it can sack these people, how independent are they really? The pressure on them will be enormous. For example, how would you apply fiscal constraint in an upturn? Taxes cannot be raised in an upturn because that would raise inflationary pressure. Reducing infrastructural expenditure would just increase the bottlenecks, which are already in place in a situation of overheating. Lowering social benefits, for instance health care, just attacks the social cohesion. At a time when other incomes go up by 5 percent or more, this is a very difficult thing to do and is bound to stir a ferocious political debate. I wonder what the support for such an independent panel could be. If politicians are not keen on taking the responsibility for those actions, who else in society will? So I think you can not do without political leadership here."

Marek Dabrowski, a former deputy minister of Finance of Poland, saw a contradiction in Wyplosz' proposal. "On the one hand, you want to impose some rules on fiscal policy, which I am very sympathetic of. On the other hand, you want to leave quite substantial room for discretion, for counter-cyclical fiscal policy. To solve this contradiction, you look for a magic solution that has some characteristics of the technocratic illusion, that you can find a group of experts who will be able to solve this problem in an optimal way. In the real world, however, you have either a good track record in macroeconomic, monetary and fiscal policy, or not. If you have a good track record, this gives you a bit more room for flexibility and discretion. But then, if you have a good track record, you do not need an additional straitjacket.

In the case of developing and transition economies, discretion is not a good proposal. It is contradictory with a problem Charles addresses in his paper: the problem of expectations. If a country does not have a very good record and resorts to discretionary policy – even if it has certain rules for the discretionary policy – markets do not have to believe in the soundness of such discretion. And if the markets do not believe the soundness of discretion, they will penalise the country in a painful way. In my view, this is what happened in many emerging market crises."

A final criticism of Dabrowski on the Wyplosz proposal was that there is a problem of time lags and time horizon. "In the case of monetary policy, the longest time lags between monetary changes, interest rates, and inflation effects are 18 to 24 months, and in most countries lags are shorter. But today's fiscal decisions will have an impact on financial sustainability in 10 or 20 years. What should be the time horizon of a FPC? Wyplosz talks about the possibility of revoking, changing the committee, if it does not follow rules. That means it is no longer independent. I cannot imagine that a parliament will stop the term of the committee because it is not tough enough. Probably it will only stop it because it is too tough."

Barbara Stallings recalled that the FPC is not a new idea since it had been proposed a number of years ago by Ricardo Hausmann of the Inter-American Development Bank and was subsequently rejected by the member states. "But if we look at Charles' paper in the spirit, and not in the letter, it offers much to recommend. I think it is very useful to clearly separate at the conceptual level the deficit or surplus issue from the level of expenditure and the taxation, to say nothing of the content of expenditures and taxation. In Latin America there are vast differences, no matter what the deficit or surplus is. There are countries that are raising and spending 30 to 35 percent of GDP and there are countries that are raising and spending less then 10 percent of GDP. This makes a tremendous difference. Not separating out the issue of deficit or surplus from the level of expenditure leads us to gloss over some very important issues in the fiscal area. It is also the case that external actors, whether it is the IMF or the bond markets, are basically interested in the deficit issues. So it gives you more flexibility if you can separate those out and keep those people out of the issues of levels of expenditure and taxes and the contents of expenditure and taxes.

My conclusion is, that we should take Charles' proposal in spirit as opposed to letter. We should concentrate on an advisory board as opposed to some board that could in principle make decisions. It is important to place this advisory board in Congress, to educate the Congress about these kinds of issues. The Congressional Budget Office in the US is a good example. I would second that as a more flexible and realistic version of Charles' proposal."

In his reply, Charles Wyplosz first noted that many critics did not take to heart the importance of separating decisions on the deficit from decisions on the level and structure of spending and taxation. "Take for example the weapon acquisition issue. If the democratically-elected authorities insist that they have to spend resources on weaponry, this is their absolute right but it is not a technocratic question to ask how this item will be financed. The proper framework has to be one that requires the authorities to answer that question at the same time as the proposal is put to the parliament. One solution – not necessarily the best – may be to raise the debt ceiling, which would then be given to the FPC as a modified target. It is hard to believe that explicitly recognising the debt implication is less desirable than keeping the financing implicit as seems to be the case in the examples described by various speakers. The critics miss the simple point that for such purchases not to endanger debt sustainability, we need accounting procedures that extend over the long run, FPC or no FPC. FPC-type arrangements impose a proper accounting, and that cannot be construed as a weakness of the proposal."

Wyplosz recognised that the question of coordination between the FPC and the MPC is very important. "As noted by José Antonio Ocampo, the debt is largely endogenous to the exchange rate, which lies partly in the hands of the central bank. But let's separate the debate into two questions. The first one concerns the danger of a vicious circle that goes from market fears of debt non-sustainability to currency crashes and to effective debt non-sustainability. This is by now a classic and well understood case of self-fulfilling crisis, driven by expectations. If the markets believe that a debt default is looming, there is little that the central bank can do about it. There is much debate on the merits of an interest rate defense, if only because sharply raising the interest rate also threatens debt sustainability. There is no miracle solution, but any one will have to work on market expectations. The essential merit of an independent and powerful FPC is precisely to anchor expectations. An untested FPC may not always be able to break market concerns, but it is now increasingly recognised that adequate institutions represent our best hope to deal with market jitters. Until a better institutional proposal is put forward, the FPC idea is the one that comes closest to providing protection against this kind of crisis that has repeatedly played havoc throughout Latin America.

The second aspect is the risk that the MPC and the FPC will attempt to act as free-riders on each other. Both must be independent and democratically accountable. Being shielded from electoral pressure, they are unlikely to be major offenders, and both are likely to be exceedingly prudent. This confirms the remark by José Antonio

Ocampo that independent central banks are found to act in a pro-cyclical way. I admit that this is a structural weakness of such institutions, one that will be erased by proper political oversight within the democratic accountability framework. Until that happens, there might well be some degree of pro-cyclicality. Bad as it may be, it is better than runaway inflation and debts, which is what we have seen over the last decades."

Wyplosz finally addressed the "technocratic illusion" problem mentioned by Marek Dabrowski and others. He noted first that the only item removed from the realm of politics is the deficit, not the other more sensitive aspects of the budget. He then observed that, like price stability, debt sustainability requires some limit on the deficit process. "A rule does just that, and no one objects to it. A FPC is only an intelligent, i.e. feed-back rule. So the problem is the feed-back, the fact that someone can realise that blindly applying a rule can be counter-productive. Yet, this has become acceptable for monetary policy, so the real problem is to go one step further in the same direction. What may seem unrealistic today may become reality tomorrow. Just remember when we started to talk about monetary union at a similar table 15 years ago, everybody was laughing, saying it is politically unacceptable. I remember having discussed the idea of independent central banks with the authorities of a number of countries, and people were laughing at me. They said, 'you can't start thinking about that, it is politically unacceptable'. About capital account liberalisation, Jürgen Stark said, 'We changed our mind'. I predict you will change your mind faster than you think."

Part II

Central and Eastern Europe: The EU Convergence Challenges

6

Banking Sector Development and Financial Stability in the Run Up to EU Accession

Henk Brouwer, Ralph de Haas and Bas Kiviet[1]

The countries in Central and Eastern Europe (CEE) that are negotiating their entry into the European Union have seen their financial landscape change dramatically over the past decade. With the breakdown of the system of central planning, the need for an effective and efficient system of financial intermediation became apparent. Since banks were already present during the communist era, the transition countries took their monobanks as the starting point for creating bank-based financial systems. Although these systems in the EU accession countries are currently not yet on par with their western peers, remarkable progress has been made. In many countries almost all of the large state banks have by now been privatised. Foreign strategic investors, mostly Western European and American banks, have been among the most important buyers. Preceding or simultaneous with this privatisation process, governments have – to various degrees – started to deal with the problem of bad loans. Progress has also been made with regard to supervision and regulation, in part stimulated by the requirements of EU accession. All these restructuring efforts with regard to the banking system and its regulatory environment may have contributed

[1] The authors would like to thank Martin Admiraal and Henk van Kerkhoff for research assistance and several colleagues for useful comments and suggestions.

to the fact that CEE has proven to be rather resilient during recent periods of international financial instability, such as the Asian and the Russian crises. Of course, this relative immunity can also be partly attributed to the fact that in many CEE countries (some) capital controls were still in place. In addition, the local banking systems – let alone bond and stock markets – are still relatively underdeveloped. A lot of work remains to be done to improve the accession countries' financial systems.

At present the banking sector is by far the most important part of the financial system in all transition economies and is, as a consequence, also the main source of risk for financial stability in this region. This is all the more so because the lack of well-functioning equity markets confronts banks with relatively high credit risks, as bank credit must to some extent substitute for equity. In order to consistently survey the risks for banking system stability, we apply the framework as described by Goldstein and Turner (1996). Whereas this framework mainly draws lessons from earlier banking crises, we use a more forward-looking approach by taking stock of the potential risks that may accompany a further development of the CEE banking sectors, taking into account the specific challenges posed by the EU accession process. Addressing such risks is probably the best method authorities of CEE countries can use to stimulate the development of the banking sector as well as financial markets. Given our focus on the specific issues related to transition countries, we will touch only briefly on the other two accession countries, Cyprus and Malta. Section 1 contains our assessment of the potential risks for the CEE banking sectors. Section 2 concludes and gives policy recommendations.

1 Financial Stability and EU Accession: An Assessment

Based on the framework as set out by Goldstein and Turner (1996), this section takes stock of what appear to be the main sources of risk for the accession countries' banking sectors during the pre-accession period. Of course, the characteristics of the transition countries' banking systems are to a large extent specific, the transition process being a unique historical process. Yet, on the other hand, the opening up of the still relatively underdeveloped markets in CEE also shares some important features with earlier experiences of connecting countries to the global economic system. In the following, we take the relevant themes identified by Goldstein and Turner as a starting point to explore the specific conditions and challenges associated with the stable development of the banking sector in the CEE countries.

1.1 Macroeconomic Stability

A stable macroeconomic environment is important for banking sector stability, mainly because uncertainty about macroeconomic policies and fluctuating fundamentals, such as economic growth and inflation, makes it harder for banks to assess credit risks accurately.[2] Besides from its negative influence on the banking sector, (macro) economic uncertainty may also inhibit economic growth more generally. Lensink (2001) shows for instance that uncertainty with regard to inflation and government expenditures leads to lower per capita economic growth. Importantly, this negative effect of uncertainty appears to be less severe in countries with a more developed financial sector. Yet, subdued economic growth, due to macroeconomic uncertainty or for other reasons, may feed back to bank soundness as it reduces the debt servicing capacity of firms and households.

Table 1 shows the differences between the accession countries and the current EU members with regard to the volatility of both their GDP growth and inflation-rate. Over the period 1995-2001, macroeconomic volatility has been considerably higher in the accession countries, creating a relatively difficult environment for the local banking sector. On average, the difference in volatility has been more pronounced with regard to inflation than with regard to growth. Table 1 shows that, when excluding the outliers Romania and Bulgaria, there is a significant negative correlation between on the one hand the level of GDP per capita and on the other hand, respectively, the volatility of GDP growth and the volatility of inflation. As the convergence process progresses and sound economic policies are continued, macroeconomic volatility will therefore probably decrease further. Still, the convergence process implies that growth rates will stay at a higher level compared to the current EU

---

2 Van der Zwet and Swank (2000). See also Boyd, Levine and Smith (2001) on the negative impact of inflation on the functioning of the banking sector.

Table 1 Volatility of Growth and Inflation in EU and Accession Countries: Standard Deviation of Yearly GDP Growth and Inflation over 1995-2001

	Growth	Inflation		Growth	Inflation
Austria	0.9	0.6	Bulgaria	6.1	360.5
Belgium	1.0	0.6	Czech Rep.	2.6	3.1
Finland	1.7	0.7	Estonia	3.1	9.3
France	0.8	0.5	Hungary	1.5	6.9
Germany	0.8	0.6	Latvia	3.1	8.2
Greece	0.8	2.3	Lithuania	3.2	13.8
Ireland	1.8	1.2	Poland	1.7	7.2
Italy	0.6	1.2	Romania	4.7	40.1
Luxembourg	2.2	0.8	Slovak Rep.	2.1	2.3
Netherlands	1.1	1.1	Slovenia	0.7	2.3
Portugal	0.9	0.9			
Cyprus	1.4	0.8	Spain	0.8	
1.0					
Malta	0.9	0.7	Denmark	0.6	0.3
Sweden	1.2	1.0	UK	0.4	0.3

Note:
Correlation coefficient with level of GDP per capita: -0.45 and 0.67 percent respectively (both significant at 5 percent level).

Source: IMF, *World Economic Outlook*.

members. Volatility of these growth rates will depend, among other things, on the credibility of government policies and the ability of authorities to prevent boom-bust cycles on domestic credit and asset markets.

It is also important to keep in mind that the level of inflation is likely to remain significantly above the EU level in the years to come. One reason for this is the Balassa-Samuelson effect, or the fact that during the catching-up process, faster productivity growth in the tradables sector will push up wages and prices in all sectors. Unfortunately, estimates of the size of this effect in accession countries vary widely because of data problems and theoretical limitations in the model that make it hard to quantify the relative importance of the effect.[3] However, other reasons for inflation differentials may be even more important. In a process of structural convergence, the structure of relative prices will have to change as well. Such relative price changes are important as they stimulate a more efficient (re)allocation of production factors. In particular, prices of (new) products and services that are in demand have to rise vis-à-vis those of old and less sought-after products. Since the latter prices may to some extent be sticky downwards, relative price adjustments will often take place through price increases for new products and services. Consequently, a rise in inflation can be the result. Also, the carry-on effect of high inflation rates observed in the past disappears only gradually, while the continuing liberalisation process of administered prices puts upward pressure on the price level as well.[4] It should be noted that pure Balassa-Samuelson inflation will not harm a country's competitiveness, as the inflationary pressure is confined to the non-tradables sector. However, the other sources of inflationary pressure mentioned above can lead to a deterioration of competitiveness. Still, it is questionable whether these sources of inflation warrant restrictive policies aimed at short-term stabilisation, as they are natural elements of the transition process. An inordinate strict policy to fight such inflation may impede the much needed structural convergence process. An independent central bank is the obvious institution to assess the appropriate policies in this respect. By means of its policies an independent central bank will then contribute to a stable environment for the banking system. Whereas independence will eventually be guaranteed through its inclusion in the *acquis communautaire*, no single accession country has implemented all requirements up until now. Progress is especially needed in the personal independence of the members of the decision making bodies and in central banks' financial independence.

---

[3] Pelkmans *et al.* (2000) estimate an average effect of 3.8%-point for all candidate transition countries, whereas De Broeck and Sløk (2001) estimate an effect of 0.8 to 1.6%-point for these same countries. The Balassa-Samuelson effect critically depends on the assumption of nominal wage convergence – wages in the non-tradables sector follow those in the tradables sector – as a result of complete labour mobility within a country. Insofar as labour mobility is limited, the Balassa-Samuelson effect will thus be less pronounced.

[4] On average, administered prices still have a weight of around 18% in the HICP baskets in accession countries (ECB – unpublished document).

1.2 Managing Capital Inflows and Preventing Lending Booms

In the coming years, as remaining entry barriers will be removed and investor confidence in the region increases, EU accession countries will most likely continue to receive significant capital inflows. In principle, such capital inflows (FDI, bank loans, debt issues and portfolio investments) will contribute to economic development by providing funding for investment projects that cannot be financed domestically. In this way, capital flows contribute to an improved resource allocation. At the same time, such inflows and the associated structural convergence, may lead to real exchange rate appreciation, which can be considered a normal "side-effect" of the convergence process. The same goes for the current account deficits that accompany substantial capital inflows (Table 2). Such deficits reflect the surge in aggregate domestic demand, for both investments and consumption, that results from the inflow of capital.

However, the Asian experience has shown that capital inflows, and particularly sudden reversals in such flows, may cause significant risks for the banking system. From a financial stability perspective it is therefore important that current account deficits remain within sound limits and are financed prudently, so as to minimise the likelihood of potentially harmful capital flow reversals. This likelihood increases as a larger proportion of total inflows originates from investors that are not so much interested in providing finance for long-term investments, but are rather focussed on exploiting short-term gains. Generally, it is assumed that investments with a short-term maturity, such as portfolio investments and short-term bank loans, are more often related to the latter motive, whereas long-term bank lending and especially FDI more often concern the former.[5] During recent years the financing of the current account deficit has been relatively prudent, as foreign direct investments (FDI) have played an important role. Still, short-term (portfolio) investments were significant as well in some countries, at least for a number of years (Table 3).

In the run-up to EU accession, the composition of capital inflows may change substantially. First, once the present privatisation wave

[5] Garibaldi *et al.* (2002) show that between 1991 and 1999 portfolio investment inflows into CEE were much more volatile than foreign direct investments, whereas bank lending took an intermediate position.

Table 2 Current Account in Accession Countries
(as percentage of GDP)

	1993	1994	1995	1996	1997	1998	1999	2000
Bulgaria	-11.0	-0.3	-0.2	0.2	4.2	-0.5	-5.6	-5.8
Czech Rep.	1.3	-2.0	-2.6	-7.1	-6.8	-2.5	-2.9	-4.4
Estonia	1.3	-7.3	-4.4	-9.1	-12.1	-9.2	-5.8	-6.3
Hungary	-11.0	-9.8	-5.7	-3.7	-2.1	-4.9	-4.4	-3.3
Latvia	19.3	5.5	-0.4	-5.4	-6.1	-10.7	-9.9	-6.9
Lithuania	-3.2	-2.2	-10.2	-9.2	-10.2	-12.1	-11.2	-6.0
Poland	-6.7	1.0	0.7	-2.3	-4.0	-4.3	-8.1	-6.3
Romania	-4.7	-1.5	-5.0	-7.3	-6.1	-7.0	-3.7	-3.7
Slovak Rep.	-4.6	4.6	2.1	-10.6	-9.6	-10.0	-5.9	-3.6
Slovenia	1.5	4.0	-0.5	0.2	0.1	-0.8	-3.9	-3.4
Cyprus	1.7	1.0	-1.8	-5.3	-3.9	-6.7	-2.3	n.a.
Malta	-3.4	-4.9	-11.0	-12.1	-6.1	-6.4	-3.3	-14.7

Source: International Financial Statistics (IMF).

comes to an end, FDI may decline in importance.[6] It remains to be seen whether the FDI flows attracted by the privatisation process will be fully substituted by FDI targeted at financing green field investments.[7] Secondly, the prospect of EU accession may lead to a significant increase of portfolio investments into the region, as the confidence of investors and international portfolio managers increases. The abolition of the remaining (short-term) capital controls will only facilitate this process.[8] Thirdly, the average maturity of foreign bank debt may decline as well. As a matter of fact, this has already happened to a certain extent during the last decade.

6 An example is Latvia, where the current account deficit amounted to 10.1% of GDP in 2001, partly as a result of strong consumption growth. In that same year, FDI was only sufficient to cover approximately 25% of this deficit (Bank of Finland, 2002).

7 Green field investments concern investments in new projects and firms that have to be started up from scratch (as opposed to taking-over already existing enterprises).

8 Garibaldi *et al.* (2002) show that portfolio investment into transition countries has been mainly determined by the quality of the financial infrastructure and by property rights protection. In as far as these institutions will further improve during the run up to EU accession, an additional inflow of portfolio investments might be expected.

Table 3 Private Net Capital Flows to Selected Accession Countries
(percentage total net inflow)

	Poland	Hungary	Czech Republic	Baltic States
		Bank loans		
1996	-1	-16	31	14
1997	28	38	32	34
1998	25	16	-1	32
1999	23	4	-2	-15
2000	-1	44	5	-12
2001*	—	-5	11	7
		Direct Investment		
1996	101	140	41	59
1997	57	108	44	44
1998	58	43	54	68
1999	70	47	78	65
2000	74	65	88	78
2001*	—	54	81	70
		Portfolio Investment		
1996	0	-24	27	27
1997	15	-46	24	22
1998	17	41	48	-1
1999	7	49	24	50
2000	27	-8	7	34
2001*	—	51	8	23

Note:
* First three quarters.
Sources: BIS, IMF. Bank loans could not be split in short-term and long-term loans.

The first pane of Figure 1 shows that, on average, the accession countries have significantly increased their short-term debt owed to foreign (BIS-reporting) banks.[9] As a share of total bank debt, this short-term debt has increased from 34 percent in 1985 to 41 percent in 2001. As a percentage of GDP, short-term debt owed to foreign banks has risen even stronger: from a low of 37 percent in 1994 to 83 percent in 2001 (pane 2). A growing share of total foreign bank debt

[9] Short-term debt as a percentage of GDP has been *declining* in the Czech and Slovak Republic since 1999 and is now back on the average level.

is directed to the accession countries' non-bank private sector, while less credit goes to the public sector or to the local banking system (pane 3). Local banks have thus become less important as intermediaries in allocating foreign banks' funds to local businesses. Foreign banks increasingly allocate their resources directly to local firms, making use of the local branches and subsidiaries they have acquired during recent years.

In sum, it can be stated that in many accession countries current account deficits are substantial, while there is a tendency for the financing of these deficits to be increasingly short-term in nature. As this would make countries more vulnerable to sudden reversals in capital-flows, it is of great importance that their banking systems are adequately prepared for the consequences of such changes. In many accession countries significant progress has been made in financial reforms, often stimulated by the growing importance of foreign banks. Foreign (owned) banks intermediate an increasing share of external bank debt to local enterprises, which is an important difference with "pre-crisis" Asia, where the role of foreign banks in intermediating capital inflows was only very limited.[10] Furthermore, financial intermediation in transition countries has been expanding

Figure 1 External Debt Accession Countries: Liabilities to BIS Reporting Banks

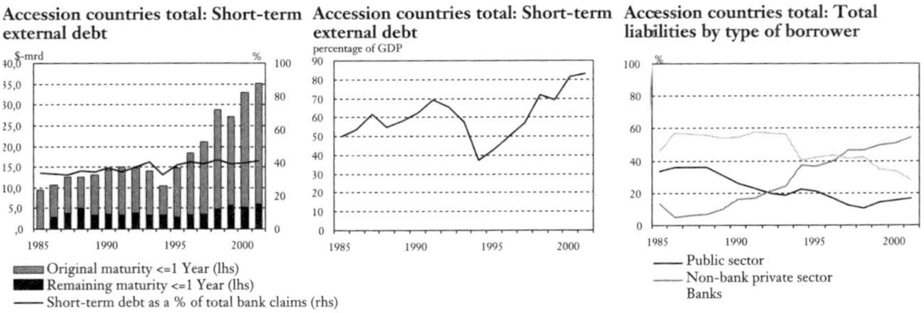

10 McKinnon and Pill (1997) stress that emerging markets may be particularly prone to overborrowing as a result of excessive optimism. Consumers and investors then want to increase consumption and investment beyond sound levels, and banks, confronted with increased possibilities of foreign funding, may be willing to finance this. Up until now, this scenario has not materialised in the accession countries, partly due to the importance of foreign banks. By "importing" sound lending policies, foreign banks have thus to some extent contributed to a higher degree of financial stability.

fairly gradually from very low levels, in spite of good prospects of convergence towards EU levels of income. While too little credit growth might be an impediment to change in transition economies, at least the gradual growth of credit has given the accession countries some time to strengthen their banking sectors. Nevertheless, capital outflows could be triggered when markets no longer perceive the current account deficits and accompanying real appreciation as a sign of strength and structural convergence, but rather as a weakness and as a sign of badly intermediated foreign capital.

1.3 Suitable Exchange Rate Regimes

The accession countries are currently employing a broad range of exchange rate strategies, each with their own specific challenges in maintaining stability. The Czech Republic, Poland, Romania, Slovakia and Slovenia have opted for, either free or managed, floating arrangements. On the other end of the spectrum, Bulgaria, the Baltic States and Malta maintain either conventional fixed peg or currency board arrangements. Cyprus and Hungary are taking an intermediate approach by mirroring the ERM-II arrangement with 15 percent fluctuation bands around a central rate to the euro. The wide degree of regime diversity partially reflects historical factors,[11] but it also indicates that there is no single exchange rate regime that is optimal for all accession countries. Whereas a country's banking sector would be served best by a certain degree of exchange rate stability,[12] apparently both flexible and fixed exchange rate regimes have their advantages and disadvantages, and the specific circumstances in each country define the best choice.

A fixed peg arrangement provides the advantage of nominal exchange rate stability, but this stabilisation anchor comes at a price. As is well-known, countries with a fixed peg cannot use monetary policy, or nominal exchange rate changes, to counter an asymmetric economic shock or to maintain their competitiveness. Such a decline in competitiveness can for instance result from an appreciation of

---

[11] Bulgaria, for instance, installed its currency board as a means to stabilise its economy during the crisis of 1996/97.

[12] Substantial exchange rate volatility can inflict severe damage on bank balance sheets through the adjustment of the real value of assets that have been financed in foreign currencies (cf. Section 1.4).

their real exchange rate caused by a comparatively high rate of inflation. Subsequently they will have to remain fiscally prudent, and have to rely on wage and price flexibility as the sole adjustment mechanisms. At the same time, the perpetuity of a fixed exchange rate can never be guaranteed. Speculative attacks on the peg can be triggered by a sudden loss of confidence or other negative shocks. These can be costly in terms of reserves spent on defence, while a disorderly exit from the fixed regime, entailing a large shift in the exchange rate, can have severe economic repercussions, in particular for the banking sector. When such a scenario would unfold, it may turn out that the risks to banking sector stability have actually been augmented by the fixed peg, especially since a pegged currency can discourage hedging against currency risk, thus stimulating the build-up of unbalanced portfolios.

Whereas flexible arrangements cannot prevent damaging exchange rate volatility triggered by volatile capital flows, they do offer the potential benefits of an active monetary and exchange rate policy that can be used to manage these flows, to spur disinflation, maintain competitiveness and to support economic growth. And whereas fiscal prudence and structural flexibility will support the economic well-being of all accession countries, their importance increases along with the degree of invariability of the exchange rate. The Asian experience has shown that a pegged currency combined with large reversals in capital flows may lead to significant problems, as it is very painful and costly to adjust a fixed exchange rate regime in an orderly fashion. Flexible exchange rates are better able to adapt themselves to changes in capital flows and other economic shocks, and it seems therefore sensible for accession countries not to rush themselves in fixing their exchange rates as quickly as possible. Only countries that are confident that they can maintain strict fiscal prudence and that their wages and prices are flexible enough to safeguard competitiveness and to cope with asymmetric shocks, should consider a fixed rate regime.[13]

---

[13] The Baltic States are archetypal examples of countries that have many characteristics that will help to sustain a successful currency board arrangement. Up until now, their pegs have not come under severe stress, despite the facts that they already liberalised their capital accounts in the early 1990s and that they have shown large current account deficits over the past years. Sutela (2001) ascribes their success to both sound fundamentals and unintended consequences of policy decisions. On the one hand they have pursued sound fiscal policies and have

A new challenge for exchange rate policy will arise after the candidates have acceded to the European Union. Before a country can fully participate in EMU and introduce the euro, it will have to pass the test that was laid down in the Maastricht Treaty. Its public finances (deficit and debt), its levels of interest rates and inflation and its exchange rate will have to meet transparent criteria that help forestall inflationary tendencies within the monetary union and that can prevent tensions that might arise when the common monetary policy would fail to meet the needs of all individual participating member states. The exchange rate policy test that has to be passed, is successful participation in the ERM-II for at least two years, during which the exchange rate should remain within a band of +/- 15 percent around a central rate that has to be commonly agreed upon. In effect, ERM-II can be regarded as a relatively fixed exchange rate regime, as adjustments of the central parity will in practice be painful decisions which are not taken easily. On the other hand, the broad band around the central rate provides for some flexibility. Membership of ERM-II can thus be a useful tool to avoid excessive exchange rate fluctuations by anchoring exchange rate expectations, while at the same time providing the (limited) exchange rate flexibility needed to safeguard real convergence. It can also be a useful tool in identifying an equilibrium exchange rate that can be expected to be sustainable over the long term and that is supported by market forces. Still, already before entering ERM-II the central rate in this regime should be well-considered. Nevertheless, it cannot be excluded that – given the remaining large structural differences – the chosen rate may have to be adjusted at some point. As such adjustments are potentially painful processes, countries should be careful in giving up their exchange rate flexibility too early.

---

created a high degree of structural flexibility in their economies. On the other hand exchange rate stability was supported by the fact that their financial markets are very small, leaving little room for capital flow reversals, and the fact that almost all of their banks were sold to solid foreign institutions. Despite their successful track-record, consistent good policies – especially a prudent fiscal policy – remain vital for the sustainability of these arrangements, given their relatively high current account deficits.

1.4 Limiting Currency Mismatches in the Banking System

Banks denominating part of their assets and/or liabilities in a foreign currency will be subject to risks arising from exchange rate changes. In principle, two cases can be distinguished. First, when a bank denominates more liabilities than assets in a foreign currency (or vice versa) it will be subject to a currency mismatch. When domestic compared to foreign interest rates are high, banks may for instance be tempted to use foreign currency denominated liabilities to fund their local currency denominated activities. Such a currency mismatch will subject banks to a substantial devaluation or depreciation risk, as in that case their foreign currency denominated liabilities will increase in value, eroding the bank's capital base.[14] The second case concerns banks that denominate the same amount of assets and liabilities in a foreign currency in order to avoid a currency mismatch.[15] Even then, the bank remains subject to risks linked to exchange rate fluctuations. On the asset side, currency risk is shifted to debtors with foreign currency denominated loans, and currency risk will accordingly be substituted by credit risk. After all, banks' customers may not be able to pay off such loans, the value of which will rise sharply in terms of the local currency after a downward exchange rate correction. Firms may be overly optimistic in assuming that the current exchange rate will also hold in the future, and thus demand a relatively high proportion of foreign currency debt. In Poland, Hungary and the Czech Republic, the importance of foreign-currency denominated lending to the corporate sector has indeed risen.[16] At the same time, the share of foreign currency denominated deposits has declined in these countries. As a result, the corporate sector has increased its net foreign exchange position against the domestic banking sector and may therefore be more vulnerable to downward corrections in the exchange rate.

During the run-up to E(M)U accession, it is conceivable that the importance of euro-deposits will increase. This may increase

---

[14] Additionally, a maturity mismatch will increase the bank's interest rate exposure or, more specifically, its exposure to changes in the yield curve.

[15] An alternative would be to use off balance sheet hedging instruments such as forward contracts.

[16] In these three countries, foreign currency denominated credit amounted to 24%, 38% and 19%, respectively, of total credit granted by the domestic banking system to the corporate sector in 2000 (Reininger *et al.*, 2001, pp. 13-14).

depositors' sensitivity to interest rate differentials between euro-deposits at home, international euro-deposits and local currency deposits. As a result, both cross-border and within-border capital mobility may intensify. With regard to the former, the threshold for depositors to shift from domestic euro-deposits into foreign euro-deposits may decline, leading to more volatile cross-border capital movements reacting to changes in international interest rate differences. Within borders, depositors may start to shift more frequently between local currency and euro-deposits depending on the interest rate differential. Insofar such shifting takes places within the same bank, risks will be limited. However, depositors will also take into account the safety of euro-deposits by (their estimate of) the capital adequacy of the bank and the ability of this bank to tap the international financial markets and to return deposits in euros. The ownership structure of a bank may be important in this regard, as depositors may find foreign-owned banks to be more reliable. Shifts between local currency deposits and euro-deposits may then boil down to shifts between local banks and foreign owned banks. This would imply an increase in liquidity risk for especially the local banks, stressing the need for the monitoring of banks' net open currency positions, both on and off balance sheet. Especially during crisis periods, depositors could decide to shift their deposits with local banks (both in local currency and in euro) to foreign owned banks, thus "doing their capital flight at home". Insofar that is the case, international capital mobility may actually decline.

Besides carefully monitoring banks open currency positions, risks can also be limited by making sure that banks do not try to reduce the currency risk associated with deposit euroisation by extending euro credit to customers who will not be able to service their debt obligations in case of sharp depreciations or devaluations. Finally, bank regulators can prevent undue transformation of currency by placing limits on banks' open foreign exchange positions when deemed necessary (see also Section 1.7).

1.5 Adequate Preparations for Financial Liberalisation

Financial liberalisation covers a whole range of deregulatory measures that loosen the constraints on the financial activities of banks and other economic actors, varying from lending restrictions to capital account liberalisation. Although financial liberalisation can generate substantial long-term benefits, the new environment inevitably presents banks with new risks, which, without the proper precautions, may pose a threat to banking sector stability. The Asian experience has shown that getting the sequence right can be important in this regard. The positive effects of financial liberalisation will come within reach at a lower cost if banks and supervisory capacity are strengthened before reforms are implemented.

The CEE accession countries have come a long way in liberalising their financial systems since the beginning of the transition period, to a large extent stimulated by the institutional requirements of the EU accession process. Full liberalisation of the capital account is a part of the *acquis communautaire*, introduced to ensure a more efficient allocation of resources. However, even though EU rules allow for the temporal reintroduction (6 months maximum) of some capital restrictions under exceptional circumstances, full liberalisation might not necessarily benefit the accession countries at all times. It could be beneficiary to initially postpone the liberalisation of the most fluid capital flows, and thus liberalise longer-term flows before short-term flows, and direct investment before portfolio investment.[17] Thus, short-term capital controls might fulfil a positive role during the catching-up process when a country's credibility has not yet increased sufficiently to prevent large capital flow reversals due to speculative investors. Nevertheless, no country has requested any transitional periods for the liberalisation of short-term capital movements. Instead, the focus has often been on the postponement of the politically sensitive liberalisation of real estate purchases. The chapter on capital movement has now been closed by all accession countries, except Poland and Romania, and implementation of the liberalisation of capital movements has come a long way in most countries. Only Romania, Malta and Cyprus still maintain significant restrictions. Despite the fact that the adoption of the full *acquis communautaire* by new member states is an essential precondition for

[17] Although it may be unattainable to adequately distinguish between "productive" and "speculative" capital flows, making an – imperfect – distinction between short-term and long-term capital flows is in many cases possible. Limiting short-term capital flows will then inevitably also hinder productive short-term investments, such as trade credit. The resulting loss in allocative efficiency then has to be weighed against the increased financial stability that is gained by imposing the capital flow restrictions.

the continued success of European integration, a temporary derogation allowing the accession countries to maintain some barriers to short-term capital flows, might actually have been beneficiary.

With liberalisation of capital movements being reality in most of the accession countries at present, the most important instrument available to prepare the financial sector for EU accession is now the framework of prudential regulation and supervision. Banks could be encouraged to increase their loan-loss provisions and enhance their know-how in the fields of credit assessment, liquidity management and the pricing of risks. This last point goes in principle also for banks' clients and other (end) users of (intermediated) foreign capital, who will also need time to adapt their risk management systems. Additionally, banks' capital levels should be high enough to be able to cope with a more liberalised and market-based operating environment. When the capacity of banks to take on risks of various sorts is expanded, the capacity of supervisors to monitor these changes has to increase commensurately. The accession countries have generally introduced adequate laws and regulations to promote the soundness of individual banks, but that does not necessarily guarantee their actual implementation. It is also important that supervisors and the judiciary have adequate resources to perform their tasks (cf. Section 1.7). The development of the institutional capacity that is necessary to ensure the well-functioning of the prudential framework requires substantial financial resources and, inevitably, time.

1.6 Reducing Government Involvement and Connected Lending

Excessive government involvement in banks' credit decisions as well as connected lending to bank insiders, such as management or shareholders, may harm bank profitability and in the end, bank stability. After all, such lending is unlikely to be based on a commercial evaluation of risk and return, but rather on political objectives. Not surprisingly, recent research shows that related loans have higher default rates and lower recovery rates (La Porta, López-de-Silanes and Zamarripa, 2002). Government ownership in the accession countries has decreased remarkably during recent years, even compared with several EU member states (Table 4).

Table 4 Asset-Share of State-Owned Banks 1996-2001
(in percentages)

Country	2000	1996
Bulgaria	20	82
Czech Republic*	28	17
Estonia	0	7
Hungary	9	16
Latvia	3	7
Lithuania	39	54
Poland	24	70
Romania	50	81
Slovak Republic	49	54
Slovenia	42	41

Note:
* Excludes Ceska Sporitelna and Komercni Banka.
Source: EBRD, *Transition Report*, 2001.

During communist times, governments were in complete charge of banks' credit granting process. A first step in reducing this involvement was the privatisation of state banks. However, stakeholders in these newly privatised banks were often former members of the communist nomenclature. Insofar that was the case, the privatisation process was partly a substitution between government involvement and connected lending. Hersch *et al.* (1997) show for instance that former nomenclature members in Hungary had a higher chance of receiving bank credit than other firm managers. An important second step in reducing unsound lending practices, which in some countries partly coincided with the first one, was the selling of majority stakes in the largest banks to foreign strategic investors. With this, the problem of connected lending has most likely become less pressing as well.

The establishment of foreign bank branches and subsidiaries, whether through green field investments or by taking over local banks, has generally led to a higher efficiency of the domestic banking system.[18] Foreign bank penetration will for example lead to

[18] See for instance Claessens *et al.* (2001) for a comprehensive study into the effects of foreign bank entry on local banking markets.

improved bank management, the introduction of new financial services and the "import" of better regulation. However, for transition economies that open up their banking markets to foreign competition, the challenge lies in achieving such higher long-run efficiency without creating financial instability in the short run. Such instability may for instance be the result of very fragile local banks – burdened by large amounts of bad debt – that default when confronted with foreign competition.[19] In such cases, foreign bank liberalisation can best be preceded or combined with the cleaning and reforming of the local banking system and, importantly, the strengthening of the local supervisory authorities (cf. Section 1.5).

Strong and independent supervisory authorities are extremely important from the viewpoint of reducing connected lending and government involvement. Some authors even argue that regulatory and supervisory independence is important for financial stability just as central bank independence is important for monetary stability.[20] Only when regulators are independent – but at the same time sufficiently accountable – may they withstand political interference in the supervisory process. Supervisors may for instance consider to place tough limits on lending to insiders, as such lending is likely to lead to conflicts of interest. Strict enforcement of these connected exposure limits will be at least as important as the exact size of the limits.

---

[19] Also, foreign banks may be inclined to reduce their credit supply during adverse economic times, leading to increased credit volatility in the host country. Results for Latin America show that even though cross-border foreign bank credit may indeed be withdrawn during an economic downturn, foreign bank subsidiaries' credit is much more stable and even increased during such a period (Peek and Rosengren, 2000). Comparable research for CEE suggest that this conclusion holds for this region as well (De Haas and Lelyveld, 2002).

[20] See Quintyn and Taylor (2002) who distinguish four dimensions of regulatory and supervisory independence. Firstly, regulators should have sufficient autonomy in setting rules and regulations, within the confines of the law (regulatory independence). Secondly, supervisors should be able to inspect, monitor, sanction and enforce sanctions without interference by the government or the supervised institutions (supervisory independence). Thirdly, the supervisory agency should be separate from the executive and legislative branches of government (institutional independence). Fourthly, the supervisory agency should be able to decide independently over the size and use of its budget (budgetary independence).

1.7 *Strengthening the Legal, Supervisory and Accounting Framework*

Adequate institutions, such as a legal framework that specifies the "rules of the game" for a market economy, are crucial for the development of a deep, stable and efficient banking sector. Legal rules provide for instance for creditor protection in case debtors default and collateral has to be liquidated. Without such protection banks may not be incited to expand their credit supply, as they hesitate to lend funds to any enterprise that is even slightly risky, and may instead seek recourse in investing in government bonds or other risk-free assets.[21] Likewise, banks will tend to ration credit if they have to operate in an environment with intransparent and unclear accounting rules as they cannot adequately judge the risks involved in lending. An incomplete implementation of internationally acceptable accounting standards and the subsequent low quality of consolidated accounts makes it difficult for supervisors as well to assess inter-affiliate lending and relationships between banks.

The challenges accession countries face over the coming years in improving their legal, supervisory and accounting frameworks are basically twofold. Firstly, the lack of sound creditor protection has been an important impediment for banks in transition economies to start lending to small, new and innovative enterprises, even when risk-return characteristics were satisfactory in themselves. A sound legal framework that effectively protects creditors when making loans to the private sector, would thus ensure that banks do not overprice the risks of private investments. It will then be conducive to the development of a local banking system that is able to efficiently allocate domestic resources to long-term productive investments. Additionally, an adequate supervisory framework ideally fulfils a complementary role in making sure that banks do neither start to invest funds in overly risky projects. Effective supervision thus warrants that banks do not underprice risks, for instance due to perverse incentives that lead to moral hazard. By providing banks with the right incentives, financial laws and supervision thus enable the banking system to deepen and to allocate the available resources more efficiently. The second, though related, challenge for the

[21] See also the contributions by La Porta, Lopez-De-Silanes, Shleifer and Vishny (1997, 1998 and 2000).

accession countries relates to the role of laws and supervision with respect to exogenous shocks, such as sudden reversals in capital flows. Effective legal and supervisory institutions contribute to a solid banking system that is able to efficiently intermediate the increasing flow of (short-term) foreign funding which will likely be the result of the full liberalisation of the capital account. These challenges may be more or less urgent for different countries, depending on both the expected amount of capital inflow during the coming years and the progress that has already been made in strengthening the legal and supervisory systems.

Since the beginning of transition, many EU accession candidates have shown a substantial improvement in their commercial laws, consisting of pledge, bankruptcy and company laws. As a result, the legal protection of creditors has advanced considerably in most of the countries. Although financial laws have been improved, the enforcement or effectiveness of such laws still leaves to be desired and has in some cases even worsened lately (EBRD, 2001). Table 5 illustrates that in recent years, in some countries both the effectiveness and the extensiveness of commercial law has slightly decreased again. For example, banks that want to liquidate collateral in some countries still have to wait a considerable amount of time before they are actually able to do so. Such inefficiencies are partly caused by ineffective courts and slow legislative systems and processes, as day-to-day legal practice has not been able to adapt itself to the rapidly changing legal environment.

Empirical results suggest that such poor law enforcement indeed hinders the development of the banking sector in transition economies (Pistor, Raiser and Gelfer, 2000). Simply "copying" western laws and aligning supervision with EU standards is thus not enough. This goes as well for improvements in the quality of bank regulation. Reiniger, Schardax and Summer (2001) find that formal supervisory power to prevent and correct problems in the banking sector are relatively high in Hungary, Poland and the Czech Republic when compared with the EU average. However, supervisory resources turn out be used rather inefficiently, as on-site examinations are rather infrequent and forbearance discretion is relatively high. Additionally, Neyapti and Dincer (2001) find a positive (negative) relationship between good bank regulation and supervision and growth (inflation), but also conclude that this relationship is stronger when countries have changed or improved

Table 5 Changes in Legal Transition Indicators 1997-2001: Commercial Law

	2001			1997		
Country	Extensive-ness	Effective-ness	Total	Extensive-ness	Effective-ness	Total
Bulgaria	4	4–	4–	3	3	3
Czech Republic	3	3	3	4	4	4
Estonia		3+	4	4–	4	4
4						
Hungary	4–	4–	4–	4	4	4
Latvia	4–	4	4–	3+	3	3
Lithuania	4–	4–	4–	4	3	3
Poland	4–	3	3+	4	4+	4
Romania	4	4	4	3	3	3
Slovak Republic	3+	3+	3+	3	3	3
Slovenia	4–	4–	4	3	4	3

Note: Scores range between 1 and 4+ (maximum) and are based on EBRD survey results which reflect how lawyers and region experts perceive the state of legal reform.
Source: EBRD, *Transition Report 1997* and *Transition Report 2001*.

their supervisory framework more than once since the beginning of transition. Apparently, legal institutions become more effective when they are adapted to the particular economic situation. Therefore, not only a better enforcement of legal and supervisory frameworks is of great importance for accession countries, but also further improvements to better embed these frameworks into their specific economic and institutional background. This is all the more important since some of the current weaknesses in financial market regulation in CEE, such as a lack of resources to monitor compliance, have been identified as having contributed to the Asian financial crises before (Ramasastry and Slavova, 1999).

1.8 Well-Balanced Incentive Management

A final point of interest in the quest for banking sector stability entails the need to instil the proper incentives in bank owners, managers and depositors. Such "incentive management" confronts policymakers with conflicting objectives. On the one hand, excessive risk taking by banks can be discouraged when owners, depositors and others involved in a bank's business stand to lose from its bankruptcy. On the other hand, there are strong arguments to not always let unsound banks fail, nor to let depositors pay the price for their choice of bank. The fact that banks are important to the economy as a whole and that their failure may have severe repercussions for specific parts of the economy, argues for the more or less explicit existence of a lender of last resort. Likewise, the prevention of bank-runs, the difficulty depositors may face in distinguishing the best banks and the need to protect the public from bank failures, are all valid reasons for establishing a deposit insurance scheme. Nevertheless, the existence of a public safety net also creates moral hazard, as it incites actors to behave less responsible than they would have done otherwise.

Taking the above considerations into account, the members of the European Union have agreed to certain rules for deposit insurance in order to establish minimum prudential standards within the single market. They include a minimum level of protection of 20.000 euro per deposit and the principle that all branch depositors should be protected by the state where the head office is located (home country principle). As these agreements are part of the EU *acquis communautaire*, the candidate countries that have not yet done so, will have to harmonise their practices to meet EU standards before accession. However, this regulation might not be optimal for the accession countries. Demirgüç-Kunt and Detragiache (2000), and also Hermes and Lensink (1997), argue that whereas the moral hazard problem caused by explicit deposit insurance tends to be detrimental to bank stability in general, this is even more so in countries where the institutional environment is still relatively weak. They also conclude that the adverse impact of deposit insurance on bank stability tends to be stronger when the coverage offered to depositors is more extensive. The fact that accession countries lag behind the EU in terms of the development of the institutional environment and income levels, means that compliance with the EU regulation may actually raise moral hazard problems. A case in point is the minimum protection level of 20.000 euro in the current EU deposit insurance scheme, which is relatively high for the accession countries given their much lower income levels as well as average size of deposits. This stresses once more the importance of effective prudential regulation and banking supervision, in order to minimise moral hazard behaviour resulting from a relatively extensive deposit insurance system.

After the candidates have acceded to the EU, the lender of last resort function will remain a national responsibility. Just like the other member states these countries will (continue to) apply a strategy of 'constructive ambiguity' to minimise moral hazard problems. A related issue is the fact that many banks in the accession countries have been acquired by financial institutions from current EU member states. This may have complicated the execution of the lender of last resort function as well as the practice of deposit insurance (but possibly made it less necessary as well). Both the home country principle for deposit insurance and similar EU regulations that stipulate that full responsibility for prudential supervision belongs to the 'home country', mean that important responsibilities for the financial stability of the accession countries will have to be borne by the authorities of other member states. Subsequently, to safeguard financial stability, it is of the utmost importance that the incentives of the home and host country supervisory authorities are fully aligned, and that both parties keep each other sufficiently informed. In order to achieve this, deepened bilateral and multilateral cross-border cooperation between the relevant authorities in different countries, as has been recommended by the Economic and Financial Committee (2000 and 2001) is essential.[22] Such cross-border cooperation becomes even more important as the number of EU banks of whom the headquarters are located in other member states increases during the accession process. Within the EU, Memoranda of Understanding form the main basis of bilateral cooperation. Whereas in the run-up to accession similar agreements are also becoming more commonplace in the relations between the financial authorities of accession countries and individual EU member states, more progress in this field is needed to instil the necessary incentives in all financial authorities involved in cross-border issues.

2 Conclusions and Policy Implications

The structural changes and adjustments that the EU accession candidates have made during recent years, party speeded up by the

---

22 See also Enria and Vesala (2001).

accession requirements, have in many cases been impressive. Notwithstanding this progress, the financial and regulatory infrastructure in many accession countries still considerably lags behind the prevailing levels within the present Union. The much needed further development and deepening of the CEE banking systems may therefore also pose some risks to the stability of these systems as well as to the wider economy. These risks include for instance an unfavourable operating environment for the banking sector due to considerable macroeconomic volatility. Such volatility can result from consistently large current account deficits coupled with increasing short-term financing, such as portfolio investments and short-term bank debt. In addition, (unexpected) exchange rate changes may lead to substantial currency and credit risks in the banking system. Related lending and government involvement, especially when combined with a deficient regulatory and supervisory environment, will make banks more vulnerable as well.

Countries on the road to E(M)U-accession can take some important policy measures to limit the probability of the materialisation of the above-mentioned risks. In general, sound macroeconomic policies tailored to country-specific circumstances, combined with a further strengthening of the supervisory and institutional environment are key. More specifically, current account deficits should be kept in limits within which sound, long-term financing can be ensured to limit the vulnerability of the financial sector to international contagion and sudden sizeable outflows of foreign capital. In addition, the choice of the exchange rate regime should explicitly take into account the risks for financial stability, both in the run-up to EU and to EMU accession. The advantages of preserving some exchange rate flexibility during the coming years should not be underestimated, especially as many countries have already completed the liberalisation of (short-term) capital flows. As regards the institutional environment, the independence of the central bank is crucial, as is the independence of the supervisory authorities. Adequate cooperation of the central bank and banking supervisors, and possibly combining both within one organisation, is imperative as well, as in many accession countries financial knowledge is still relatively scarce and should thus be used as efficiently as possible. Consistent national and cross-border efforts are needed to continuously improve supervision and to keep up with the rapid developments in the financial sector. This should help safeguard the general soundness of banks by stimulating the development of good risk management practices, for example in the field of currency risk. Finally the legal environment needs further strengthening, and enforcement should be tightened up.

The strengthening of the legal system and supervisory authorities will prove all the more important and pressing as there is in some areas an unequivocal tension between the requirements for EU accession and the lagging behind of the financial infrastructure. More precisely, the pursuit of banking stability in the short and medium term might be rendered more difficult by a premature and rash adoption of all EU requirements when striving for (too) speedy E(M)U-accession. An example is the fact that the adoption of the *acquis communautaire* implies that the accession countries have to liberalise their capital accounts in a dynamic economic environment where macroeconomic volatility and capital flow reversals cannot be excluded. Other examples include the adoption of relatively extensive deposit insurance schemes, which may encourage moral hazard, and the early (though voluntary) giving up of exchange rate flexibility. In the coming years all accession countries will face important decisions relating to their upcoming accession to the EU and EMU, ranging from the decision on when to fully liberalise the capital account, to the decision on when to adopt the euro. It is important that the possible implications of these decisions for banking sector stability are always considered carefully.

References

Bank of Finland (2002), *Russian and Baltic Economies: The Week in Review*, No. 15, Helsinki.

Boyd, J.H., R. Levine, and B.D. Smith (2001), "The Impact of Inflation on Financial Sector Performance", In: *Journal of Monetary Economics*, Vol. 47, pp. 221-248.

Broeck, M. de, and T. Sløk (2001), "Interpreting real exchange rate movements in transition economies", IMF Working Paper No. 56, Washington D.C.

Claessens, S., A. Demirgüç-Kunt, and H. Huizinga (2001), "How Does Foreign Entry Affect Domestic Banking Markets?", In: *Journal of Banking and Finance*, Vol. 25, pp. 891-911.

Deutsche Bundesbank (2001), "Monetary Aspects of the

Enlargement of the EU", Monthly Report, October, pp. 15-30.

Demirgüç-Kunt, A. and E. Detragiache (2000), "Does Deposit Insurance Increase Banking Sector Stability?", IMF Working Paper No. 3, Washington D.C.

Economic and Financial Committee (2000), *Report on Financial Stability*, Brussels.

Economic and Financial Committee (2001), *Report on Financial Crisis Management*, Brussels.

Enria, A. and J. Vesala (2001), "Externalities in Financial Supervision: the European Case", Paper prepared for the conference on "Financial Supervision in Europe", The Hague, June.

European Bank for Reconstruction and Development (1998), *Transition Report 1998: Financial Sector in Transition*, London.

Garibaldi, P., N. Mora, R. Sahay and J. Zettelmeyer (2002), "What Moves Capital to Transition Economies?", IMF Working Paper No. 64, Washington D.C.

Goldstein, M. and P. Turner (1996), "Banking Crises in Emerging Economies: Origins and Policy Options", BIS Economic Papers No. 46, Basel.

Haas, de, R.T.A. and I.P.P. van Lelyveld (2002), *Foreign Bank Penetration and Bank Credit Stability in Central and Eastern Europe*, Research Series Supervision No. 43, De Nederlandsche Bank, Amsterdam.

Hermes, N. and R. Lensink (1997), "Can Deposit Insurance Help to Establish a Stable Banking System During the Transition Process?", In: *Financial Reform in Emerging Market Economies: Quantitative and Institutional Issues*, Poznan University Press, Poznan, pp. 67-92.

Hersch, P., D. Kemme and J. Netter (1997), "Access to Bank Loans in a Transition Economy: The Case of Hungary", In: *Journal of Comparative Economics*, Vol. 24, pp. 79-89.

La Porta, R., F. López-de-Silanes, A. Shleifer and R.W. Vishny (1997), "Legal Determinants of External Finance", In: *Journal of Finance*, 52, pp. 1131-1150.

—— (1998), "Law and Finance", In: *Journal of Political Economy*, Vol. 106, pp. 1113-1155.

—— (2000), "Investor Protection and Corporate Governance", *Journal of Financial Economics*, Vol. 58, pp. 3-27.

La Porta, R., F. López-de-Silanes and G. Zamarripa (2002), "Related Lending", NBER Working Paper No. 8848, Cambridge MA.

Lensink, R. (2001), "Financial Development, Uncertainty and Economic Growth", In: *De Economist*, Vol. 149, No. 3, pp. 299-312.

Lipschitz, L., T. Lane and A. Mourmouras (2002), "Capital Flows to Transition Economies: Master or Servant?", IMF Working Paper No. 11, Washington D.C.

McKinnon, R. I. and H. Pill (1997), "Credible Economic Liberalizations and Overborrowing", In: *American Economic Review Papers and Proceedings*, Vol. 87, No. 2, pp. 189-193.

Neyapti, B. and N. Dincer (2001), "Measuring the Quality of Bank Regulation and Supervision and Its Macroeconomic Effects – an Application to Transition Economies", Working Paper, Bilkent University, Bilkent Ankara.

Peek, J., and E.S. Rosengren, (2000), "Implications of the Globalization of the Banking Sector. The Latin American Experience", In: *New England Economic Review*, September/ October, Federal Reserve Bank of Boston, Boston, pp. 45-63.

Pelkmans, J., D. Gros and J. Ferrer (2000), *Long-Run Economic Aspects of the European Union's Eastern Enlargement*, Dutch Scientific Council for Government Policy (WRR), The Hague.

Pistor, K., M. Raiser, and S. Gelfer (2000), "Law and Finance in Transition Economies", In: *Economics of Transition*, Vol. 8, pp. 325-368.

Quintyn, M. and M.W. Taylor (2002), "Regulatory and Supervisory Independence and Financial Stability", IMF Working Paper No. 46, Washington D.C.

Ramasastry, A. and S. Slavova (1999), "Market Perceptions of Financial Law in the Region – EBRD Survey Results", In: *Law in Transition*, Spring, EBRD, London.

Reininger, T., F. Schardax and M. Summer (2001), "The Financial System in the Czech Republic, Hungary and Poland after a Decade of Transition", Discussion Paper No. 16, Economic Research Centre of the Deutsche Bundesbank, Deutsche Bundesbank, Frankfurt am Main.

Sutela, P. (2001), "Managing Capital Flows in Estonia and Latvia", BOFIT Discussion Paper No. 17, Bank of Finland, Helsinki.

Zwet, van der, A.M.C. and J. Swank (2000), *Financial Fragility and Macroeconomic Performance: A Comparison of Emerging and Highly Developed Countries*, DNB Staff Reports No. 52, De Nederlandsche Bank, Amsterdam.

7

Postscript to Henk Brouwer, Ralph de Haas and Bas Kiviet

Mark Teunissen

In December 2002, the European Council in Copenhagen concluded that ten candidate countries would be able to accede to the EU in 2004. In the history of the EU enlargement process, this is undoubtedly a unique step. The decision has intensified the debate on how quickly these countries should join the EMU after their accession to the EU. To be able to join the EMU, countries must comply with the (nominal) convergence criteria for inflation, public finances, long-term interest rates and the exchange rate, as laid down in the Treaty of Maastricht. The latter criterion stipulates that a country should observe the normal fluctuation bands within the European Exchange Rate Mechanism (the so-called ERM-II) for at least two years without devaluing against the currency of any other member state. In the ERM-II, the exchange rates of the currencies of the accession countries are pegged to the euro, with a standard fluctuation band of +/- 15 percent and with the possibility of realignments of this central rate. This minimum period of two years implies that the ten candidate countries would be able to join the EMU at the end of 2006, or early 2007, at the earliest. With this formal timeframe in mind, the authorities of most candidate countries, supported by several academics, seem to be in favour of entering the EMU as quickly as possible. On the other hand, the eurosystem authorities have been especially reticent to the idea of rapid EMU accession.

The Road to EMU: Short Cut or Detour?

The proponents of rapid EMU accession generally base their view on three arguments. A first argument is that most candidate countries are already highly integrated with the euro area in terms of financial and trade flows, and as a consequence have more or less similar business cycles as compared to the euro area. As such, the common monetary policy of the eurosystem would not be inappropriate for the candidate countries. A second argument is that the prospect of rapid accession to the EMU would stimulate governments of the candidate countries to implement necessary, but painful reforms. Also, with EMU accession ahead, such reforms would likely be more acceptable to parliaments and the public at large. A third argument relates to the general antipathy towards the ERM-II. This mechanism is considered to be a mere waiting room before the adoption of the euro, while at the same time creating possible risks to financial stability. In fact, some academics even refer to the ERM-II as purgatory! One important reason for this view is that trying to maintain a fixed, but adjustable exchange rate in the context of large and volatile capital inflows, would unavoidably lead to speculative attacks on the new EU members' currencies. While fighting off such attacks is costly, giving in to them might be even more costly in terms of financial instability. Therefore, the quick adoption of the euro will eliminate exchange rate risk and, as such limit financial stability risks. Moreover, no exchange rate risk means lower risk premiums. This would of course be beneficial for trade and investment, which in turn would enhance the growth potential of the accession countries. All together, although acknowledging the formal requirement of the ERM-II participation after EU accession, most accession countries are likely to limit their stay in ERM-II to the shortest period possible. As they aim for rapid EMU accession, they might well consider the central parity chosen in the ERM-II to be the conversion rate for euro adoption.

The arguments against (too) rapid EMU accession are basically two-fold. First, rapid EMU accession would require the new EU member states to comply with the nominal convergence criteria at rather short notice. One could question the feasibility of such a steep adjustment path, especially with regard to the criterion for public finances. Currently, the budget deficits, particularly in the Central and Eastern European accession countries, are still significant.

Moreover, substantial budgetary risks may emerge in the near future. For instance, the completion of the transition process and of the accession to the EU will entail significant government outlays. In the three Baltic countries, for example, annual public expenditures due to complying with the environmental requirements stemming from the EU *acquis communautaire*, are estimated to reach 2 percent of GDP. Although most of the current accession countries have made remarkable progress in inflation reduction, major risks in this area still lie ahead. In addition to the well-known Balassa-Samuelson effect, inflationary pressures might also arise from EU accession itself. For instance, regulated prices in the accession countries still constitute around 20 percent of the consumer price index on average. As most of these regulated prices are set below cost-recovery level, the process of price liberalisation as required by EU accession, will have an upward effect on price dynamics in the accession countries. Besides the question of feasibility, one could wonder whether a very ambitious nominal convergence path is desirable. In some countries, this adjustment path is only possible with very tight budgetary and monetary policies, which could slow down their already limited progress in real convergence towards the euro area.

A second argument against rapid adoption of the euro is that maintaining their currencies through participation in the ERM-II could be beneficial for the new EU member states. The ERM-II provides both stability and flexibility, and as such can foster the combination of nominal and real convergence. The exchange rate peg vis-à-vis the euro offers the new EU member states an anchor for macroeconomic stability in general, and for containing inflation in particular, as in a number of these countries with relatively limited financial markets, the exchange rate channel is the most effective monetary transmission channel. At the same time, the ERM-II offers flexibility through the relatively large bandwidth and the possibility of realignments, which could be advantageous for the new member states. After all, most of these countries are small open economies, which are still in the process of rapid structural transformation and catching-up. In this environment, nominal exchange rate flexibility could serve as a useful instrument to accommodate economic shocks or an appreciation of the real exchange rate. As such, *ex ante* guarantees about the euro conversion rate are impossible to give, even more so as last minutes revaluations are still possible – see, for instance, Ireland and Greece. If used in this way, the ERM-II could both foster economic stability as well as provide an anchor for nominal stability.

To conclude, it is clear there is more than one ground for arguing both in favour and against rapid EMU accession by the new EU member states. It is important to note that the ERM-II is a multilateral arrangement with responsibilities for the authorities of both the participating country and the euro area. Therefore, in advance of accession of the new EU member states to the ERM-II, intensive discussions between these parties on the modalities of operating in this exchange rate mechanism seem warranted. Obviously, once participation in the ERM-II becomes a fact, both parties should carefully monitor the sustainability of the central rates.

8

Comment on Henk Brouwer, Ralph de Haas and Bas Kiviet

György Szapáry

In my comment, I would like to touch upon three characteristics of the financial sector of the Central and Eastern European Countries of transition (CEECs), namely, the relatively low degree of financial intermediation, the dominance of the banking sector over the capital markets, and the high degree of foreign ownership. To a large extent, these features are a direct consequence of the transition process. I agree with the authors of the chapter that macroeconomic stability and a strong independent regulatory and supervisory authority are essential for reducing the potential risks to financial stability. However, the special features of the CEECs financial system need to be considered, since in some cases they mitigate, while in others they exacerbate the commonly known potential risks. To make my arguments, I will refer to the experience of Hungary, the country with which I am the most familiar, but most of the points I make are also relevant for the other CEECs.[1]

Low Degree of Financial Intermediation

A typical characteristic of the CEECs is the low level of bank intermediation. In the CEECs-10,[2] banking assets average about 50

[1] For details of the banking sector reform in Hungary see György Szapáry, "Banking Sector Reform in Hungary: What Have We Learned and What Are the Prospects?", In: *Comparative Economic Studies*, XLIV, No. 1, Spring 2002.

percent of GDP, compared with an average of 240 percent in the euro area. In Hungary that number is 70 percent. Even in Greece, where the depth of the financial sector is the lowest among EMU members, the corresponding figure is twice as high. The low ratio in Hungary is explained by the low level of credit to the private sector. As can be seen from Chart 1, loans extended by the banking sector to the corporate and household sectors totalled about 30 percent of GDP in 2000. That figure in the euro area ranges form close to 50 percent in Finland to almost 120 percent in the Netherlands and Portugal, the weighted average for the whole area being over 80 percent.

Several factors account for the low level of credit in Hungary. First, as a result of the privatisation of enterprises to strategic owners and the inflow of FDI to greenfield projects, a major part of the Hungarian GDP is produced by foreign invested companies, which account for about 70 percent of Hungarian exports, a main driving force behind the dynamic economic growth. These multinational companies tend to borrow from their mother companies or from

Chart 1 Credit to the Private Sector in the Euro Zone and in Hungary, 2000

(in percentages of GDP)

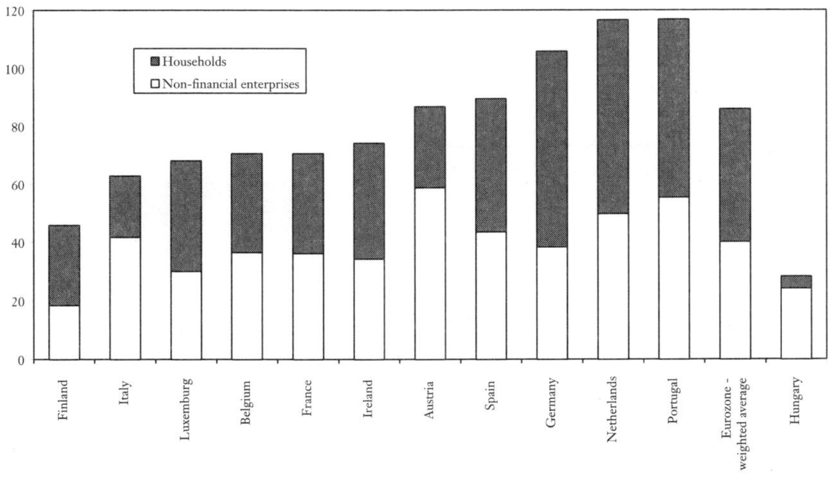

Source: National Bank of Hungary, *Report on Financial Stability*, June, 2002.

2 All accession counties except Cyprus, Malta and Turkey.

their banks abroad, bypassing the domestic banking system. Second, as illustrated in Chart 2, lending to the household sector is very low by comparison to the euro zone. In the euro area, such loans average 46 percent (weighted) of GDP, while in Hungary they represent a mere 6 percent. Lending to households has been constrained by the low level of incomes and the high risks involved in lending to this sector. Third, the access to bank credit by domestic private firms has been impeded by the lack of sufficiently long track record that would make them acceptable credit risks for banks.

The low level of bank intermediation raises a number of issues from the point of view of potential risks. That situation is partly explained by the fact that banks have shied away from lending to the riskier small and medium-sized enterprise and household markets, concentrating on the more stable corporate sector. This sector is better capitalised and hence more able to withstand the fluctuations in market conditions. Therefore, there are less potential risks to banks from shifts in market conditions. On the other hand, the low level of credit also means that there is "room to expand" into the more risky market segments. This is already happening in Hungary, as the increased competition encourages banks to extend their activities into new markets, particularly the household market. Currently, the capital adequacy ratio of banks in Hungary is satisfactory (12,3 percent in 2001) and the bad loan portfolio is less

Chart 2 Credit to Households in the Euro Zone and in Hungary, 2000
(in percentages of GDP)

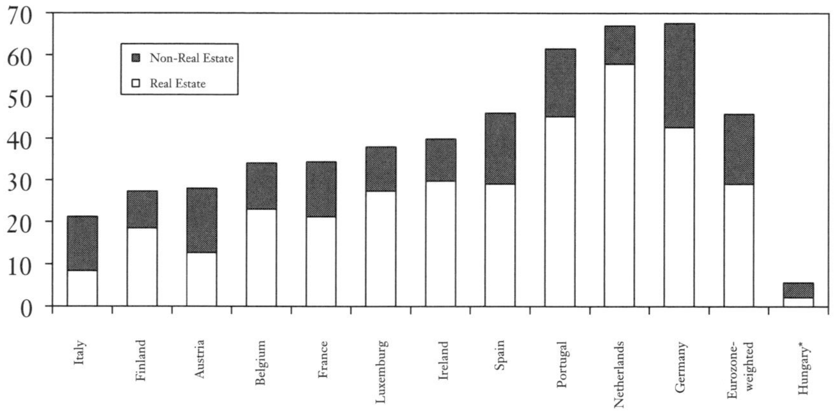

Source: National Bank of Hungary, *Report on Financial Stability*, June, 2002.

than 4 percent. As banks extend their activities to riskier markets, the quality of the loan portfolio might worsen and there might be a need to increase the capital of the banks in order to avoid an undue decline in the capital adequacy ratios. In this respect, it can be considered as an advantage that all but two of the 31 commercial banks are subsidiaries of well known foreign banks. However, there is no guarantee that the mother banks will not get into trouble, in which case they might be less willing to put additional capital into their subsidiaries abroad. Foreign ownership of banks can not, therefore, be an excuse for lax supervision at home.

The foreign currency denominated loans of the banks represent a relatively large proportion (38 percent) of total credit extended by banks in Hungary. Under the narrow-band preannounced crawling peg, there was an incentive to borrow in foreign currency to take advantage of lower interest rates. Since the widening of the exchange rate band in May 2001, foreign currency borrowings have been reduced in response to the appreciation of the Hungarian forint and to the increased exchange rate risk. As a prudential measure, the foreign currency open positions of banks are subject to limits imposed by the authorities, but the foreign currency exposure of domestic borrowers represent a potential risk for banks. That risk is mitigated by the fact that most of the foreign currency borrowing is done by exporting companies whose receipts are in foreign exchange. Nevertheless, the situation needs to be closely monitored since a depreciation of the currency can create problems for the borrowers with attendant implications for banks.

Dominance of the Banking Sector

In Hungary, as in the other CEECs, the financial sector is dominated by the banking sector. The average market capitalisation of the CEECs-10 amounts to 16 percent of GDP, compared to the euro area average of 84 percent. The turnover of the stock exchanges in the Czech Republic, Hungary and Poland *per year* is roughly equivalent to 2, 3 and 5 *days* of turnover at the stock exchanges of Paris or Frankfurt, respectively.[3] One reason for the low market

[3] See, European Central Bank, "Financial Sector Development and Convergence in Accession Countries: An Overview", Background Paper for the

capitalisation is the feeble income levels, another is the low level of institutional savings (e.g. pension funds, insurance companies). While these constraints are expected to loosen with the growth in incomes and the development of the private pension fund and insurance markets, there are impediments to the growth of the stock markets that will take longer to disappear. These impediments reflect the dominance of the Hungarian corporate market by multinational companies, which are naturally listed on the stock exchanges of London, Frankfurt, New York, etc. and not on the stock exchange of Budapest. This means that firms representing dynamic sectors of the economy are not present in the Hungarian stock market. Domestic firms which have the necessary size and a sufficient track record to borrow on the capital market are few and those which do borrow are often also listed on stock exchanges abroad. Another feature of the Hungarian stock markets is that non-residents account for about 70 percent of the market capitalisation, again a reflection of the low level of incomes and institutional savings. It is my view that the above constraints will slow down the development of the equity market in Hungary and the other CEECs for a long time to come.

The small size of the equity market and its dominance by non-residents means that the wealth effects due to equity price fluctuations are limited. The potential risks to banks associated with price bubbles – overconsumption, overinvestment, excessive credit expansion – are thus reduced. On the other hand, the large share of non-residents renders the markets more easily subject to contagion, which can induce greater volatility in exchange rates and interest rates.

Foreign Ownership

As shown in Chart 3, foreign ownership of banks is important in most CEECs. In Hungary, it is one of the most important, with foreign ownership representing about 70 percent of the banking sector's registered capital. This is the result of both privatisation and the greenfield establishment of banks. By increasing competition, foreign ownership led to a remarkable improvement in services and to a

---

Eurosystem Seminar with Accession Countries' Central Banks, Berlin, December, 2001.

Chart 3 Foreign Ownership of Banks
(in percentages of GDP)

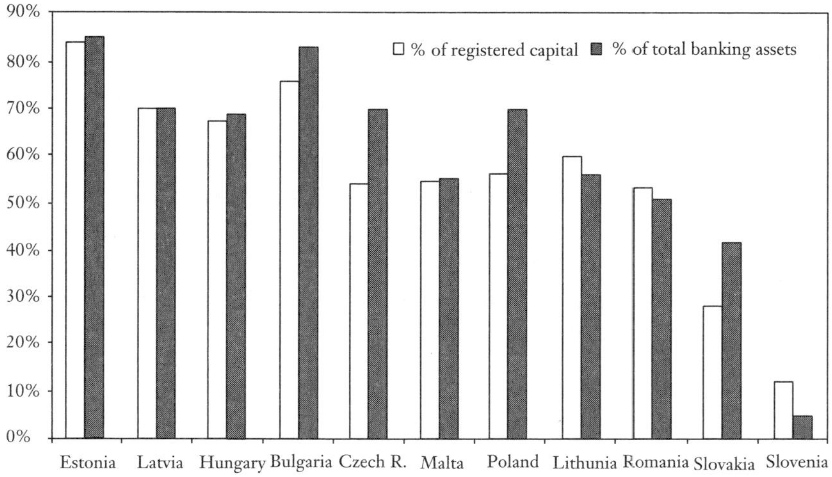

Source: European Central Bank, "Financial Sector Development and Convergence in Accession Countries: An Overview", background paper for the Eurosystem Seminar with Accession Countries' Central Banks, Berlin, December, 2001.

Chart 4 Hungary – Return on Equity of Commercial Banks
(in percentages)

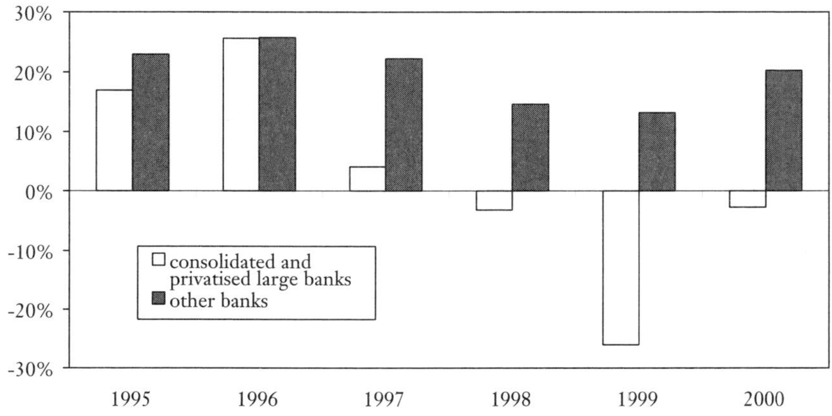

Source: National Bank of Hungary, *Report on Financial Stability*, June, 2002.

compression of the spreads between deposit and lending rates. This has also helped to improve the monetary transmission process. An interesting lesson from the Hungarian experience is that the profitability of banks, as measured by the pre-tax return on equity (ROE), evolved very differently for large privatised banks and for banks established as greenfield projects (Chart 4). For the latter, the ROE fluctuated but remained positive throughout the period of 1995-2000. For the former, the ROE fell sharply and turned negative during 1998-2000, indicating that the foreign owners face a difficult task in restructuring the former state-owned banks. Bank supervision can play an important role in preventing that a protracted restructuring does not lead to more serious problems, a danger that foreign ownership does not necessarily eliminate.

9

Sources of Financial Fragility in the EU Candidate Countries

Marek Dabrowski

Although countries of Central and Eastern Europe have made impressive progress during the last decade in the sphere of both macroeconomic and microeconomic reforms, they cannot be considered fully mature market economies. In addition, their increasing openness connected with progressing integration of financial markets (globalisation) and the EU accession process brings, apart from obvious benefits, some additional risks.

Generally speaking, the potential financial fragility of the EU candidate countries can originate from microeconomic sources, including banking sector instability, corporate sector non-transparency and over-borrowing; and macroeconomic sources, including fiscal imbalances, inflation differentials, current account imbalances, and intermediate exchange rate regimes.

Banking sector instability can be caused either by political influence on lending decisions (mainly in the state-owned banks) or by connected and imprudent lending (mainly in the private and newly privatised banks). Both phenomena usually originate from the flawed ownership structure, insufficient prudential regulation and weak banking supervision. Remedies should be seen mainly in privatisation involving the key role of the first-class transnational financial institutions, avoiding government bailouts and building strong banking supervision and prudential regulations.

Problems in a non-financial corporate sector usually come from soft-budget constraints leading to over-borrowing ('too big to fail' approach or political sensitivity of some sectors), imprudent corporate and business practices (for example, lack of transparency) and currency mismatches in the corporation balance sheets. These unfavourable phenomena are usually concentrated in state-owned enterprises and conglomerates, but not exclusively. The experience of many emerging markets demonstrates the case of big private owners having an influence on government and its decisions and extracting various kinds of rent from this political connection.

Like the case of the banking sector, remedies can be seen mainly in avoiding government intervention and bailing-out practices (which lead to soft budget constraints and moral hazard behaviour), sound privatisation involving the first-class international investors and improving corporate governance, protecting property-rights, reporting and accounting standards. However, it is difficult to find a good remedy for currency mismatches in economies that lack sufficient macroeconomic credibility and, therefore, are unable to borrow internationally in their own currencies (the so-called 'original sin' problem – see Hausmann, 2001).

This leads us to the analysis of macroeconomic sources of financial fragility. The biggest danger of instability originates from fiscal imbalances, which in some EU candidate countries – particularly those belonging to the so-called Visegrad group[1] – have become chronic (see Table 1).

Table 1 General Government Balance (Cash Basis)
(in percentage of GDP)

	2000	2001	1997-2001[a]
Bulgaria	-0.7	1.7	0.5
Czech Rep.	-4.2	-5.5	-3.8
Estonia	-0.7	-0.4	-0.5
Hungary	-3.1	-4.1	-5.4
Latvia	-2.7	-1.6	-1.7
Lithuania	-3.3	-1.9	-2.9
Poland	-3.5	-3.9	-2.8
Romania	-3.8	-3.4	-4.0
Slovakia	-6.7	-5.6	-7.0
Slovenia	-2.3	-2.5	-2.3

Note:
[a] Average 1997 - 2001.
Sources: EU (2001), Annex 2; EU (2002), Annex 7.

As EU candidate countries continued substantial deficits in years of relatively high growth rates, their fiscal situation will further deteriorate when growth slows down for any reason (the recent example of Poland). Although for obvious methodological reasons it is almost impossible to estimate cyclically adjusted deficits in transition economies there are no doubts that their fiscal positions are very vulnerable to changes in real GDP growth rates.

In addition, the fiscal position of the EU candidates can deteriorate further in the first two years of their EU membership as the result of several accession-related factors such as:

1. Additional fiscal burden in national budgets coming from adoption of some specific *acquis communautaire*, particularly in such fiscally burdening areas as environmental protection, infrastructure, transportation, public administration, social policy, etc. On the other hand, one may expect some additional revenues coming from indirect tax harmonisation (increasing VAT and excise tax rates for certain groups of products).
2. Giving up part of the budget revenues (custom duties and part of the VAT) in favour of the EU budget, but these losses can hardly be compensated by the expected transfers from the EU budget since the latter relate mostly to items and programmes, that were not previously financed by the EU applicants from their national budgets. In addition, some of the EU funded programmes need co-financing of the national budgets.
3. Transition problems connected with launching the EU funding mechanisms in the first year (two years) of the membership. They will originate from a time mismatch between contribution to the EU budget (which must be done up front) and incoming transfers (*ex post* reimbursement of incurred expenses). Also, the institutional capacities of the new members to absorb EU structural funds will be very limited in the beginning.

Fiscal imbalances increase the country's financial fragility in various ways. First, a deteriorating fiscal balance must lead to a deterioration of the current account balance, other things being unchanged. Second, a fiscal deficit in period t automatically narrows the fiscal room of manoeuvre in periods $t+1$, $t+2$, etc., as it contributes to an increasing debt burden and higher debt service

---

[1] The Visegrad group consists of the Czech Republic, Hungary, Poland and Slovakia.

costs in the future. Finally, a higher fiscal deficit and a higher public debt increase the perception of country risk among investors and make them more reluctant to lend both to the government and private borrowers.

The available empirical experience shows the dominant role of fiscal imbalances in causing financial crises in transition economies (Dabrowski *et al.*, 2003). Hopefully, the disciplining mechanism of *The Stability and Growth Pact* and interest of most EU candidates to meet Maastricht criteria in order to enter the EMU at earliest possible date (see below), will force them to carry out serious fiscal adjustment in the coming years.

The role of inflation differentials is perhaps less obvious but certainly not less important. Moderate or high inflation discourages savings and distorts the allocation process. Under open capital accounts, it increases the international perception of country macroeconomic risk, particularly currency depreciation or devaluation risk, provoking sudden changes in direction of capital flows (closely related to changes in demand for local currency). Real interest rates are usually higher than in countries with a sustainable low inflation level.

Most of the EU candidate countries have experienced serious problems with breaking a well-rooted inflationary inertia (see Table 2). However, the last two years have brought some progress in this area. This progress will be even more visible if we consider the continuous disinflation trend in 2002 which is not reflected in

Table 2 End-of-Year Inflation in EU Candidate Countries, 1994-2001

	1994	1995	1996	1997	1998	1999	2000	2001
Bulgaria	121.9	32.9	310.8	578.6	0.9	7.0	11.2	4.8
Czech Republic	9.7	7.9	8.6	10.1	6.8	2.6	4.0	4.1
Estonia	41.6	28.8	15.0	12.5	4.5	3.8	5.0	4.2
Hungary	21.2	28.3	19.8	18.4	10.3	11.2	10.0	6.7
Latvia	26.2	23.3	13.2	7.0	2.8	3.2	1.8	3.1
Lithuania	45.0	35.5	13.1	8.5	2.4	0.3	1.4	2.0
Poland	29.5	21.6	18.5	13.2	8.6	9.8	8.6	3.7
Romania	61.7	27.8	56.9	151.6	43.8	54.8	40.7	30.3
Slovakia	11.7	7.2	5.4	6.4	5.6	14.2	8.4	6.6
Slovenia	18.3	8.6	8.8	9.4	5.7	8.8	10.6	7.0

Source: IMF.

Table 2. The progress in the EU accession process radically improved the financial markets' perception of the macroeconomic fundamentals of the future EU members, stimulating increased capital inflows, appreciation pressure on national currencies, and convergence of nominal interest rates and inflation levels.

However, the disinflation trend cannot be considered sustainable as long as the currency depreciation or devaluation risk remains. And this risk is justified (in the eyes of financial market players) both by the remaining uncertainty concerning the timetable of the EU/EMU accession and by the expected high current account deficits.

High current account deficits can originate from many factors, including historically low domestic savings-to-GDP ratios in several countries, a negative rate of government savings (the consequences of fiscal deficits analysed above) and prospects of the EU accession itself. This last factor needs some additional comment.

Perspective of the near EU membership can stimulate additional capital inflows (a better perception of country risk and future rate of return) on the one hand, and discourage domestic savings (through a consumption smoothing effect) on the other. Both trends must lead inevitably to higher current account deficits and increasing appreciation pressures (see Rostowski, 2002a). From the long-term perspective, high current account deficits should not be considered the danger because the current EU candidates will eventually become members of the euro zone and balance-of-payments constraints will disappear. However, the transition period can be extremely difficult and risky, increasing the candidates' macroeconomic vulnerability and the danger of a sudden currency crisis.

Empirical observations support the concern related to current account imbalances and their possibly risky consequences. Most of the EU candidates record high current account deficits (Table 3). The above mentioned nominal convergence, which achieved momentum in Central Europe in 2002,[2] may involve elements of a speculative bubble, particularly in the case of Czech Republic, where short-term interest rates came down below the euro zone level.

---

[2] The intensive convergence play has been caused not only by the ongoing accession process but also by the very low level of interest rates in developed countries and high uncertainty in several emerging markets (Latin America, Turkey, and South Africa), that increased additionally attractiveness of Central Europe for potential investors.

While the balance of public savings (in fact, fiscal balance) can and should be subject of policy targeting, two other discussed factors, i.e. the rate of domestic private savings and capital inflows, are largely out of the control of national economic policies, at least in the short term. Moreover, defining what is the 'safe' level of a current account deficit is an intellectually tricky task, and the financial markets' perception of what level is 'safe' can easily change over time. Thus, the only way to eliminate the danger of a balance-of-payment (currency) crisis forever is to give up the national monetary policy and join one of major currency areas. If such a solution is not possible (for any economic and political reason), the current account balance and the factors influencing its changes must be subject to very careful monitoring.

However, keeping a current account deficit under control (i.e. limiting its magnitude) involves serious economic costs such as a lower rate of economic growth, as the recent experience of Poland (2001-2002) and the earlier experience of the Czech Republic (1997-1999) confirms.

These arguments should be considered in the debate on the timing of the EMU accession by the current candidates. While membership in the Economic and Monetary Union is not automatic upon joining the EU, the new EU members will have to do it at some point. The Maastricht Treaty did not grant them the same opt-out option as the UK and Denmark. However, as Sweden's case

Table 3 Current Account Balance in EU Candidate Countries
(as percentage of GDP)

	2000	2001	1997-2001[a]
Bulgaria	-5.0	-6.0	-1.5
Czech Republic	-4.7	-4.7	-4.3
Estonia	-6.7	-6.1	-7.8
Hungary	-3.3	-2.2	-3.4
Latvia	-6.9	-9.7	-8.6
Lithuania	-6.0	-4.8	-8.9
Poland	-6.3	-4.1	-5.4
Romania	-3.7	-5.9	-5.3
Slovakia	-3.7	-8.8	-7.4
Slovenia	-3.3	-0.4	-1.7

Note:
[a] Average 1997 – 2001.
Sources: EU (2001), Annex 2; EU (2002), Annex 7.

demonstrates, the EU member can effectively postpone the date of the EMU accession if it is not economically or politically ready to accede..

Another question relates to a specific EMU accession path which the future member can choose. Theoretically, there are four possible variants of transitional exchange rate regimes which the candidate can consider: (i) fixed but adjustable peg in the +/- 15 percent band (the 'classical' ERM variant); (ii) managed float; (iii) currency board; and (iv) earlier unilateral euroisation

The third and fourth option mean *de facto* earlier unilateral entering the euro zone although not the EMU because of the lack of influence on the ECB decisions and opportunity to use its 'lender of last resort' facility. While the third option is officially accepted by the European Commission and the European Central Bank, they oppose the idea of the unilateral euroisation as illegal or inappropriate (see Rostowski, 2002c). Formally speaking, these kinds of arguments do not sound convincing since the euro is a fully convertible and internationally tradable currency, and some small Balkan countries (Montenegro, Kosovo and partly Bosnia and Herzegovina) already use the euro as the official legal tender even though they are not, yet, EU candidates. The real arguments against a quick entry into the euro zone by the current EU candidates have a different character and are discussed below.

The two first variants of transition to the EMU represent the so-called intermediate or hybrid exchange rate regimes where the monetary authority tries to simultaneously manage both the exchange rate and the money supply. This kind of monetary/ exchange rate arrangement violates the principle of 'impossible trinity'[3] (see Frankel, 1999) and is particularly vulnerable to speculative attacks (see Obstfeld and Rogoff, 1995; McCallum, 1999; Eichengreen and Hausmann, 1999; IIE, 1999). Thus, this kind of arrangement does not eliminate sources of financial fragility in the economies of the future EU members.

Looking at the current arrangements (Table 4), six out of the ten candidates continue evident hybrid regimes. Romania, Slovakia and Slovenia do not have a clear nominal anchor at all. The Czech

3 According to this principle a country must give up one of the following three goals: exchange rate stability, monetary independence, and financial market integration. It cannot have all three simultaneously.

Table 4 Monetary Regimes in EU Candidate Countries

	Monetary regime
Bulgaria	Currency board
Czech Rep.	DIT (managed float)
Estonia	Currency board
Hungary	DIT (horizontal band; narrow crawling band until 2001)
Latvia	Stable horizontal peg to SDR
Lithuania	Currency board
Poland	DIT (independent float from April 2000)
Romania	No clear nominal anchor (managed float)
Slovakia	No clear nominal anchor (managed float)
Slovenia	No clear nominal anchor (informal crawling band)

Sources: IMF Country Reports, central bank websites, author's own observation.

Republic and Hungary formally follow direct inflation targeting but have not fully abandoned the exchange rate targets – ad hoc anti-appreciation foreign exchange market intervention in the former and horizontal exchange rate band in the latter. Latvia consequently follows an exchange rate peg to SDR (which will require a re-pegging to the euro in some point) but does not abandon open market operations regulating domestic liquidity. Poland represents the case of a really free (independent) float under a direct inflation-targeting (DIT) regime. Estonia, Lithuania and Bulgaria run euro-denominated currency boards (Lithuania after successful re-pegging it from dollar to euro in early 2002).

The question of how quickly to join the euro zone is a subject of hot economic and political debate. While the idea of rapid euro zone accession becomes increasingly popular in the candidate countries, there is a lot of reservation on the EU side.[4] It seems that the main fears of the incumbents relate to the danger of weakening the euro, eliminating or limiting the policy conditionality related to the EMU accession of the new EU members and the fact that the ECB is not institutionally prepared to deal with 20+ members.[5]

4 Brouwer, de Haas, and Kiviet's chapter in this book seems to be a good example of the western scepticism related to fast EMU enlargement.

5 Rostowski (2002b) formulates additional hypotheses: (i) fear that new, fast growing euro zone members will create additional inflation pressure and (ii) some aspects of the discussed EU institutional reform (particularly strengthening prerogatives of the Euro Ecofin group).

Looking at the timing of the EMU accession from the candidates' perspective, the potential disadvantages of giving up monetary independence early relate to abandoning devaluation as a stimulating and corrective mechanism and increasing competitive pressure on several sectors of real economy. However, the big question is to what extent a small open economy can use exchange rate and national monetary policy as a shock absorber and anti-cyclical tool in an environment of free capital mobility and competition between currencies (see Dabrowski, 2001; Dabrowski, 2002). Obviously, national monetary and fiscal policies are not effective in influencing real exchange rate and current account deficits in such an environment (see Rostowski, 2002a; Dabrowski 2002).

On the other hand, one can list several potential advantages of rapid entry to the euro zone by the current EU candidates. First, it will forever eliminate the danger of a currency crisis by removing balance-of-payments constraints. Second, it will decrease the candidate countries' risk premiums, helping in sustainable interest rate and inflation convergence (by importing credibility). Third, it will force the governments and parliaments of candidate countries to carry out serious fiscal adjustments. Lower real interest rates will make this adjustment easier, particularly in countries with high public debt burdens (Bulgaria, Hungary, Poland and Slovakia). Fourth, early monetary unification will promote further trade and investment integration between new and incumbent members.

Incumbents can also gain from an early EMU enlargement. It will eliminate the danger of competitive devaluation and decrease the possibility of macroeconomic and financial instability inside the single European Market. The new members will have stronger incentives to comply with the macroeconomic convergence criteria and disciplining rules defined by the Maastricht and Amsterdam Treaties. Avoiding a long lasting phenomenon of a 'second class' EU membership in the case of new entrants will be beneficial for both sides in political and economic terms, supporting further stages of European integration.

Summing up, it is in the interest of both new members and incumbents to think about rapid accession of the former to the euro zone.

References

Dabrowski, Marek (2001), "Global Integration of Financial Markets and Its Consequences for Transition Economies", In: Lucjan T. Orlowski (ed.), *Transition and Growth in Post-communist countries. The Ten-year Experience*, Edward Elgar, Cheltenham.

Dabrowski, Marek (2002), "Which 'Corner' Solution?", Paper presented at the CASE International Conference on "Beyond Transition. Development Perspectives and Dilemmas", Falenty n. Warsaw, April 12-13.

Dabrowski, Marek (ed.) (2003), *Currency Crises in Emerging Markets*, The Kluwer Academic Publishers, Boston.

Eichengreen, Barry, and Ricardo Hausmann (1999), "Exchange Rates and Financial Fragility", NBER Working Paper No. 7418, November.

EU (2001), "Making a Success of Enlargement", Strategy Paper and Report of the European Commission on "The Progress Towards Accession by Each of the Candidate Countries", Commission of the European Communities, Brussels, October.

EU (2002), "Towards the Enlarged Union", Strategy Paper and Report of the European Commission on "The Progress Towards Accession by Each of the Candidate Countries", Commission of the European Communities, Brussels, October 9.

Frankel, Jeffrey A. (1999), "No Single Currency Regime is Right for All Countries or at All Times", NBER Working Paper No. 7338, September.

Hausmann, Ricardo (2001), "The Polish Road to the Euro: An Envious Latin American View", Paper prepared for the Conference on "The Polish Way to the Euro" organised by the National Bank of Poland, Warsaw, October 22-23.

IIE (1999), "Safeguarding Prosperity in a Global Financial System: The Future International Financial Architecture", A Council of Foreign Relations-Sponsored Report, Institute for International Economics, Washington D.C.

McCallum, Bennett T. (1999), "Theoretical Issues Pertaining to Monetary Unions", NBER Working Paper, No. 7393, October.

Obstfeld, Maurice, and Kenneth Rogoff (1995), "The Mirage of Fixed Exchange Rates", NBER Working Paper No. 5191, Cambridge MA.

Rostowski, Jacek (2002a), "The Eastern Enlargement of the EU and the Case for Unilateral Euroization", In: M. Blejer and M. Skreb (eds.), *Financial Problems and Policies for Emerging Markets*, MIT Press, Cambridge MA.

Rostowski, Jacek (2002b), "The Debate on Early EMU Accession by the Transition Applicant Countries", CASE seminar paper, preliminary draft, Warsaw, October 1.

Rostowski, Jacek and Andrzej Bratkowski (2002c), "Why Unilateral Euroization Makes Sense for (some) Applicant Countries", Paper presented at the conference on "Dollarization and Euroization: Viable Policy Options?" held at the London School of Economics on 24-25 May.

Part III

Asia: A New Agenda of Financial Reform and Regional Cooperation

10

Financial Liberalisation and Integration in East Asia

Yung Chul Park and Kee Hong Bea

A number of studies on the European economic integration process have shown that an expansion of trade among a group of countries over time could lead to synchronisation of business cycles across the members of the group.[1] Synchronisation of business cycles would be more pronounced, if intra-industry trade accounts for most trade. This finding suggests that regional trade integration within similar industries could then develop conditions favourable for establishing a common currency area for the regional trading partners. A similar development has taken place in East Asia, where the ongoing trade liberalisation has contributed to a substantial increase in intra-regional trade, raising expectations that the recent movement toward free trade would generate market pressures for policy coordination for stable exchange rates of regional currencies and eventually for adopting a common currency for the region.

With the spread of the liberal ideology of the Washington Consensus, many countries in East Asia, in particular more advanced ones including Thailand, Indonesia, and Malaysia, have been reducing restrictions on capital account transactions and barriers to entry of foreign financial institutions into local markets and to trade in financial services since the early 1990s (Eichengreen and Mussa 1998). After the 1997-98 crisis, the speed and scope of penetration of foreign financial institutions, except for Malaysia, has increased in

1 See, for example, Rose and Frankel (1998).

East Asia.[2] In removing restrictions on entry, these East Asian countries have been motivated by their desire to build efficient and stable financial systems befitting an open foreign trade and investment regime that are resilient enough to forestall future crises. According to the IMF (2000), the removal of entry restrictions have also been triggered by the need to help reduce the costs of restructuring and recapitalising banks following a major crisis (p.158). If indeed this was one of their objectives of liberalisation, it appears few of the crisis countries in East Asia have succeeded in this regard.

In view of the thrust of financial liberalisation that has been directed to market opening since the 1997-98 crisis, one would presume that greater capital mobility through capital account liberalisation and opening of financial services industries may have tightened financial linkages between individual countries, thereby promoting the creation of integrated regional financial markets in East Asia.

The purpose of this chapter is to analyse East Asia's experiences with financial liberalisation and innovation with a view to assessing the extent to which liberal financial policies have contributed to economic integration in East Asia. Section 1 discusses some of the reasons why financially integrated countries would be more disposed to joining a common currency area. Section 2 analyses the progress East Asian countries have made in liberalising and opening their financial markets. It will be shown that when financial markets are liberalised and open, countries with different structural characteristics or asynchronous business cycles would have more incentives to integrate with one another than countries with similar characteristics have. This leads to the conclusion that the ongoing capital account liberalisation is likely to develop closer ties between East Asian and global financial markets (globalisation), rather than between the markets of individual countries in the region. Section 3 then examines empirically whether East Asian countries have gravitated to regional or global integration. Our conclusion is that East Asian countries have developed stronger financial ties with advanced countries than with one another in the process of financial

---

2 The IMF (2000) argues, however, that the degree of foreign participation in domestic financial markets has been lower than originally expected in Korea and Taiwan.

opening. Section 4 provides some of the reasons for East Asia's global financial linkages, one of them being penetration by western financial institutions of East Asian financial markets. Section 5 analyses causes of the dominance of western financial institutions in East Asia. This is followed in Section 6 by a discussion of future prospects for regional integration in East Asia. Concluding remarks are in a final section.

1 Financial Market Integration and Common Currency Area

Benefits of Financial Liberalisation

Trade liberalisation is likely to result in more closely correlated business cycles across countries, especially if the liberalisation promotes trade within similar industries. Therefore, countries that establish close economic ties through trade liberalisation are likely to be members of a common currency area in the sense that the similar business cycles make it easier for them to accommodate a common monetary policy regime.

There is general consensus that economic liberalisation in emerging market economies should begin with trade liberalisation, to be followed by deregulation of domestic financial markets, before lifting restrictions on capital account transactions and on entry of foreign financial institutions. This sequencing strategy suggests that countries would go through the process of financial market integration before adopting a common currency: that is, creation of a common currency area would take place at the last stage of full economic integration in any region or a group of countries.

However, there is no theory predicting that liberalisation of the trade regime would subsequently produce market pressure for liberalisation of financial markets and capital account transactions to follow. Indeed, East Asian countries started lowering tariffs and non-tariff barriers long before taking steps to liberalise and open their financial markets. Furthermore, the sequencing strategy does not explain whether financial deregulation and opening among a group of countries such as the ASEAN+3 will also pave the way for financial and monetary integration within the group. As will be shown below, countries that establish close financial linkages through financial market liberalisation would benefit from joining a common currency area. However, these financially integrated countries do not necessarily satisfy the traditional criteria for potential candidates of a common currency area.

Financial market deregulation and opening facilitate migration of real capital in the long run and cross-border financing of current account imbalances in the short run, thereby reducing the costs of adjustment to shocks to demand and supply. Financial liberalisation also allows extensive sharing of the risks associated with macroeconomic shocks across countries, as it broadens the range of portfolio diversification by including foreign bonds and equities in individual portfolios. It follows then that the countries with close financial ties would benefit more from financial liberalisation by forming a common currency area among them, as monetary integration lowers costs of financial transactions and eliminates exchange rate risks. However, the financially integrated countries are likely to be heterogeneous in terms of their economic structures and exposed to asymmetrical shocks. One important implication of financial liberalisation and integration is that contrary to the traditional argument, heterogeneous countries are as well qualified as potential candidates for a common currency area as countries are.

Capital Mobility and External Financing

An increase in capital mobility (factor migration in general) between countries could relieve a country's external deficit as well as unemployment that reflect its internal imbalance. An adverse demand or supply shock to a given industry of a country may require shifts in labour and capital to other industries. After all adjustments have been made within the country including a fall in factor prices, some factors of production are likely to remain unemployed. In this case, capital account liberalisation facilitates migration of capital to other countries, thereby mitigating the burden of adjustment through changes in factor prices and employment. That is, real capital mobility can be a partial substitute for price-wage flexibility.[3]

[3] Financial market liberalisation and opening facilitate real capital mobility as it increases the availability of external financing for trade in both used and new capital goods. Some of the firms in a country that sustains a demand or supply shock may move their production facilities such as machines and equipment to other countries. Alternatively, some of the investment planned by these firms may

However, in the short run, real capital mobility is low and as a result only in the long run could ease difficulties of adjustment to demand and supply shocks. In the absence of price and wage flexibility, an adverse supply shock such as an oil price increase may result in a deficit on the current account in addition to both an increase in unemployment and decrease in factor prices. Countries with an open financial regime have better access to both regional and global capital markets, so that it would be easier and less costly for them to borrow to finance their current account deficits. External borrowing could make the real adjustment smaller or unnecessary if the deficit is transitory and hence reversible.[4]

Risk Sharing Through International Portfolio Diversification

With financial market opening, domestic residents can diversify their portfolios in terms of assets issued by firms and financial institutions of other countries in addition to domestic ones. This possibility of enhancing portfolio diversification across a large array of assets means that a country suffering an adverse terms of trade shock could share some of the loss with other countries to the extent that it holds claims on their output. The amount of the loss that could be shared would increase, if this country holds diversified portfolios of bonds and equities of those countries with different structural characteristics, that is, with lower business cycle correlations of macroeconomic variables.

The presence of currency risk under free floating, however, increases the cost of international portfolio diversification in terms of foreign securities: free floating would inhibit countries from cross-holding of securities, thereby bottling up the cost of the shock in the country in which the shock originated.

---

be relocated in other countries in the form of foreign direct investment as a result of the adverse shock, a possibility that is rather limited in a controlled capital account regime.

4 If the deficit reflects changes in economic fundamentals instead, external borrowing would simply mask the imbalances that require real sector adjustments.

Does Homogeneity Really Matter for a Common Currency Area?

Financial liberalisation and integration may call in question some of the criteria for a successful common currency area focusing on similarity of business cycles. In contrast to the earlier literature, the benefits of financial liberalisation imply that countries with asymmetric shocks and dissimilar structural characteristics may find it easier to integrate financially with one another and can be potential candidates for a common currency area.

Mundell (1973) showed, contradicting his earlier argument, that reserve pooling and international portfolio diversification could mitigate asymmetric shocks, because a country suffering an adverse shock could minimise its loss by drawing down on its claims on or borrowing from other countries in the common currency area. Portfolio diversification for risk sharing could then be better served by establishing a common currency area that includes a large number of structurally heterogeneous countries.[5]

To elaborate further on this point, consider a group of economies in which business cycles are synchronised across countries. The traditional argument is that the member countries in such a group may readily yield their monetary independence to a supranational authority, because they are likely to pursue a similar monetary policy. However, once financial integration is taken into consideration, synchronisation of business cycles may no longer be a critical criterion for identifying potential common currency area candidates, as the following example illustrates.

Suppose the group of countries with symmetric shocks is hit by an adverse shock such as an oil price increase. Because of the similarity of their economic structures, all of the countries in the group will suffer from the shock with the consequence of a group-wide slowdown. This group-wide slump then leads to a decrease in intra-group trade, which in turn aggravates further the downturn in each country. That is, the slump in one country amplifies output contraction in other countries through the trade channel.[6] Since all of the member countries suffer from the same shock, they cannot

---

[5] For a recent analysis on risk sharing through international portfolio diversification, see McKinnon (2001).

[6] The effects of the supply shock in one country could be much more contagious to other countries when they are more homogeneous (Park and Song, 2001).

supplement their output and income losses by liquidating their claims on the other countries. Under these circumstances, there is also little room for capital to move between countries.

Most of the countries in the group may also experience deterioration in their current accounts. As a result, the deficit countries may find it difficult to borrow from the other countries in the group. For the group as a whole, the deficit financing to be secured from outside of the group would be larger and hence more costly. This example therefore implies that the impact of the shock would, other things being equal, be much less severe and hence more manageable, if the members of the group have different structural characteristics. That is, heterogeneity of the members of a common currency area could reduce the burden of adjustment to external shocks because it increases the scope of factor mobility and also eases financing of current account deficits from the countries unaffected by the shock. The risk sharing through asset diversification also suggests that countries with similar economic structures would not gain from joining a common currency area. This is because the adverse supply shock is likely to impinge on most of the firms in the group, and thus market values of securities issued by them will fall at the same time.

From the point of view of portfolio diversification in a liberalised and open financial environment, larger currency unions with more heterogeneous countries are likely to be more successful than smaller ones with homogeneous members: as far as financial integration is concerned, countries with asynchronous macroeconomic shocks would make better candidates for a common currency area. In searching for potential partners for a common currency area, therefore, emerging market economies would prefer tying themselves up with advanced countries whose bonds and equities are relatively more secure and carry high rates of return adjusted for default and liquidity risks, such as US Treasury bonds. That is, globalisation may be a better strategy than regionalisation including forming a common currency area for a large number of small countries: dollarisation, or euroisation, may make more sense to many emerging market economies than forming a currency union among them.

In a recent paper, Heathcote and Perri (2002) argue that the decline in the correlations of output, investment, employment, and consumption between the United States and the rest of the world comprising Europe, Japan, and Canada between the two post-

Bretton Wood periods they observe (1972-86 and 1986-2000) could in part be explained by a decrease in the correlation of exogenous shocks, but also by financial globalisation. The emergence of global financial markets increases opportunities for inter-temporal specialisation in production that, in turn, contributes to lowering the correlation of factor supplies as the globalisation increases the scope of international portfolio diversification.

In terms of an infinite horizon model, Heathcote and Perri (2002) demonstrate that a decline in the correlation of shocks leads to greater international portfolio diversification, which then further reduces international correlations of macroeconomic variables. Calibrating the model, the authors also show that a combination of the decline in the shock correlation and the resulting endogenous growth in international trade in financial assets, jointly accounts for most of the observed decline in the correlation of international business cycles during the post-Bretton Wood period between the United States and the rest of the industrial countries.

One of the implications of the analysis of Heathcote and Perri (2002) is that capital account liberalisation – an exogenous development – could reduce the business cycle correlation of output, investment, and employment in East Asia, if it has not already. Another implication is that growing similarity of business cycles among the East Asian countries through trade expansion may encourage global diversification of portfolios including assets issued by corporations and financial institutions of advanced countries and hence integration of East Asian financial markets into global financial markets.

How significant are then the benefits associated with financial market opening such as the international risk sharing quantitatively? There are few empirical studies that shed light on this question. The well-known home bias in asset holding suggests that the benefit would not be as large as the theory would predict. Despite the ongoing financial liberalisation stretching over more than two decades, the increase in international diversification in assets, in particular bonds, across countries has been relatively small. McKinnon (2002) points to the principal-agent problem as the main cause of limited global portfolio diversification.

In a recent study, however, Park and Bea (2002) present empirical evidence that since the early 1990s most East Asian countries embarked on deregulation of capital account transactions and entry

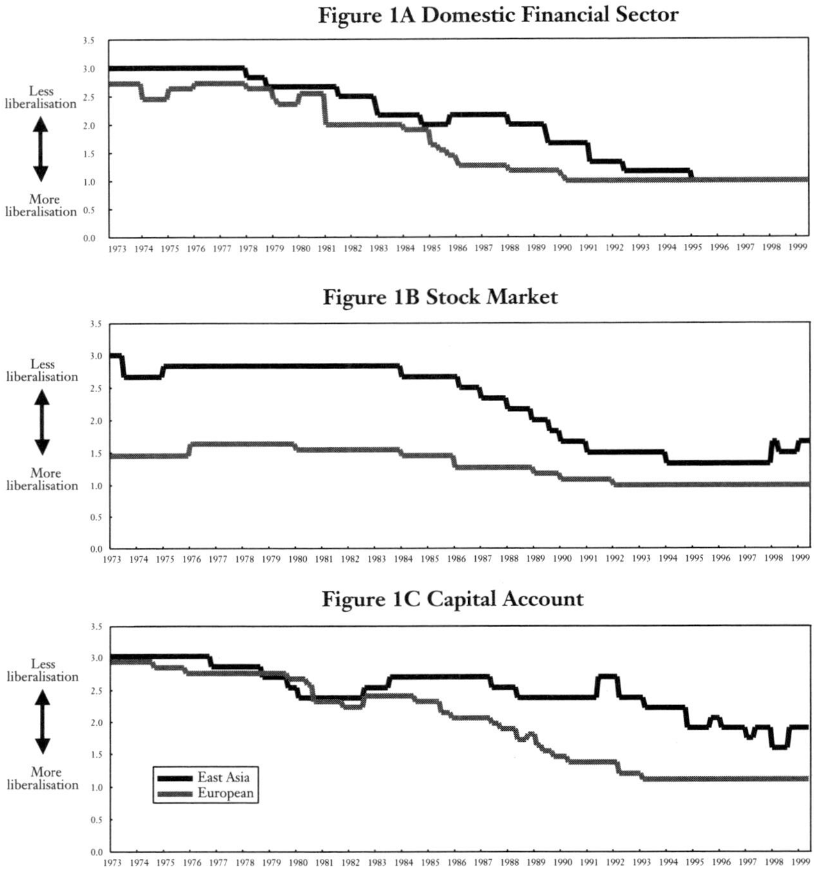

of foreign financial institutions. East Asian capital markets have been integrating into global financial markets rather than forging clear linkages with one another. This development has become more pronounced after the 1997-98 financial crisis.

2 Financial Liberalisation and Integration in East Asia

Liberalisation

Financial liberalisation often refers to: (i) domestic financial market deregulation such as decontrol of the interest rate; (ii) removal of restrictions on capital account transactions that will increase mobility of capital between countries; and (iii) opening of the financial services industry to foreign competition. In a recent paper, Kaminsky and Schmukler (2002) devise a monthly index for overall financial liberalisation, which jointly evaluates the liberalisation of the capital account, the stock market, and the domestic financial sector. The index takes values between 1 and 3: fully liberalised (1), partially liberalised (2), and repressed (3). To measure the extent of financial liberalisation, the authors track the evolution of the regulatory regime covering all three sectors over the 1973-99 period. The East Asian countries covered in their study include: Hong Kong, Indonesia, Malaysia, the Philippines, Korea, Taiwan, and Thailand.

As shown in Figures 1A-1C, the indices for the East Asian countries show that they made considerable progress in deregulating their domestic financial sectors and the stock market, but only partially in liberalising capital account transactions. By 1995, compared to the nine sample European countries, the seven East Asian economies achieved on average the same level of domestic financial sector liberalisation. As for the stock market, the sample East Asian countries were slow in market deregulation, reaching the European level of liberalisation in the mid-1980s, and the same is true for capital account deregulation.

Financial Integration

From the perspective of this study, the usefulness of the indices of the degree of overall financial liberalisation and capital account liberalisation is rather limited in that these measures by themselves

Figure 1 Indices of Financial Liberalisation by Sector

Figure 1A Domestic Financial Sector

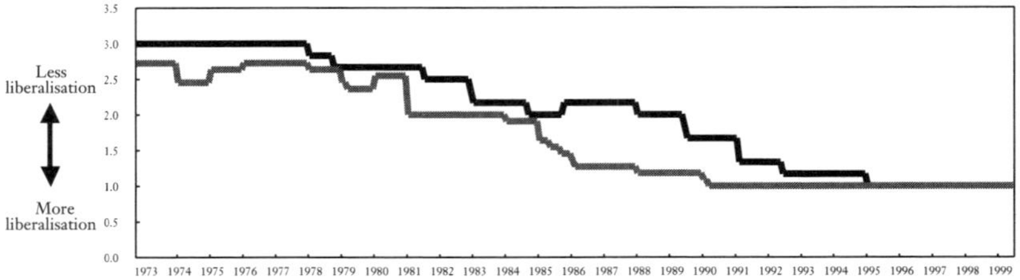

Figure 1B Stock Market

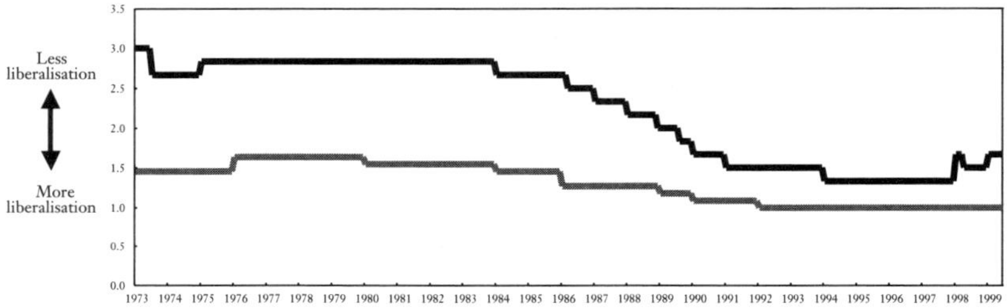

Figure 1C Capital Account

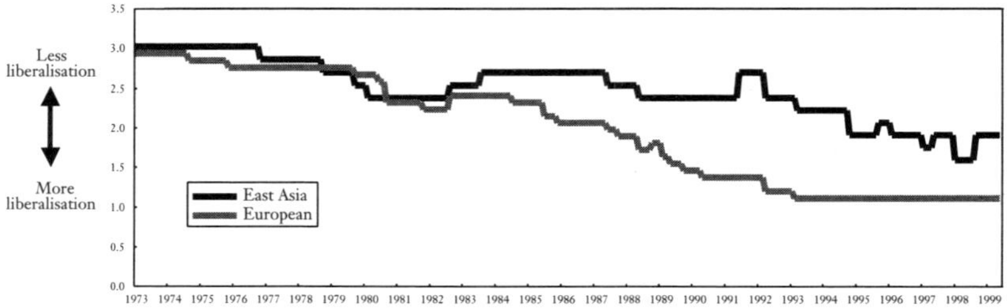

Notes:
Liberalisation index: 3 = high restrictions, 2 = partial liberalisation, and 1 = full liberalisation.
European countries include: Denmark, Finland, France, Germany, Ireland, Italy, Portugal, Spain, Sweden.
East Asian emerging market economies include: Hong Kong, Indonesia, Korea, Malaysia, the Philippines, Taiwan, and Thailand.
Source: Kaminsky and Schmukler (2002).

do not indicate whether capital account deregulation has been associated with financial integration at the regional level in East Asia or at the global level. One of the conclusions of the preceding section is that financial liberalisation in East Asian countries would steer in the direction of developing closer financial linkages between East

Asian and global financial markets rather than similar linkages among financial markets of individual countries in the region. This and the following two sections are devoted to an empirical examination of this hypothesis.

Before turning to this issue, conceptual clarification of regional versus global financial integration in the East Asian context may be in order. Suppose that financial markets of individual East Asian countries are being integrated into global financial markets as a result of financial liberalisation. Does this development not bring about the concomitant financial integration in the region? In our view it does not, in the sense that financial market liberalisation in individual countries may not support the development of regionally integrated financial markets where financial instruments denominated in regional currencies are traded; in fact, it is likely to encourage and expand financial transactions between these countries through global financial markets located in New York and London. In a graphic sense, New York and London are the financial hub whereas individual financial markets of East Asia are spokes.

In order to determine the direction of financial integration in East Asia (regional vs. global), we present three types of evidence:

1. Capital flows within East Asia and between East Asia and other regions, to examine the extent to which East Asian portfolios have been globally diversified (this section);
2. Decomposition of error variances of stock returns and interest rates in both East Asia and Europe, to gauge the relative significance of global capital markets in influencing stock prices and interest rates in East Asia (Section 3); and
3. The degree of commercial presence of foreign financial institutions in East Asia, as a measure of globalisation of East Asian financial markets (Section 4).

Intra-Regional Capital Movements in East Asia

For a measure of regional integration in East Asia, one would need information on intra-regional capital flows in East Asia relative to inter-regional flows between East Asia and the rest of the world. Reliable data on intra- or inter-regional capital flows are not available. As East Asia is defined to include the ASEAN members, Taiwan, Hong Kong, China, Korea, and Japan, it has always been a net saver to the rest of the world. This balance of payment characteristic, together with underdevelopment of financial markets, which we discuss in Section 5, suggests that the level of financial transactions, including bank lending and trade in regional securities, between different countries in East Asia is likely to have been relatively small, in particular when Japanese bank lending to and direct investment in other East Asian countries are excluded.

Furthermore, since the outbreak of the 1997-98 crisis, Japanese bank lending and FDI to other East Asian countries have fallen dramatically (see Table 2 and 3; all tables are at the end of this chapter). Korea's and Taiwan's FDIs in other East Asian countries also decreased sharply (see Table 4 and 5). Singapore's FDI data are rather sketchy, but its FDI in Malaysia and Indonesia declined during the post-crisis period from 1997 to 1999 (see Table 6). As a result, it would be reasonable to assume that intra-regional financial flows in East Asia have been smaller than inter-regional flows between East Asia on the one hand and North America and Europe on the other. This feature of inter-regional capital movements has become more visible with the increase in current account surpluses of Indonesia, Malaysia, Korea, and Thailand (see Table 1) and provides a piece of indirect evidence that East Asian countries have forged tighter financial links with North America and Europe than with their neighbouring economies in the process of financial liberalisation.

Throughout the 1980s and until the mid-1990s the ASEAN members and Korea were net borrowers, as they were running deficits on their current accounts. China, Taiwan, and Japan were, on the other hand, accumulating huge amounts of current account surpluses, which made East Asia as a whole a net lender financing the bulk of current account deficits of the US and the rest of the world. External financing for East Asia's deficit countries therefore ultimately came from the three East Asian surplus countries (on a net basis). However, the East Asian deficit countries borrowed in part from regional but mostly from global financial markets to finance their current account imbalances. This pattern of external financing established East Asian linkages with global financial markets well before the region went on to liberalise and open its financial markets.

Since the 1997 crisis, all four East Asian crisis countries have generated large surpluses on their current accounts and are likely to continue to do so for the next several years (see Table 1). Together with China, Taiwan and Japan, East Asia as a whole has become a larger net saver of the global economy than before. Current account surpluses have been added to foreign reserve holdings of these countries. In managing their reserve portfolios, the East Asian countries have traditionally preferred liquid and safe foreign securities such as US Treasury bills in addition to holding major international currencies.

However, some of these countries have in recent years sought to diversify their reserve portfolios by adding short-term European government bonds and even private bonds and equities. And the growing surplus position in recent years has increased opportunities for diversification of foreign reserves in East Asia through the international financial hub in New York and London. This increase is likely to have contributed to East Asia's tighter financial links with developed countries. It is also reasonable to assume that East Asian savers have been placing an increasing share of their savings in bonds and equities issued by western corporations and financial institutions in diversifying their portfolios.

3 Decomposition of Error Variances

The Model and the Data

Given the extent to which the East Asian countries have managed to liberalise their capital account transactions in recent years, one might expect that financial markets of these economies may have become more closely linked with one another than in the past. However, the available empirical evidence does not support this expectation. Regionally integrated financial markets are yet to emerge and prospects for further financial liberalisation in East Asia are not promising (Park and Song 2001).[7]

---

[7] A World Bank study (1997) uses three different measures to determine the extent to which countries are financially integrated. In constructing an overall index of integration the World Bank study uses the access to international financial markets, the ability to attract private external financing, and the level of diversification of financing in terms of the composition of financial flows. The same study shows that changes in the degree of financial integration between 1992-94 were high in Indonesia, Korea, Malaysia, Philippines, and Thailand, but it does not examine whether these countries were more integrated financially with one another than before.

The Model

In a given region, financial liberalisation and market opening would, other things being equal, lead to an increase in cross-border banking and securities transactions between the countries of the region as well as those between the region and the rest of the world. According to our discussion in Section 1, with deepening financial liberalisation, financial prices in East Asia would react more sharply to shocks originating in the global rather than regional markets. In order to examine whether the financial data of East Asia and Europe bear out this prediction, this section analyses the extent to which financial prices such as the interest rate and stock return are influenced by shocks that are global, regional, or country specific in the two regions.

For this purpose, changes in the interest rate and stock return of each country in East Asia and Europe are decomposed into three components: a world-common, a region-common, and a country-specific component. The world-common component is a factor that affects changes in the financial variables of all countries in both regions; a region-common factor influences only the countries belonging to either region; and the effect of the country-specific factor is restricted to a country in question. The decomposition is carried out in terms of a structural Vector Autoregression (VAR) model, which is described in Appendix 1 at the end of this chapter.

More specially, in this empirical test, the error variances of the stock market return (the US dollarised total market return index) and the interest rate of each of the 7 sample East Asian and 13 European countries for one through four-week ahead forecasts are explained by domestic, regional, and global factors. Regional factors are represented by the shocks originating in the Japanese market for East Asia and in the EMU market for Europe (a value weighted return index for the EMU). Global factors are the shocks from the US market. In order to examine whether there has been any change in the relative importance of both regional and global factors, the sample period is divided into two sub-periods before and after the 1997-98 crisis in East Asia.

The Data

Empirical estimation of the model uses weakly stock market price index data of seven East Asian and 13 European countries plus Japan and the US from DataStream International for the period from 1/3/90 to 8/21/02. In this estimation, a weakly interval is chosen, because daily price data suffer from market frictions such as bid-ask bounce and non-synchronous trading hours between the East Asian countries and the US. All price series are adjusted for dividends and expressed in the US dollar. Weakly compounded stock returns are then estimated by taking the log of price ratios.

As for the interest rates, this study uses daily interest rates of all sample countries plus Japan and the US from DataStream International (see Appendix 2). A daily interval is chosen to minimise the effects of changes in the exchange rate on the interest rate.

Estimation Results

Stock Returns

Table 7 presents a decomposition of the error variance of the dollarised stock market index return of each East Asian country for one-week_through four-week ahead forecasts. The first column is the forecast period. The second through fourth columns represent proportions of the forecast error variance of an East Asian country explained by the performance of the market returns of the US (global factor), Japan (regional factor), and the East Asian country itself (local factor) respectively before the 1997-98 crisis (1/3/90–4/30/97) and the fifth through seventh after the crisis (1/6/99–8/21/02). The explanatory power of each shock is measured in percentage so that the horizontal sum of each row is 100.

The results show that, in all seven markets, forecast error variances of the market index returns are largely explained by local markets' own performance in both periods. However, the dominance of the local market performance declined during the post-crisis period in East Asia except for Malaysia. In both periods, the shocks originating in the US market played a more significant role than that in Japan in explaining variations of all East Asian market returns over a four-week horizon.

On average, 89.5 percent of forecast error variances of the East Asian market index returns are attributable to the innovations in the local markets, 7.8 percent to the US market, and 2.6 percent to the Japanese market, respectively, during the pre-crisis period. Since the outbreak of the 1997-98 crisis, the relative importance of the three factors has changed considerably. During the post-crisis period (1/6/99–8/21/02), the proportion of the local factor fell by more than 8 percentage points to 81 percent, giving rise to the gains of both the global and regional factors. In all East Asian sample countries except for Malaysia, the relative share of the US factor rose during the post-crisis period. The East Asian average of the share of the US factor almost doubled to 14.2 percent, whereas the same figure for the Japanese factor went up by about 2 percentage points to 4.5 percent.

Except for Indonesia and Malaysia, all other sample East Asian countries saw a large increase in the share of the US factor during the post-crisis period. In the case of Korea, the proportion jumped to 18.6 percent from 2.0 percent before the crisis. For Hong Kong, the increase was more pronounced to 30.9 percent from less than 12 percent. In contrast, however, the Japanese influence declined in Malaysia, the Philippines, and Singapore, although the region's average has risen as a result of the large increase in Hong Kong and Korea. These results suggest that changes in the US market exert a stronger influence on the East Asian stock markets than the Japanese one, supporting in part our argument that financial market opening has led to growing integration of East Asian financial markets into global financial markets.

It would be reasonable to assume that unlike in East Asia, in Europe the regional factor figures more importantly in influencing stock prices than the global factor (represented by the shock originating in the US market) in view of the long and carefully managed process of economic integration that culminated in the creation of a common currency area in Europe. This assumption is borne out by the data (in Table 8). The results of the variance decomposition of stock returns for Europe reflect the consequences of the successful financial integration in the region. Except for Ireland, Sweden, and the UK, regional shocks measured by a value weighted return index for the EMU markets as a whole dominate error variances of the dollarised stock returns of the sample European countries.

Interest Rates

The variance decomposition analysis is carried out for the interest rates of the sample East Asian and European countries. The results of this estimation are presented in Table 9. Unlike in the case of the stock market, the influences of foreign market shocks on the interest rates are very low in all East Asian countries except for Hong Kong before or after the crisis. In fact, the local factor accounts on average for more than 95 percent of forecast error variances in East Asia during both sub-periods.

For the region as a whole, the importance of the US factor rose to 3.9 percent after the crisis from 2.3 percent before, but the increase is negligible to have any implications for financial integration in East Asia. The insignificance of the external factors in influencing interest rates in East Asia is not surprising. As will be discussed in a later section, bond markets of individual East Asian countries are fragmented, narrow in terms of maturity and variety and closed to foreign investors compared to their equity markets. Furthermore, the short-term interest rates are intermediate targets of monetary policy, which are frequently adjusted for the attainment of domestic policy objectives in these countries. The Japanese interest rate, which is used to represent changes in the regional factor, has been very low and showed little fluctuations during much of the post-crisis period in East Asia. These developments may account for the relative insulation of East Asian markets for financial assets other than equities from external shocks.

The Maastricht Treaty of 1991, which was an important step toward the formation of the European Monetary Union, may have affected the nature of financial integration in Europe. To account for this change, this study examines the relative importance of the global and regional factor in influencing European interest rates in two sub-periods, before (1/1/85–12/31/90) and after (1/1/94–8/30/02) the Maastricht Treaty. Because of the unavailability of reliable data, a similar test cannot be done for the stock markets.

As shown in Table 10, compared to East Asian countries, in Europe both the global and regional factors are more important in explaining error variances of the interest rates, although the domestic factor still dominates. Table 10 also shows that the relative influence of global and regional factors has risen in the 1990s, but the increase is not large enough to indicate any significant changes in the financial market structure of Europe.

4 Financial Liberalisation and Penetration of Foreign Financial Institutions of East Asian Financial Markets

According to the definition of the General Agreement on Trade in Services (GATS), financial services include commercial banking, investment banking, securities brokerage, insurance, and insurance-related services. The financial services industry is in general made up of activities in various fields of finance including commercial banking, investment banking (notably underwriting and trading), insurance, derivatives, merger and acquisition, financial leasing, management consulting, asset management, accounting and auditing, financial data processing, and even law and telecommunication. Listing the full range of financial services is almost an impossible task as new financial services are being created and provided. It will be shown that few of the East Asian financial institutions appear to have comparative advantage in supplying these variegated and sophisticated services.

Banking Institutions

As shown in the IMF survey of international capital markets (2000), there has been a dramatic increase in foreign ownership of banks in most emerging market economies during the second half of the 1990s. Due largely to severe restrictions on entry, foreign banks penetration was traditionally low in East Asia. However, this has changed since the 1997-98 crisis (see Table 11). Notwithstanding the initial low degree of penetration, foreign bank control over assets of local banks jumped to 4.3 percent in 1999 from less than one percent in Korea in 1994. In Thailand, it rose by more than ten times to 11.5 percent during the same period. On average, the foreign control in Korea, Malaysia and Thailand shot up to 6 percent in 1999 from 1.6 percent five years earlier.

A similar development can be found in the lending behaviour of BIS reporting foreign banks in East Asia. Lending in both local and foreign currencies of BIS reporting foreign banks in the nine East Asian countries are shown in Figures 2 to 4. As shown in Figure 2, between 1991 and 2001, foreign banks' credit as a share of total bank credit more than doubled in Malaysia: it rose to more than 40 percent after the 1997 crisis from an average of less than 20 percent over the 1990-96 period. In the Philippines the share jumped to 35.5 percent in 2001 after a sustained decline during the first half of the 1990s. In Thailand, the increase in foreign banks' share has been rather gradual.

Figure 3 depicts a substantial gain of foreign banks' loan market share, which reached almost 30 percent in Malaysia in 2001. Only in Taiwan and Korea, foreign banks have not been able to increase their loan market shares. Much of the increase in the market share of foreign banks in the South-East Asian countries has come from the large increase in their local currency lending, as shown in Figure 4. Except for Malaysia, in all of the East Asian countries the absolute amounts of international claims of the foreign banks have declined, thereby lifting the ratios of local currency to international claims.

Provision of Capital Market Services

While foreign bank penetration in East Asia is still lagging behind that in other emerging market economies, western investment banks, in particular American and European ones, have established a monopoly position in providing two major services in the capital markets in East Asia: (i) underwriting in the primary market and (ii) trading and consulting in the secondary market. While there are many areas of financial services other than securities underwriting and trading, it is hard to quantify the value of financial services

Figure 2 Foreign Bank Credit / Total Bank Credit
(in percentages)

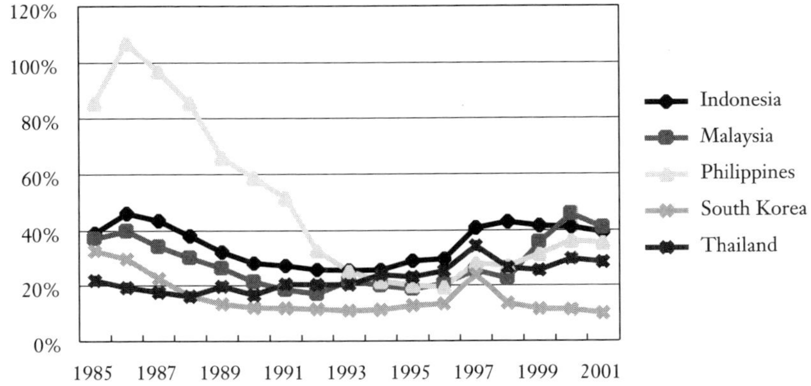

Source: BIS (2002).

Figure 3 Foreign Banks Local Claims / Domestic Bank Credit (in percentages)

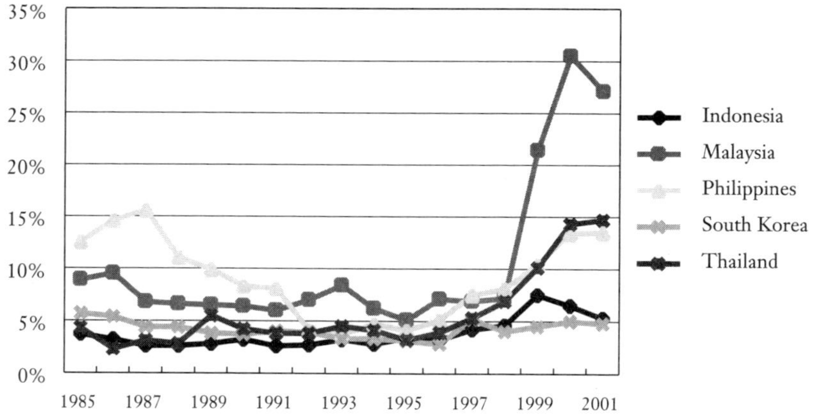

Source: BIS (2002).

Figure 4 Foreign Banks Local Claims / International Claims (in percentages)

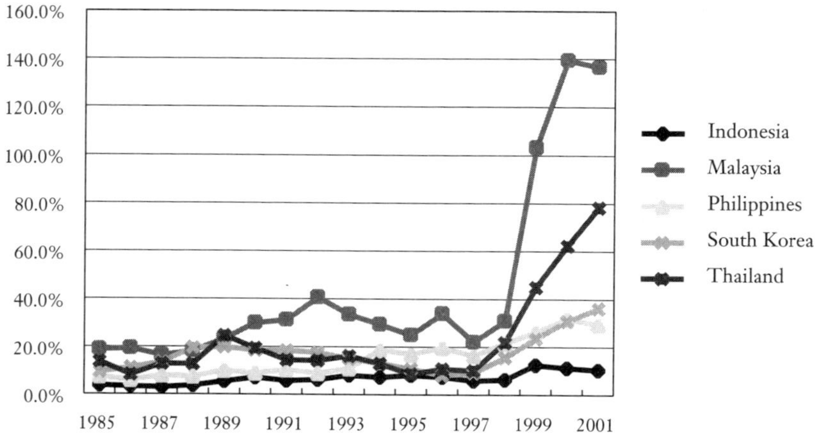

Source: BIS (2002).

provided by financial institutions and in many cases relevant data are difficult to find. For these reasons, the data related to the investment banking are presented to show the dominance of American and European capital market financial institutions in providing capital market services in East Asia.

Western financial institutions, in particular American ones, have been by far the largest providers of financial services in global investment banking. This was confirmed by Euromoney's 1996 poll of polls, which selects the top 20 investment banks on the basis of 70 Euromoney polls and league tables produced in 1995: 18 out of the 20 selected investment banks were either American or European, the other two were Japanese. Six years later, this dominance remained; only one Japanese investment bank made it to the list. In fact, American and European institutions held dominance in providing the entire range of financial services. US-based financial institutions led in every category of services, followed by British-based ones. Not one single financial institution was based in Asia with the exception of Japan, and even then, the Japanese institutions were ranked dead last. According to the Euromoney polls in 2002, American investment banks have solidified their dominance further; Japanese investment banks have been largely driven out of the market for capital market services since 1995.

From the perspective of East Asia, a more pertinent issue to examine in regard to the role of western investment banks is their dominance in East Asian international financing. The amount of international financing for East Asian countries before the crisis grew rapidly (Table 13-1), but it was not local financial institutions but rather American and European financial institutions which managed to control the vast share of the market for underwriting and distribution of the new issues. Table 1 classifies the capital market instruments issued in the five Asian countries during the 1991-2001 period by nationality of the lead managers or book runners who sponsored the new issues. It can be seen that out of US$31.96 billion that was financed through capital markets for the 1998-2001 period by the six countries, 74 percent was undertaken by American and European investment banks, and 6 percent by Japanese institutions. The cumulative figures for the 1991-1997 period show that western institutions managed 69 percent of the capital market financing, compared to 31 percent managed by East Asian investment banks.

As shown in Table 15, the distribution of lead managers by their parent country and each type of instrument issued in the six Asian countries during 1991-2001 period is also lopsided: American and European institutions accounted for more than 70 percent of all capital market financing, while Japanese institutions for only 9 percent. Table 16 lists the top 20 lead managers or book runners in the management of debt and equity issues. The total amount underwritten shows a similar pattern of western dominance, the American and European institutions representing 90 percent and the East Asian institutions only 10 percent. Table 17 divides the list of top 20 lead managers into the two sub-periods, before (1991-97) and after (1998-2001) the crisis; there was little change in the dominance of western lead managers.

Financial institutions and corporates worldwide are making increasing use of financial derivatives. Exchange-traded derivatives are currently estimated to be in the magnitude of several trillion dollars, compared with several hundred billion dollars in the late 1980s. Trading volume of over-the-counter derivatives is even larger than exchange-traded derivatives. Financial institutions and corporates in East Asian countries are also increasingly relying on the use of derivative products to meet their diverse needs for hedging instruments.

It is, however, American and European institutions that dominate in the roles of brokers and dealers of derivative transactions. This is so even in the transaction of East Asian derivatives including Asian interest rate swaps, and currency swaps, currency options, not to mention the derivative products traded in more developed markets. According to *Risk Magazine* (November 1996), most of the first-tiered derivative broker and dealer were either American or European institutions when evaluated on the basis of pricing ability, market-making reliability, liquidity, innovation and speed of transactions before the 1997-98 crisis.

In fact, it was reported that no local financial institution was ranked as active brokers or dealers of Asian derivatives. Moreover, the role of providing tailor-made derivative products according to customer's needs, which requires highly developed financial expertise and sophisticated financial technology and becomes an increasingly important area of financial service industry, is entirely played by American and European institutions. The East Asian financial crisis and the non-performing loan problems of Japanese banks have curtailed so much the lending and provision of capital market services by East Asian financial institutions, that western financial institutions could enter the East Asian market without encountering much competition in recent years.

5 Causes of Foreign Dominance in Capital Market Services in East Asia

Overview

The discussion in the preceding section raises important questions as to how western financial institutions have been able to establish such a dominant commercial presence in East Asian finance and what effects this dominance would have on efficiency and stability of East Asian financial systems. More than anything else, the dismal state of East Asian finance in the aftermath of the 1997-98 crisis has combined with market deregulation to increase opportunities for western financial institutions to carve out a large share of the East Asian financial services industry. Saddled with large amounts of non-performing loans, many banks and non-bank financial institutions have been forced to curtail their lending operations and supply of other financial services At the end of 2000, in Indonesia more than 70 percent of the assets of financial institutions was held by state-owned institutions; in Korea this was roughly 50 percent. Prospects of these countries for privatising the state-owned financial institutions are not promising because viable buyers, foreign or domestic, have yet to be found. Institutional reform for the improvement of risk management and corporate governance of financial institutions has been carried on intermittently and by and large at the snail's pace. Financial markets have displayed considerable instability and remain susceptible to swings in investor sentiment. To complicate the difficulty of East Asian finance, there appears to be no end in sight for the resolution of the Japanese banking crisis.

As shown in the preceding section, however, even before the crisis, western financial institutions had already controlled a commanding market share in the provision of a number of financial services, in particular capital market related ones. From a longer-term perspective, therefore, underdevelopment of financial markets and institutions, in particular capital markets, in an environment of rapid financial globalisation, has given a large competitive edge to foreign institutions in serving East Asian local customers. Finally, many East Asian countries have been running large surpluses on their capital accounts. In providing services for investing these surpluses in foreign securities, western financial institutions have been able to win over their East Asian counterparts as they have more experience and expertise in placing funds in global financial markets.

Financial Globalisation

To western market participants, the growing presence of western financial institutions in East Asia may be a natural consequence of financial globalisation. An overwhelming share of East Asia's international financial transactions is denominated in terms of key currencies, mostly the US dollar, and conducted through the international financial hub of New York and London. Except for Japanese banks, most of the banks in other East Asian countries have a limited access to international capital markets, relatively limited experience in international corporate banking, and a small region wide branch network in East Asia. By and large, their customer bases are confined to domestic borrowers and lenders. Bond markets still remain relatively small in size and narrow in terms of maturity and issues. And the markets for financial derivatives have only recently begun to emerge. There are few domestic investment banks, securities firms, and mutual funds that are efficient enough to compete with their counterparts from the developed countries in international financial markets.

In the absence of these securities market institutions, therefore, it comes as no surprise that American and European investment banks have been able to dominate underwriting securities in international capital markets, organising large syndicated loans, and negotiating multinational mergers and acquisitions and the provision of other financial services in East Asia, and more so since East Asian countries took steps to open their financial markets in the early 1990s.[8]

The financial services industry is an industry that is very intensive

---

[8] Even in banking, Japanese banks, which were active in lending to other East Asian countries and accounted for the bulk of syndicated loans to these countries before the crisis, have withdrawn drastically their lending to Asian countries: East Asia accounted for less than 6% of their total external lending in 2001 (see Table 2).

in information, communication, and computation. The ongoing IT revolution has formed the basis of numerous innovations in financial technology; the costs of supplying financial services have in turn declined dramatically, thereby creating economies of scale and scope in the financial services industry. In order to take advantage of scale and scope economics, financial institutions including banks and securities institutions throughout the world have come under increasing competitive pressure to capture a large market share, leading them to diversify their activities geographically and also to move into new service areas.

Financial market deregulation and opening in both developed and developing countries that began in the 1980s has also increased substantially the share of capital market financing relative to bank lending in global financial markets. Beginning in the early 1990s, emerging market economies in East Asia have increasingly sought to raise funds from capital markets rather than relying on syndicated loans or interbank short-term loans. This change in the financing structure has led to a large increase in the demand for capital market services. Trade and financial liberalisation in East Asian emerging market economies has also increased the demand for new financial services and products such as instruments for hedging exposure to currency and commercial risks and derivative products – options, swaps, and futures – for portfolio diversification and better risk management.

However, after long periods of financial repression, which had inhibited development of capital markets, East Asian economies did not have any comparative advantage in supplying capital market and other new financial services when their financial markets were opened. As a result, financial institutions in East Asia have been losing out in competition vis-à-vis their competitors from the West, despite the fact that they enjoy information and home bias advantage in local finance. Even in commercial banking where the home bias is of significant advantage, East Asian countries have seen their banking market share chipped away, albeit slowly, largely because East Asian banks have not been able to move out of traditional deposit taking and lending business into capital market, insurance, and other new services. That is, East Asian banks have been slow and inefficient in adapting to universalisation of banking services. In recent years, western financial institutions have increasingly filled up the vacuum of services created by this slow adjustment.

Under these circumstances, it is not surprising that large corporations with an investment grade rating in East Asia have migrated to the international financial hub where they could tap into wider investor bases and also obtain funds at lower costs and better terms. East Asian savers have also moved to New York and London markets, as part of their international diversification strategy to add to their portfolios the stocks and banks of advanced countries, where financial markets are more open and legal systems protect shareholder rights better than in their own countries.

Several measures of internationalisation of stock market activities (the relative market capitalisation of firms listed abroad, the ratio of value traded abroad to GDP, and the ratio of value traded abroad to value traded domestically) all show the growing trend of migration of issuance and trading of equities in emerging market economies, as (Claessens, Klingebiel, and Schmukler (2002) argue. According to them, the migration of stocks from emerging market economies to international financial centres depends on the overall development of the economy, the degree of shareholder protection, and trading costs. Improvement in economic fundamentals of emerging market economies has been the major driving force behind the migration.

Services offered by stock markets in New York and London are easily accessible from anywhere in the world. Large liquidity further increases the value of transactions at these markets. Global harmonisation of accounting, auditing, disclosure, and corporate governance is likely to accelerate financial globalisation. As Claessens, Klingebiel, and Schmukler (2002) argue, in an age of financial globalisation the functions and forms of stock exchanges in many emerging economies may need to be reconsidered.

Underdevelopment of Capital Markets

There is little doubt that underdevelopment of the financial sector, in particular that of capital markets, has been largely responsible for the dominance of western financial institutions in providing capital market services in East Asia. What are then the causes of the financial underdevelopment in East Asia? They are well known and mostly pertain to financial restriction and to the bank or financial intermediary-oriented financial system that have delayed and interfered with the building of the legal, regulatory, and information infrastructure that could support the development of efficient capital markets.

Post-war financial development, prior to the 1997-98 crisis in East Asia, had been characterised by regulation of interest rates at below-market levels, restricted entry of new financial institutions, segmentation of financial markets, insularity of domestic finance from the world financial markets, and system safety at the expense of competition. The increasing complexity and technological sophistication of financial industries required a high-quality information and telecommunication infrastructure and placed new demands on the labour force. However, the intermediary orientation of the financial system coupled with the financial repression had discouraged the requisite institution building, thereby holding up the development of competitive markets for bonds, equities and financial derivatives before the onset of financial liberalisation in the early 1990s. Since the 1997-98 crisis, most of the East Asian countries have taken measures to strengthen and improve the efficiency of their capital markets, including the government bond markets, realising that resilient and efficient capital markets are key to the prevention of future crises and that they should rely less on the banking sector than before.

Legal and Regulatory Inefficiency

La Porta, Lopez-de-Silanes, and Vishny (1999) argue that the legal environment for investor protection and contract enforcement is the most critical determinant of the level and quality of financial services and that it is critical to the development of both financial intermediary and markets. One implication of this legal approach to finance is that the development of equity markets will be facilitated if the legal system provides a strong protection of shareholder rights such as the right to vote on key corporate matters, to select corporate directors, or to sue the directors and the firm. Efficient corporate bond markets would thrive if they are supported by a legal system that ensures public confidence by protecting investors from fraud, insider trading, and market manipulation and by bringing civil and criminal enforcement actions against violators of securities laws.

In a banking-oriented system, regulation is directed to discouraging and limiting excessive risk taking on the part of individual banks to prevent a systemic banking crisis. Regulations such as capital adequacy requirements and limits on loan concentration are all designed for the banking system safety and foreign currency exposure. In contrast, in a market-oriented system the regulatory system places its emphasis on enforcing compliance with the securities laws with regard to licensing of issues, ensuring due diligence process, and other rules concerning accounting, auditing, and disclosure to protect the interests of public investors. Effective enforcement rules and regulation is crucial to nurturing investors' confidence in the capital markets.

Although reform efforts have been made for improvement, the regulatory systems in many East Asian countries have not been successful in keeping abreast of rapid innovations in the financial industry, developing the necessary skills to assess the complexity and potential risks associated with new financial services, and in strengthening the regulation of securities markets. The lack of shareholder and creditor rights in most East Asian capital markets has made external reporting a low priority, which has in part been responsible for relatively low standards of accounting and disclosure systems.

Paucity of Institutional Investors

The nature of the shareholder population in East Asian countries also has constrained the development of capital markets as a source of corporate financing of the financial services industry. In financial markets of developed economies, a large proportion of listed companies tend to be owned by a diverse shareholder population, in which institutional investors such as pension funds, mutual funds and insurance companies predominate. Such a diverse shareholder population facilitates the development of well-functioning capital markets and related financial services, such as securities trading, consulting, merger and acquisition, and asset management.

In contrast, a large proportion of East Asian companies is owner-managed, or at least feature a congruence of interests of shareholders and management in the form of 'proprietor capitalism'. In Malaysia, Hong Kong, Thailand, and Indonesia, a family group – often Chinese – who staff many of the senior positions and also own a large proportion, if not the majority, of shares, usually controls many companies. In countries such as Korea and Japan, listed corporate groups tend to be large conglomerates, often far too big to be controlled by a single family. However, although the founding family may no longer have a controlling stake, this does not mean that a floating population of institutional investors, as in the West, holds the shares. Rather, the bulk of a company's shares tend to be held for the long term by friendly institutions with which strong business ties exist, such as banks, life insurance firms and other industrial companies. This ownership concentration has been one of the obstacles to the development of the requisite institutional infrastructure for capital market and related services.

Absence of Government Bond and Financial Derivative Markets and Other Market Supporting Institutions

The government bond market provides a reliable benchmark yield curve of risk-free interest rates, on which pricing of corporate bonds is based. In part because most of the East Asian governments have been able to maintain balanced government budgets, borrowing requirements have been relatively small, limiting the growth of government bond markets. Financial derivative markets such as forward, interest rate swaps, options, and bond future markets are important complements to capital market development as they facilitate risk management and also enhance market liquidity. These markets are in the early stage of their development in East Asia.

The bank dominance of East Asian financial systems has also delayed the development of such institutions as credit rating agencies, clearing and settlement systems, and investment banking firms that constitute the important elements of supporting institutions for mature capital markets. The absence of reliable credit rating agencies has meant that firms and financial institutions have not been able to obtain credit ratings. In the absence of efficient investment banking, there have been few financial institutions capable of assuming full responsibility for selling entire issues of new stocks and bonds. Firms and financial institutions wishing to raise funds through bonds thus bear all the risks of potential price fluctuations.

Integration Into Global Financial Markets

External financing for the East Asia's deficit countries it was arranged and managed in part by Japanese banks, but mostly by western financial institutions. That is, East Asian savers and investors were intermediated by western financial institutions at financial markets in New York and London.

Since the 1997 crisis, together with China, Taiwan, and Japan, East Asia as a whole has become a larger net saver in the global economy than before (Table 1). In investing their surpluses, East Asian countries have sought the services of western financial institutions, simply because institutions with a global reach and network are more efficient in allocating East Asian savings. The growing surplus position in recent years has expanded East Asia's lending to the rest of the world through the international financial hub in New York and London.

However, in diversifying their portfolios, East Asian savers seem to have been placing at least some of their savings in bonds and equities issued by other East Asian corporations and financial institutions. But again, it is reasonable to assume that the brokerage services for investing in foreign securities have been mostly provided by western financial institutions. This may be corroborated by the fact that equity markets have been expanding rapidly in terms of market capitalisation and the variety of stocks listed in most of the East Asian exchanges, and have attracted a growing number of investors from outside of the region since the early 1990s.

Hong Kong and Singapore have been two important regional financial centres in East Asia, but they do not appear to have played an important rolle in advancing financial integration in East Asia with the onset of financial liberalisation in the region. Moreover, iIt should be noted that they were serving East Asian borrowers and lenders well before financial market opening got underway in the region. These two centres are essentially outposts of major international capital markets headquartered in advanced countries. The crisis in 1997, which almost brought Hong Kong to the brink of collapse, has undermined their importance of these two centres as the a regional financial centres, as East Asian corporations and banks have increasingly migrated to the New York and London markets for their financial service needs. In this process, Hong Kong and Singapore may have gravitated more toward linking financially East Asian economies with advanced economies than integrating them with one another.

Foreign financial institutions now receive a national treatment, which provides a level playing field when they enter financial markets of East Asian countries. Many western banks have established a wide network of branches and subsidiaries throughout East Asia, and so have western securities firms, investment banks, insurance companies, and other non-bank financial institutions. There are numerous emerging market funds operating out of New York to invest in East Asian securities. There is little doubt that the hold of western financial institutions in East Asia has increased since the early 1990s. This pervasive presence of western financial institutions is likely to expand and strengthen East Asia's financial ties with advanced countries, given the continuing financial liberalisation in the region.

Over time, local investment banks and other financial institutions may become more competitive and new markets for financial derivatives may emerge to the extent that, compared to western institutions, they enjoy advantage in collecting and assessing local information. However, such an advantage will diminish with advances in information and communication technology, while the gap in financial technology and expertise between East Asian and western financial institutions will remain. As a result, borrowers and lenders from East Asia will have more incentives to go to the New York and London markets than before, thereby speeding up integration of East Asian financial markets into global financial centres.

6 Prospects for Regional Financial Integration in East Asia

Implications of Financial Liberalisation for Regional Integration

There has been a substantial increase in intra-regional trade in East Asia. Emergence of China as a major trading partner and its entry into the WTO are likely to accelerate trade integration in the region. The APEC agreement on trade liberalisation and a recent proliferation of bilateral free trade negotiations will gather forces for a further expansion of trade in East Asia. This expansion is in turn expected to lead to market pressures on East Asian policymakers for closer coordination of economic policies, including exchange rate policy.

In contrast, however, financial liberalisation and innovation in East Asia do not appear to have strengthened financial linkages among financial markets of individual East Asian countries. Instead, the financial market opening has led to global diversification of asset portfolios and strengthening of financial ties with major international financial markets in East Asia. Trade liberalisation has unleashed market forces gravitating East Asian economies to regional integration; financial liberalisation has led to global financial integration. The difficulty of harmonising and coordinating institutional reform has slowed down further financial integration in East Asia.

While individual East Asian countries have made considerable progress in deregulating and opening their financial markets, collectively they have achieved little in harmonising the legal systems for bankruptcy procedures and protection of minority stockholders, regulatory systems for financial stability and soundness, and tax treatments of cross-border financial transactions. Equally slow has been the setting of common standards of banking, accounting, auditing, disclosure, and corporate governance at the regional level. In the meantime, East Asian countries have come under pressure to adopt codes and standards for financial sector regulations, accounting and corporate governance set by advanced countries. Whatever its rationale, the effort of the advanced countries to graft the western systems and standards on East Asia may have contributed to East Asia's integration into global financial markets.

In the long run, financial liberalisation would facilitate the mobility of real capital between countries in East Asia, as evidenced by a large increase in intra-regional foreign direct investment prior to the 1997 crisis, in particular Japanese investment, in China and ASEAN states. At the same time, however, the growing dominance of western financial institutions, together with the benefits of globalisation of finance, would diversify and deepen the region's ties with global financial markets. Combining these two developments, it is difficult to predict whether the collective efforts at financial cooperation through the Chiang Mai Initiative could be sustained in East Asia.

In fact, financial market opening in East Asia in itself may not produce incentives to establish regional financial arrangements such as the Asian Monetary Fund and to replicate the European monetary integration. As far as finance is concerned, most of the East Asian countries may benefit more from joining the US dollar bloc than an East Asian currency union. Realisation of this possibility may in part explain why the ASEAN+3 have not been able to make much progress in their negotiations for increasing the number of bilateral swap contracts, casting clouds over the prospects for further expansion and consolidation of the Chiang Mai Initiative.

As in trade, however, causality may run from currency union to financial integration: that is, a political decision to consolidate the Chiang Mai Initiative or to form a common currency area could anchor exchange rate expectations so that it could deepen financial integration as it creates incentives to establish regional capital markets, thereby forging closer financial linkages among East Asian countries. However, these cooperative efforts are not likely to weaken East Asia's financial linkages with global financial markets. In deciding whether to expand the Chiang Mai Initiative or to form a regional common currency area, East Asian countries may therefore have to examine closely whether their cooperative efforts would lead to the development of stable and efficient regional financial markets that could survive competition with other global financial markets.

Benefits and Costs of Establishing Regional Financial Markets

Since the 1997-98 crisis, there have been repeated calls for promoting regional financial markets in East Asia, where bonds and equities denominated in local as well as key international currencies are issued and traded, as part of the strategy to deepen financial integration in the region. This movement has raised two fundamental questions related to benefits and costs of building regional financial institutions and markets. Will the proposed regional capital markets help improve allocation of resources in East Asia? Will they reduce the likelihood of recurrence of financial crises in the future?

As noted earlier, the lack of professional expertise in securities business, the poor financial infrastructure including legal and regulatory systems, inadequate standards of accounting, auditing and disclosure systems, and non-transparent corporate governance all have plagued the development of efficient capital markets in East Asia. The cost of developing these legal, regulatory and informational infrastructures could be very high and hence may not justify the development of capital markets in small economies which are not likely to obtain scale economies and hence efficiency. The increasing migration of stocks to the main international financial centres increases the fixed overhead cost of maintaining market regulation, clearing, and settlements systems; it also reduces an order flow for local brokerage houses and business for local investment banks, accounting firms and credit rating agencies.

This cost consideration has generated interest in establishing an East Asian regional stock exchange and an East Asian regional bond market. These markets may overcome inefficiency of individual capital markets and enable some of the East Asian countries to borrow in their own currencies. At this stage, however, there is no guarantee that a regional bond market based in East Asia will be large and efficient enough to survive competition with global bond markets. Furthermore, a viable East Asian bond market will require support of a regional financial infrastructure that includes regional credit agencies, clearing and settlement systems, cross-border securities borrowing and lending mechanisms, credit enhancement and guarantee agencies, and regional trading mechanisms (ADBI, 2001). Tax treatments for securities transactions will also have to be harmonised at the regional level.

Starting from scratch it will take many years, if not many decades, for the East Asian countries with diverse legal and regulatory systems and at different stages of financial development to construct the requisite financial infrastructures for efficient regional capital markets. And many countries in East Asia will be hesitant in issuing bonds in their own currencies for fear that trading in these bonds could entail the currency mismatch problem.

In East Asia, Tokyo is a logical candidate for the location of a regional bond market, and the Japanese yen could serve as a key currency, given Japan's status as the second largest economy in the world. However, Tokyo has not been able to build the infrastructure that could support such a regional market and the prospects for internationalisation of the yen as an international transactions and reserve currency do not appear to be promising (ADBI, 2001).

There is also the question of whether the proposed East Asian bond market could be more efficient in diversifying sources of corporate financing and opening new investment opportunities than global bond markets. The presumption is that participants in this market would have better access to a large amount of more accurate information about prospects of economic and financial conditions of firms and financial institutions in the region than participants in global bond markets. However, this advantage may not be as significant as it may appear in view of the increased accessibility to not only macroeconomic but also sectoral and corporate information throughout East Asia as a result of the improvement in corporate governance, disclosure, and information technology.

While the advantage in gathering and assessing regional market information has become less important than before, the cost of raising funds through regional capital markets is likely to be higher in East Asia compared to global capital markets, as evidenced by recent developments in the Japanese Samurai (foreign and yen denominated) and Shogun (foreign currency denominated) bond markets. Although it is expected that foreign borrowers would take advantage of the low interest rates and continuing deflation in Japan, the issuance of Samurai bonds has not reached the pre-crisis peak level (¥37.9 trillion) in 1996, while no Shogun bonds have been issued since 1994. One of the most important reasons for these inactivities is simply the higher cost of borrowing through these markets than the Euro-yen, Euro bond, or Yankee bond markets. Rhee (2001) shows that the difference in all-in-cost to a sovereign borrower of ¥20 billion between the Samurai and Euroyen bonds is about 7 basis points (¥14 million). The lead time required from mandate to launch takes a few days in the Euro-yen issue, whereas it takes two to three months in the Samurai bond issue.

Inefficiency of the clearing and settlement process is another reason for the high cost of borrowing through the Samurai bond market. The Euro-yen bond market can clear through international clearing houses such as EURO-CLEAR and CEDEL, whereas the Samurai bond market is not eligible for such a global clearing. Furthermore, a regional clearing network in East Asia is yet to be created to link the Tokyo's clearing system with the region's financial centres such as Hong Kong and Singapore. As Rhee (2001) points out, one of the key issues related to the development of a regional bond market in East Asia may be the creation of a single central securities depository in East Asia for safekeeping, clearance, and settlements for all securities traded in the region.

There is also no reason to believe that the East Asian bond market will be better placed to safeguard the countries in the region from the recurrence of financial crisis in the future, unless it can be shown that this market will be less susceptible to speculation, herding and other market failures than international financial markets. Finally, efficiency considerations may in the end require integration of the East Asian regional bond market with global bond markets. Given the size and efficiency disadvantages, it is difficult to argue that such a regional bond market could weather through the competitive pressure of global bond markets.

As noted earlier, for smaller emerging market economies in East Asia, the cost of developing legal, regulatory, and other supporting infrastructure for efficient capital markets would be prohibitively expensive. Claessens, Klingebiel, and Schmakler (2002) show that the process of developing capital markets itself could increase access for domestic firms to international financial centres, where the investor base is large, market liquidity is abundant, and the cost of capital is relatively lower. With the continuing deregulation of capital account transactions, a growing number of large and efficient firms will migrate to international financial centres for their capital market services. This migration will result in a smaller availability of liquidity to the firms remaining in local markets and hence reducing incentives further to develop local bond and equity markets: a vicious circle could set in.

With the improvement in access to information, harmonisation of legal and regulatory systems and standards, and advances in financial technology that allow remote access to capital market services offered by international financial centres, future prospects for developing robust capital markets in East Asian countries are not promising. One of the implications of globalisation of finance is that East Asian countries will find it difficult to convert their bank-oriented financial systems into market-oriented ones. Another implication is that these bank-oriented systems will be increasingly specialised in catering to the credit needs of small and medium-sized firms and households. This is because a growing number of firms will leave the banking sector as they gain access to local capital markets. Some of these first comers will then migrate to international capital markets as they grow and meet requirements for cross-listing on and capital raising from international exchanges.

7 Concluding Remarks

One could argue that East Asia's integration into global financial markets is a natural as well as a desirable development, since the ultimate objective of economic liberalisation is, after all, the creation of globally integrated markets for goods and services, including financial services. Why should then globalisation of finance raise any consternation in East Asia, or for that matter, anywhere else? It does because globalisation has raised a number of concerns to East Asian policymakers that have not been adequately addressed in the discussion of reform of the international financial system.

One concern is that financial liberalisation may not necessarily help improve efficiency and competitiveness of the financial service industry in East Asia through the process of learning and acquiring new and more sophisticated financial technologies, certainly not in the foreseeable future. Because the gap in financial technology and expertise between East Asian emerging market economies and advanced developed countries is so large and building legal, regulatory, and other financial infrastructures is costly and takes so much time, that the East Asian countries may never be able to catch up with their western competitors, and in fact may fall in a trap of low technology banking while the provision of other more sophisticated financial services is dominated by foreign financial institutions.

This specialisation may not pose any serious problems to the East Asian countries, if efficiency and stability of the global financial system could be enhanced so as to reduce the incidence of financial crisis and help emerging market economies withstand better both internal and external shocks by instituting an effective system of liquidity provision and prudential regulation of financial institutions and markets at the global level.

Despite the long and protracted discussion of reform of the international financial system, in the eyes of many East Asian policymakers not much has been accomplished in addressing the interests of emerging market economies.[9] There is no reliable global or regional lender of last resort, which could provide liquidity support to emerging market economies in case they suffer from a short-run balance of payments problem. It is also highly unlikely that the global community could agree on establishing a global regulatory authority. From the perspectives of East Asian emerging market economies, advanced countries with developed financial markets have not devoted much effort to expanding and strengthening cross-border financial supervision and regulation.

The absence of effective cross-border prudential supervision of foreign financial institutions operating out of East Asian financial markets has created a number of problems. As the IMF (2000) report points out, there is no effective mechanism of monitoring large

---

9 On limited progress on international financial reform, see Griffith-Jones and Ocampo (2002).

foreign financial institutions providing a large number of different financial services to local customers in emerging market economies including those in East Asia. Many of the sophisticated derivative products developed by these foreign institutions could easily be used to evade taxes and regulations.

Most important of all, to East Asian policymakers, it is difficult to predict how branches or subsidiaries of foreign financial institutions and their parent institutions would behave in times of financial difficulties and crises in emerging market economies. Would they panic and move out all at once at the first sign of crisis as they did in the fall of 1997? Most of the East Asian countries have not been able to borrow from international capital markets in their own currencies although they have been removing many restrictions on capital movements, and they are not likely anytime soon. This means that they will be continuously exposed to the currency and term mismatch problems that triggered the crisis in 1997. A macroeconomic policy framework focusing on free floating and inflation targeting has not been tested for its effectiveness in sustaining financial stability with robust growth in emerging market economies.

These concerns and competitive disadvantages in producing financial services together with the region's desire to build its own mechanism of defense against future financial crises led to the discussion of establishing regional financial arrangements in East Asia, culminating in the Chiang Mai Initiative in May, 2000. As long as these issues remain unresolved, they will continue to rally East Asian countries in their ongoing movement toward financial integration.

References

Asian Development Bank Institute (2001), *Development of Capital Markets*, ADBI Executive Summary Series No. S56/02, July.

Asian Development Bank Institute (2001), "Designing New and Balanced Financial Market Structures in Post-Crisis Asia – Proposals on How to Foster Bond Markets through Strengthening the Banking Sector", Policy Proposal prepared by the Asian Policy Forum for the Evening Seminar on "Policy Recommendations", ADB Institute, Tokyo, 18 October.

Claessens, Stijn, Daniela Klingebiel and Sergio Schmukler (2002),

"Explaining the Migration of Stocks from Exchanges in Emerging Economies to International Centers", Working Paper No. 2816, The World Bank, Washington D.C., 25 March.

Eichengreen, Barry, and Michael Mussa (1998), *Capital Account Liberalization-Theoretical and Practical Aspects*, IMF Occasional Paper No. 172, IMF, Washington D.C.

Frankel, Jeffrey, and Andrew K. Rose (1998), "The Endogeneity of the Optimum Currency Area Criteria", In: *The Economic Journal*, Vol. 108, pp.1009-1025, July.

Griffith-Jones, Stephany and José Antonio Ocampo (2002), "What Progress on International Financial Reform? Why So Limited?", Paper prepared for the Expert Group on Development Issues (EGDI).

Heathcote, Jonathan, and Fabrizio Perri (2002), "Financial Globalisation and Real Regionalization," NBER Working Paper No. 9292, October.

IMF (2000), "The Role of Foreign Banks in Emerging Markets", In: *International Capital Markets Developments, Prospects, and Key Policy Issues*, Chapter VI, IMF, Washington D.C.

Kaminskey, Graciela Laura and Sergio L. Schmukler (2002), "Short-Run Pain, Long-Run Gain The Effect of Financial Liberalization", Paper prepared for George Washington University and The World Bank Joint Conferences, May 30-31.

La Porta, Rafael, Florencio Lopez-de-Silanes, Andrei Shleifer, and Robert Vishny (1999), "Investor Protection: Origins, Consequences, Reform", Financial Sector Discussion Paper No. 1, The World Bank, Washington D.C., September.

McKinnon, Ronald (2001), "Optimum Currency Areas and the European Experience", October 16 (forthcoming in *Economics of Transition*, Volume 10).

—— (2002), *The East Asian Exchange Rate Dilemma and the World Dollar Standard*, Asian Development Bank, February.

Mundell, R. (1973), "Uncommon Argument for Common Currencies," In: H.G. Johnson and A.K. Swoboda, *The Economics of Common Currencies*, George Allen & Unwin Ltd., London.

Park, Y.C., and C.Y. Song (2001), "East Asia's Experiences with the Free Floating Rates System", In: J.J. Teunissen, *New Challenges of Crisis Prevention: Addressing Global Economic Imbalances in the North and Boom-Bust Cycles in the South*, FONDAD, The Hague, pp. 134-167.

Rhee, S. G. (2001), "Further Reforms of the JGB Market for the Promotion of Regional Bond Markets," Paper presented at the 2000 ADBI/OECD Workshop on Capital Markets Reforms, Tokyo, April.

World Bank (1997), *Private Capital Flows to Developing Countries:* The Road to Financial Integration, The World Bank, Washington D.C.

World Bank (2001), "Special Focus: Financial and Corporate Restructuring – An Update", The World Bank, Washington D.C., March.

Appendix 1 A Vector Autoregression (VAR) Model

Let $R_{j,t}$, $R_{US,t}$, and $R_{JP,t}$ be the daily stock returns or interest rates at time t of the market portfolio of an East Asian or European country j, US, and Japan, respectively. Then, for each East Asian or European market, the following trivariate VAR model is constructed:

$$Y(t) = D(T) + \sum_{s=1}^{m} B(s)Y(t-s) + u(t), \quad t = 1, \ldots T \quad (1)$$

where $Y(t)$ is a 3x1 vector consisting of $R(t)$. $D(t)$ is a 3x1 vector of constants, $B(s)$ a 3x3 coefficient matrix, and $u(t)$ a 3x1 vector of serially uncorrelated random residuals with a zero mean and finite variance.

The VAR specification defines $u(t)$ as an innovation in $Y(t)$ in that it is the component of $Y(t)$ that cannot be predicted from past values of the variables in the system. The moving average representation (MAR) is obtained by a successive substitution on the right hand side of equation (1) as

$$Y(t) = F(t) + \sum_{s=0}^{\infty} A(s)u(t-s) \quad (2)$$

where $F(t)$ is the corresponding 3x1 vector of constants and $A(s)$ is a 3x3 matrix of coefficients. The MAR represents $Y(t)$ as a linear combination of current and past one-step-ahead forecast errors.

While the estimated coefficients $B(s)$ of the VAR provide little insights into the dynamic interactions among the variables, equation 2 (MAR) presents the information equivalent to that contained in the original estimates, but in a form relatively easy to understand. That is,

$$\sum_{s=0}^{\infty} A(s)u(t-s) = \sum_{s=0}^{\infty} A(s)(HH^{-1})u(t-s) = \sum_{s=0}^{\infty} C(s)e(t-s), \quad (3)$$

where $C(s)=A(s)H$, $e(t)=H^{1}u(t)$ and the matrix H are such that HH' is a factorisation of the covariance matrix $u(t)$ by the Choleski decomposition method. With daily data, the k-week ahead forecast error of $Y(t+k)$ at time t is

$$C(k-1)e(t+1)+C(k-2)e(t-2)+\ldots\ldots+C(0)e(t+k)= \sum_{s=0}^{k-1} C(s)e(t+k-s). \quad (4)$$

The variance of the *k*-week ahead forecast error is

$\sum_{j=1}^{n} \sum_{s=0}^{k-1} [C^{i,j}(s)]^2$. Then, $\sum_{s=0}^{k-1} [C^{i,j}(s)]^2 / \sum_{j=1}^{n} \sum_{s=0}^{k-1} [C^{i,j}(s)]^2$ is

a component of the error variance in the *k*-week ahead forecast of Y^i, which is accounted for by the innovation in Y^i.

Equation 1 is estimated with two lags and a constant term for the deterministic part *D(t)*. In view of the cross-equation nature of the hypothesis, it is also estimated with alternative lags of one, three, and four. The results are qualitatively similar, however. In order to find a measure of the overall relative importance of weekly returns (or daily interest rates) of the US and Japan in generating the stock market return or the interest rate of each sample country belonging to both the East Asian and European group, the variance of *k*-week ahead forecast error of the market return (or the interest rate) is computed with the MAR and decomposed into innovations in the US, Japan (an EMU market index for Europe), and the local market returns (or the interest rates). In order to isolate the shocks, they are orthogonalised. The orthogonalised innovations are uncorrelated both across time and the equation.

Appendix 2 Definition of Interest Rates

Europe	
Austria	discount 'dead' – middle rate
Belgium	euro-franc 3 month (LDN: FT) – middle rate
Denmark	euro-krone 3 month (LDN: FT) – middle rate
France	money market 3 month 'dead' – middle rate
Germany	euro-mark 3 month (LDN: FT) – middle rate
Ireland	interbank 3 month – offered rate
Italy	euro-lire 3 month (LDN: FT) – middle rate
Netherlands	Neth. corp. yield (ECON) 'dead' – middle rate
Norway	interbank T/N (nominal) – middle rate
Sweden	bond yield corporate (ECON) – middle rate
Switzerland	euro-franc 3 month (LDN: FT) – middle rate
UK	discount market overnight – middle rate
East Asia	
Hong Kong	deposit call – 3 month – middle rate
Indonesia	call money (pipu) – deposit 3 month – middle rate
Japan	call overnight – 3 month – middle rate
Korea	corp. bond AA no guarantee 3 year – middle rate
Malaysia	interbank 3 month – middle rate
Philippines	Manilla treasury bill 91 D – middle rate
Singapore	deposit call 3 month – middle rate
Thailand	interbank on call – middle rate
United States	federal funds – middle rate

Table 1 Five Asian Economies*: External Financing
(in billions of dollars)

	1978	1979	1980	1981	1982	1983	1984	1985	1986
Current account balance	-6	-7.9	-8.9	-15.5	-17.6	-18.4	-8.7	-5.3	1
External financing, net	3.4	10.6	11.3	18.1	23.4	21.2	12.8	10.2	-3.9
Private flows, net	*1.7*	*7.3*	*7.7*	*11.8*	*14.5*	*14.8*	*8.7*	*6.4*	*-5.5*
Equity investment, net	0.2	0.4	0.5	1.1	0.6	0.9	1	1	1.2
Direct investment, net									
Portfolio investment, net									
Private creditors, net	1.5	6.9	7.2	10.7	13.8	13.9	7.7	5.5	-6.6
Commercial banks, net	1.5	6.1	5.5	9.9	11.8	8.3	6.1	1.9	-6.8
Non-banks, net	0.1	0.8	1.7	0.8	2	5.5	1.6	3.6	0.2
Official flows, net	*1.7*	*3.3*	*3.7*	*6.3*	*9*	*6.4*	*4.1*	*3.7*	*1.6*
IFIs	1.4	1.3	1.9	3.2	2.1	4	1.7	1.3	0.9
Bilateral creditors	0.3	2	1.8	3	6.8	2.4	2.3	2.4	0.7
Resident lending/ other, net **	-0.7	0.5	0.8	-3.3	-8.4	-1.6	-0.5	-4.3	2.4
Reserves (- = increase)	-0.6	-3.2	-3.3	0.6	2.6	-1.2	-3.6	-0.6	0.4

Notes:
* Indonesia, Malaysia, the Philippines, South Korea and Thailand.
** Including net lending, monetary gold, and errors and omissions.
Source: Institute for International Finance (IIF) data.

Table 2 Japan's International Bank Lending
(in millions of dollars and percentages)

	1995.6		1996.6		1999.12		2001.6	
	Amount	Share	Amount	Share	Amount	Share	Amount	Share
Developed Countries	30,308	0.182	26,526	0.159	528,335	0.667	728,725	0.752
Asia	107,976	0.649	115,471	0.693	65,050	0.082	51,934	0.054
Indonesia	20,512	0.123	21,622	0.130	12,491	0.016	9,626	0.010
Korea	20,874	0.125	22,512	0.135	12,592	0.016	10,110	0.010
Malaysia	6,091	0.037	8,131	0.049	6,029	0.008	5,843	0.006
Philippines	1,147	0.007	1,402	0.008	2,921	0.004	3,066	0.003
Thailand	32,628	0.196	37,552	0.225	13,075	0.016	7,979	0.008
Sub total	81,252	0.488	91,219	0.547	47,108	0.059	36,624	0.038
Total	166,368		166,701		792,676		969,425	

Source: Bank for International Settlements, *The BIS Consolidated International Banking Statistics*, various issues.

Table 3 Japan's Overseas Direct Investment by Region*
(in millions of dollars)

	1997	1998	1999	2000	2001 (first half)
Asia	12,181	6,528	7,162	5,931	2,762
Korea	442	303	980	813	355
Hong Kong	695	602	971	936	92
Taiwan	450	224	285	510	146
Singapore	1,824	636	962	424	418
Thailand	1,867	1,371	816	931	512
Philippines	524	379	617	458	93
Indonesia	2,514	1,076	918	414	191
Malaysia	791	514	526	232	104
China	1,987	1,065	751	995	752
Vietnam	311	51	99	21	49
India	434	257	208	168	36
Sri Lanka	270	36	19	11	13
Pakistan	62	9	-	-	-
N-America	21,389	10,943	24,770	12,271	3,223
Lat.-America	6,336	6,463	7,437	5,232	2,245
Middle East	471	146	113	19	1
Europe	11,204	14,010	25,804	24,406	4,966
Africa	332	444	515	53	123
Oceania	2,058	2,213	893	667	380
Total	53,972	40,747	66,694	48,580	13,699

Note:
* Report-Accepted Basis.
Source: JETRO, *Jetro Investment White Paper*, 2000 and 2002.

Table 4 Korea's Overseas Direct Investment by Region*
(in millions of dollars)

	1997	1998	1999	2000	2001	Outstanding at the end of 2001
Asia	1,575	1,531	857	849	-317	10,882
Malaysia	-7	21	2	-13	10	323
Vietnam	92	50	15	36	31	638
Singapore	23	129	154	72	20	508
India	105	115	14	15	8	475
Indonesia	154	58	75	61	-363	1,061
Japan	62	22	34	34	75	527
China	695	665	221	307	-274	4,382
Thailand	184	89	4	17	28	500
Philippines	30	33	77	62	42	505
Hong Kong	52	371	203	239	72	1,269
Middle East	68	6	0.9	27	17	246
North America	826	686	935	1,179	342	8,286
Latin America	251	224	183	1,411	76	2,722
Europe	357	1,033	204	139	1,741	5,387
Africa	92	91	20	20	13	515
Oceania	120	102	36	61	11	669
Total	3,289	3,674	2,236	3,686	1,883	28,706

Note:
* Actual Investment.
Source: The Export-Import Bank of Korea (2002), *Overseas Direct Investment Statistics Yearbook, 2002.*

Table 5 Taiwan's Overseas Direct Investment by Region*
(in millions of dollars)

	1997	1998	1999	2000	2001
Asia	819	581	836	851	815
Hong Kong	214	69	122	111	96
Japan	32	30	122	312	169
Singapore	230	158	325	220	378
Philippines	127	39	29	13	46
Indonesia	56	20	7	34	6
Thailand	58	131	113	50	16
Vietnam	85	110	35	54	31
Korea	0.3	2	81	93	12
America	1,916	2,637	2,268	3,946	3,461
Europe	59	34	61	62	46
Oceania	28	8	41	148	63
Africa	-	36	41	7	6
Total	2,894	3,296	3,269	5,077	4,391

Note:
* Approval Basis.
Source: Investment Commission, MOEA of Taiwan. *Statistics on Overseas Chinese & Foreign Investment, Outward Investment, Indirect Mainland Investment*, 2001/12.

Table 6 Singapore's Investment Abroad, 1997-1999
(in millions of dollars)

	1997	1998	1999
Total	158,566	177,949	191,031
Total Direct investment	75,807	75,622	84,219
Direct Equity investment	57,191	53,211	58,754
Direct investment	41,478	39,899	45,293
Portfolio investment	23,277	36,155	35,965
Other Foreign Assets	59,482	66,172	70,847

Destination of Singapore's Total Direct Investment Abroad
Top 8 Investment Destination Based on 1999 (Stock as at Year-End)

China	10,477	12,186	12,625
Hong Kong	8,113	7,668	8,399
Malaysia	8,908	8,610	7,940
Belgium	1,751	3,261	6,151
Indonesia	6,519	4,485	4,517
British Virgin Islands	2,901	3,993	4,368
United States	2,905	3,064	4,285
Mauritius	2,485	3,222	4,072

Source: Singapore Department of Statistics.

Table 7 VAR Decomposition of East Asian Stock Prices
(weekly dollar index)*

Period	1/ 3/ 90 ~ 4/30/97			1/ 6/ 99 ~ 8/21/02		
Shock	Global	Regional	Country	Global	Regional	Country
			Hong Kong			
1	11.81547	0.551633	87.63290	29.37337	7.361128	63.26550
2	11.84875	0.641289	87.50996	31.28107	7.092248	61.62668
3	11.74604	0.640663	87.61330	30.90170	7.222633	61.87567
4	11.74676	0.647848	87.60540	30.89759	7.236009	61.86640
			Indonesia			
1	0.514037	0.022548	99.46341	0.153653	0.990592	98.85576
2	0.530492	0.080252	99.38926	0.180802	1.317838	98.50136
3	0.852544	1.201549	97.94591	0.188271	1.331859	98.47987
4	0.869937	1.309453	97.82061	0.189255	1.336095	98.47465
			Korea			
1	1.857645	1.290440	96.85191	16.15357	5.103949	78.74248
2	2.055302	1.469221	96.47548	18.97168	9.104634	71.92369
3	2.043870	1.966944	95.98919	18.35919	13.33941	68.30140
4	2.045702	1.969084	95.98521	18.62073	13.29491	68.08436
			Malaysia			
1	8.720180	1.796037	89.48378	6.619883	0.000570	93.37955
2	10.40599	1.900747	87.69326	6.569100	0.560231	92.87067
3	10.34695	1.991289	87.66176	6.577603	1.134615	92.28778
4	10.37380	2.013665	87.61254	6.578612	1.134506	92.28688
			Philippines			
1	4.333805	0.187880	95.47831	6.314236	0.186250	93.49951
2	6.744170	0.882054	92.37378	7.883241	0.439348	91.67741
3	6.906731	0.961260	92.13201	11.71351	0.493182	87.79331
4	6.939220	0.960077	92.10070	11.75481	0.492699	87.75249
			Singapore			
1	14.34621	7.612955	78.04084	18.51377	3.222573	78.26366
2	15.93102	7.462130	76.60685	20.31242	3.082938	76.60464
3	15.74236	8.755126	75.50251	20.67759	3.155843	76.16656
4	15.75407	8.771754	75.47417	20.67528	3.163149	76.16157
			Thailand			
1	6.180099	0.235447	93.58445	9.390497	0.358787	90.25072
2	6.813609	0.954562	92.23183	11.22046	1.338870	87.44067
3	7.107116	2.721726	90.17116	10.79652	4.871466	84.33202
4	7.106599	2.728698	90.16470	10.81709	4.872960	84.30995
			Average across countries in period 4			
	7.833727	2.628654	89.53762	14.21905	4.504333	81.27661

Note: * This table presents the results of variance decomposition of East Asian market returns using the estimates of trivariate VAR for the US, Japan, and each of the East Asian markets. Estimation is based on a weekly dollar return index of each country. The return index data are from DataStream International.

Table 8 VAR Decomposition of EU Stock Prices
(weekly dollar index)*

Forecast Period	1/3/1990~8/21/2002		
	Global shock	Regional shock	Country shock
	Austria		
1	6.647274	25.92117	67.43156
2	6.709909	25.88374	67.40635
3	7.002183	25.79909	67.19872
4	7.009582	25.79814	67.19228
	Belgium		
1	14.97513	29.29040	55.73447
2	15.00695	29.58801	55.40504
3	15.27961	29.50389	55.21650
4	15.28966	29.50303	55.20731
	Denmark		
1	10.61022	29.09709	60.29268
2	10.70731	28.92995	60.36274
3	10.90243	28.90157	60.19600
4	10.90720	28.89882	60.19399
	Finland		
1	19.29257	10.99099	69.71644
2	19.37823	11.13095	69.49082
3	19.55892	11.08780	69.35328
4	19.56437	11.08748	69.34815
	France		
1	30.53955	51.88161	17.57884
2	30.86205	51.66236	17.47559
3	31.28831	51.35359	17.35810
4	31.29836	51.34576	17.35589
	Germany		
1	28.78945	51.55460	19.65595
2	28.39232	51.43619	20.17149
3	28.50102	51.33116	20.16783
4	28.50627	51.32725	20.16647
	Ireland		
1	16.92309	17.72883	65.34808
2	17.04189	17.53927	65.41884
3	17.47764	17.46170	65.06066
4	17.48791	17.46638	65.04571

Table 8 (continued)

Forecast Period	1/3/1990~8/21/2002		
	Global shock	Regional shock	Country shock
		Italy	
1	15.53691	38.32677	46.13632
2	15.55041	38.46852	45.98107
3	15.61792	38.63925	45.74283
4	15.62166	38.63841	45.73994
		Netherlands	
1	30.55973	42.00199	27.43828
2	30.06335	41.70098	28.23568
3	30.68545	41.19582	28.11873
4	30.71460	41.17469	28.11071
		Portugal	
1	5.023863	18.90529	76.07085
2	5.035442	18.90736	76.05720
3	5.168920	19.04828	75.78280
4	5.170355	19.04948	75.78017
		Spain	
1	23.19103	38.69052	38.11844
2	23.13295	38.84912	38.01793
3	23.16078	38.82539	38.01383
4	23.16234	38.82461	38.01305
		Sweden	
1	28.86423	21.30764	49.82812
2	28.94635	21.37666	49.67699
3	29.35966	21.30291	49.33742
4	29.36817	21.30586	49.32597
		United Kingdom	
1	32.94921	25.89883	41.15197
2	32.99670	26.02761	40.97569
3	33.43264	25.91782	40.64954
4	33.44185	25.92327	40.63487
		Average across countries in period 4	
	20.580179	30.7956292	48.6241931

Note:
* This table presents the results of variance decomposition using the estimates of trivariate VAR for the US, EMU (value weighted return index), and each of the European markets estimated for the periods from 1/3/1990 to 8/21/2002. The estimation is based on a Weekly US-dollarised return index of each country. The data are from DataStream International.

Table 9 VAR Decomposition of East Asian Interest Rates*

Forecast Period	1/ 1/ 94 ~ 4/31/97			1/ 1/ 99 ~ 8/31/02		
Shock	Global	Regional	Country	Global	Regional	Country
			Hong Kong			
5	4.85	0.03	95.10	9.39	0.06	90.54
10	9.73	0.06	90.19	11.16	0.23	88.60
15	15.24	0.20	84.55	12.22	0.42	87.34
20	20.89	0.42	78.67	13.10	0.59	86.29
			Indonesia			
5	0.05	0.40	99.54	0.68	0.23	99.08
10	0.54	0.62	98.82	0.75	0.90	98.34
15	1.81	0.85	97.32	0.79	1.50	97.69
20	3.83	1.07	95.08	0.84	1.96	97.19
			Malaysia			
5	0.11	0.09	99.79	0.005	0.0007	99.99
10	0.23	0.22	99.53	0.003	0.0004	99.99
15	0.40	0.40	99.19	0.002	0.0005	99.99
20	0.61	0.61	98.77	0.002	0.0007	99.99
			Philippines			
5	0.25	0.08	99.65	0.09	0.30	99.59
10	0.37	0.11	99.51	0.07	1.23	98.69
15	0.49	0.13	99.37	0.05	2.20	97.74
20	0.62	0.16	99.20	0.04	3.03	96.91
			Korea			
5	0.02	0.12	99.84	0.11	0.01	99.87
10	0.06	0.56	99.37	0.11	0.06	99.82
15	0.19	1.32	98.47	0.12	0.13	99.74
20	0.41	2.39	97.18	0.12	0.20	99.66
			Thailand			
5	0.18	0.06	99.75	0.004	0.86	99.13
10	0.14	0.07	99.77	0.01	2.73	97.25
15	0.15	0.08	99.75	0.01	4.08	95.90
20	0.21	0.09	99.69	0.01	4.79	95.19
			Singapore			
5	0.94	0.52	98.53	0.45	0.31	99.22
10	0.92	0.47	98.59	0.88	1.09	98.01
15	0.84	0.44	98.71	1.39	1.93	96.67
20	0.72	0.40	98.83	1.99	2.66	95.33
			Average across countries in period 20			
	2.30	1.89	95.79	3.90	0.74	95.34

Note: * This table presents the results of variance decomposition of interest rates using the estimates of trivariate VAR for the US, Japan, and each of the East Asian markets. Estimation based on daily interest rate data from DataStream International.

Table 10 VAR Decomposition of the Interest Rates Before and After the Maastricht Treaty in Europe

Forecast Period	1/ 1/ 85 ~ 12/31/90			1/1/94 ~ 8/30/02		
Shock	Global	Regional	Country	Global	Regional	Country
			Austria			
5	0.04	1.84	98.10	0.431	1.48	98.08
10	0.03	4.68	95.27	0.67	5.03	94.29
15	0.09	8.62	91.28	0.92	10.09	88.98
20	0.19	13.42	86.37	1.15	15.74	83.09
			Belgium			
5	0.29	0.34	99.35	1.56	12.41	86.02
10	0.65	0.53	98.81	1.96	14.72	83.31
15	0.98	0.76	98.25	2.27	17.24	80.47
20	1.26	1.06	97.67	2.57	19.81	77.61
			Denmark			
5	1.58	0.27	98.13	0.50	1.44	98.05
10	2.74	0.48	96.76	0.72	2.16	97.10
15	3.47	0.70	95.82	0.93	3.00	96.06
20	3.91	0.92	95.16	1.17	3.94	94.88
			France			
5	0.02	3.78	96.18	1.68	2.55	95.75
10	0.08	5.00	94.91	2.07	3.06	94.85
15	0.16	6.18	93.64	2.31	3.56	94.11
20	0.25	7.47	92.26	2.52	4.09	93.37
			Ireland			
5	0.04	0.35	99.60	1.98	1.08	96.93
10	0.07	0.54	99.37	2.36	1.11	96.52
15	0.14	0.72	99.13	2.58	1.15	96.26
20	0.18	0.91	98.89	2.77	1.19	96.03
			Italy			
5	0.21	0.06	99.72	0.07	0.003	99.91
10	0.97	0.04	98.98	0.09	0.01	99.88
15	1.75	0.03	98.20	0.11	0.04	99.83
20	2.39	0.03	97.57	0.14	0.07	99.77
			Netherlands			
5	0.05	0.47	99.47	7.95	22.12	69.92
10	0.10	0.87	99.01	9.09	23.15	67.75
15	0.22	1.42	98.35	9.58	23.89	66.51
20	0.36	2.13	97.50	9.93	24.53	65.52

Table 10 (continued)

Forecast Period	1/ 1/ 85 ~ 12/31/90			1/1/94 ~ 8/30/02		
Shock	Global	Regional	Country	Global	Regional	Country
			Norway			
5	1.63	0.01	98.34	0.04	0.03	99.92
10	4.24	0.05	95.69	0.03	0.02	99.93
15	5.38	0.17	94.43	0.03	0.02	99.94
20	5.78	0.38	93.83	0.02	0.02	99.95
			Sweden			
5	0.23	0.15	99.60	1.56	0.39	98.04
10	0.73	0.09	99.17	1.76	0.53	97.69
15	1.15	0.07	98.76	1.85	0.68	97.45
20	1.46	0.09	98.44	1.92	0.86	97.21
			Switzerland			
5	1.14	20.91	77.94	2.58	3.23	94.17
10	1.70	23.54	74.75	3.04	3.78	93.17
15	2.13	25.76	72.10	3.34	4.29	92.35
20	2.47	27.91	69.61	3.62	4.79	91.57
			United Kingdom			
5	1.87	0.74	97.37	4.47	0.84	94.67
10	3.81	2.74	93.44	5.18	0.88	93.93
15	4.67	5.35	89.97	5.61	0.88	93.49
20	4.98	8.13	86.87	5.98	0.87	93.13
			Average across countries in period 20			
	2.11	5.68	92.20	2.89	6.90	90.19

Note:
* This table presents the results of variance decomposition of daily interest rates using the estimates of trivariate VAR for the US, Germany, and each of the European markets estimated for each of the two sub periods (before 1/ 1/ 85 ~ 12/31/90, and after 1/1/94 ~ 8/30/02), respectively. The interest rate data are from DataStream.

Table 11 Foreign Bank Ownership in Selected Emerging Markets[1]
(in millions of dollars and percentages)

	Total Assets December 1994	Foreign Control[2] December 1994	Total Assets December 1999	Foreign Participation December 1999	Foreign Control[3] December 1999	Foreign Control[4] December 1999
Central Europe						
Czech Republic	46.6	5.8	63.4	47.3	49.3	50.7
Hungary	26.8	19.8	32.6	59.5	56.6	80.4
Poland	39.4	2.1	91.1	36.3	52.8	52.8
Total	112.8	7.8	187.1	44.0	52.3	56.9
Latin America						
Argentina	73.2	17.9	157.0	41.7	48.6	48.6
Brazil	487.0	8.4	732.3	18.2	16.8	17.7
Chile	41.4	16.3	112.3	48.4	53.6	53.6
Colombia	28.3	6.2	45.3	16.2	17.8	17.8
Mexico	210.2	1.0	204.5	18.6	18.8	18.8
Asia						
Korea	638.0	0.8	642.4	11.2	4.3	16.2
Malaysia	149.7	6.8	220.6	14.4	11.5	11.5
Thailand	192.8	0.5	198.8	6.0	5.6	5.6
Total	980.5	1.6	1061.8	10.9	6.0	13.2

Notes:
[1] Ownership data reflected changes up to December 1999 while balance sheet data are the most recent available in Fitch IBCA's BankScope.
[2] Ratio of assets of banks where foreigners own more that 50 percent of total equity to total bank assets.
[3] For central Europe and Asia available balance sheet data are in most cases for December 1998.
[4] Same as footnote 2 but at 40 percent level.
Source: IMF (2000).

Table 12 The Top 20 Investment Banks by Parent Country
(numbers in parentheses are percentages)

Function	Overall Results		Underwriting		Trading		Advisory	
Parent Country of Investment Banks	1996	2002	1996	2002	1996	2002	1996	2002
US	8	11	8	9	8	10	8	10
	(40)	(55)	(40)	(45)	(40)	(50)	(40)	(50)
UK	3	3	2	3	5	3	6	3
	(15)	(15)	(10)	(15)	(25)	(15)	(30)	(15)
Europe	7	5	7	6	6	7	6	7
	(35)	(25)	(35)	(30)	(30)	(35)	(30)	(35)
Japan	2	1	3	2	1	0	0	0
	(10)	(5)	(15)	(10)	(5)	(0)	(0)	(0)
Total no. of Investment Bank	20	20	20	20	20	20	20	20
	(100)	(100)	(100)	(100)	(100)	(100)	(100)	(100)

Source: Euromoney, January 1996 and 2002.

Table 13-1 Distribution of International Financing by Country and by Financial Instrument

(in millions of dollars and percentages)

	1991	1992	1993	1994	1995	1996	1997	1998	1999	2000	2001	Total	%
Capital market financing (A)													
Indonesia	242	100	285	1591	1545	1232	3223	0	767	76	450	9511	8.7
Malaysia	0	0	475	1325	3509	749	3000	89	591	556	1600	11894	10.9
Philippines	12	403	928	1112	1543	3020	2644	1919	623	1431	700	14335	13.2
South Korea	693	1179	2938	3214	9644	8533	4769	2137	4166	4304	3302	44880	41.2
Taiwan	139	1131	0	1766	1634	1051	1484	682	1502	3448	1693	14530	13.3
Thailand	1378	84	2095	1782	1809	1358	3421	708	661	0	555	13852	12.7
Total (A)	2464	2897	6722	10790	19683	15943	18543	5535	8310	9814	8300	109002	100.0
Loan financing (B)													
Indonesia	2171	2903	1652	5600	6255	5792	7094	0	0	0	0	31467	25.8
Malaysia	1161	1994	3493	1913	4227	5315	2975	600	0	0	0	21678	17.8
Philippines	0	57	1486	578	471	2402	2269	0	0	0	0	7263	6.0
South Korea	3369	1246	701	4772	3046	4467	5058	0	0	0	0	22658	18.6
Taiwan	850	498	611	270	1152	4075	7479	995	0	129	0	16058	13.2
Thailand	1559	2840	5326	2809	4975	3764	1531	0	0	0	0	22804	18.7
Total (B)	9110	9538	13268	15942	20126	25815	26405	1595	0	129	0	121928	100.0
Total													
Total (C)=A+B	11574	12435	19990	26732	39809	41758	44948	7130	8310	9943	8300	230929	
Proportion of capital market financing A/C	21.3	23.3	33.6	40.4	49.4	38.2	41.3	77.6	100.0	98.7	100.0	47.2	

Note:
The table presents the distribution of international financing proceeds financed in six Asian countries during the period of 1991-2001 by country and by instrument. The financing schemes are categorised into capital market financing and loan financing. Capital market financing instruments include: (i) Bond (bond with warrants, convertible bond, plain bond); (ii) Medium Term Note; and (iii) Equity (ordinary shares, preference shares, warrants). Loan financing instruments include syndicate loans.
Source: Thomson Financial SDC database.

Table 13-2 International Financing by Year and Financial Instrument
(in millions of dollars and percentages)

	1991	1992	1993	1994	1995	1996	1997	1998	1999	2000	2001	Total
Capital Market Financing												
Bond	866	929	5058	7065	9177	3835	8818	2551	2460	4721	7177	52657
%	7.48	7.47	25.30	26.43	23.05	9.18	19.62	35.78	29.60	47.48	86.47	22.80
Equity	1598	1919	764	3568	5713	6962	2298	2976	3850	3584	989	34221
%	13.81	15.43	3.82	13.35	14.35	16.67	5.11	41.74	46.33	36.05	11.92	14.82
MTN	0	50	900	157	4794	5146	7427	8	2000	1509	133	22124
%	0	0.40	4.50	0.59	12.04	12.32	16.52	0.11	24.07	15.18	1.60	9.58
Total	2464	2898	6722	10790	19684	15943	18543	5535	8310	9814	8299	109002
%	21.29	23.31	33.63	40.36	49.45	38.18	41.25	77.63	100	98.70	99.99	47.20
Loan Financing												
Loan	9110	9538	13268	15942	20126	25815	26405	1595	0	129	0	121928
%	78.71	76.70	66.37	59.64	50.56	61.82	58.75	22.37	0	1.30	0	52.80
Total												
Total	11574	12435	19990	26732	39809	41758	44948	7130	8310	9943	8300	230929
%	100	100	100	100	100	100	100	100	100	100	100	100

Table 14 Distribution of Lead Managers by their Parent Countries and Year

	1991	1992	1993	1994	1995	1996	1997	'91-'97	1998	1999	2000	2001	'98 -2001	Total
							Capital Market Financing							
US	100	0	756	412	2589	4614	5230	13700	1665	3469	4299	1396	10829	24529
UK	576	1790	2460	6102	8009	4298	8656	31890	1595	1668	3068	2995	9327	41217
Swiss	108	83	129	359	153	50	356	1238	18	0	0	0	18	1256
Other Europe	70	533	911	185	867	2412	1027	6005	252	543	556	2117	3468	9473
West Total	854	2406	4256	7058	11618	11374	15268	52834	3530	5680	7923	6508	23641	76475
%	34.65	83.08	63.31	65.41	59.02	71.34	82.34	68.58	63.77	68.35	80.72	78.40	73.97	70.16
Japan	114	0	1592	494	2528	1616	1832	8177	100	781	200	919	2001	10177
Singapore	15	0	102	179	698	943	150	2087	317	385	1211	224	2137	4223
Hong Kong	724	406	722	2327	2115	1194	819	8308	231	692	259	175	1356	9664
Other Asia	758	84	50	732	2725	815	473	5637	1357	772	222	475	2825	8462
Asia Total	1611	490	2466	3732	8066	4568	3274	24208	2005	2630	1892	1793	8319	32527
%	65.35	16.92	36.69	34.59	40.98	28.66	17.66	31.42	36.23	31.65	19.28	21.60	26.03	29.84
Total	2465	2896	6722	10790	19683	15942	18543	77042	5535	8310	9815	8301	31960	109002
%	100	100	100	100	100	100	100	100	100	100	100	100	100	100
							Loan Financing							
US	597	458	2556	1047	253	932	1371	7213	0	0	0	0	0	7213
UK	2342	2342	655	1211	1004	1298	697	7391	0	0	0	0	0	7391
Swiss	0	80	25	220	291	2451	0	3068	0	0	0	0	0	3068
Other Europe	556	663	1053	3046	4297	4297	3685	16526	0	0	0	0	0	16526
West Total	3495	1384	4288	5525	5845	7908	5753	34197	0	0	0	0	0	34197
%	38.36	14.51	32.32	34.66	29.04	30.63	21.79	28.45	0	—	0	—	0	28.05
Japan	630	3081	4496	879	1172	2317	2864	15440	0	0	0	0	0	15440
Singapore	1200	2150	1186	2080	3047	3228	2181	15072	0	0	0	0	0	15072
Hong Kong	1385	1664	2511	4461	3128	2904	2114	18167	0	0	0	0	0	18167
Other Asia	2400	1259	786	2998	6935	9457	13492	37328	1595	0	129	0	1724	39052
Asia Total	5615	8154	8980	10417	14281	17907	20652	86006	1595	0	129	0	1724	87730
%	61.64	85.49	67.68	65.34	70.96	69.37	78.21	71.55	100	—	100	—	100	71.95
							Total							
Total	9110	9538	13268	15942	20126	25815	26405	120204	1595	0	129	0	1724	121927
%	100	100	100	100	100	100	100	100	100	—	100	—	100	100

Note:
Distribution of international financing proceeds financed in six Asian countries during the period of 1991-2001 by parent country of a lead manager. The financing schemes are categorised into capital market financing and loan financing. Capital market financing instruments include i) Bond (bond with warrants, convertible bond, plain bond), ii) Medium Term Note, iii) Equity (ordinary shares, preference shares, warrants). Loan financing instruments include syndicate loans.
Source: Thomson Financial SDC database.

Table 15 Distribution of Lead Managers by their Parent Country and Financial Instrument
(in millions of dollars and percentages)

	Capital market financing				Loan financing	
	Bond	Equity	MTN	Total	Loan	Total
US	12234	7795	4500	24529	7213	31742
UK	18268	9849	13100	41217	7391	48608
Swiss	1019	237	0	1256	3068	4324
Other Europe	3864	1691	3917	9472	16526	25998
West Total	35385	19572	21517	76474	34197	110671
%	67.20	57.19	97.26	70.16	28.05	47.92
Japan	8841	1337	0	10178	15440	25618
Singapore	1209	3015	0	4224	15072	19296
Hong Kong	5207	3908	550	9665	18167	27832
Other Asia	2014	6390	57	8461	39052	47513
Asia Total	17271	14650	607	32528	87730	120258
%	32.80	42.81	2.74	29.84	71.95	52.08
Total	52657	34222	22124	109003	121927	230930
%	100	100	100	100	100	100

Note:
The distribution of international financing proceeds financed in six Asian countries during the period of 1991-2001 by the parent country of a lead manager. The financing schemes are categorised into capital market financing and loan financing. Capital market financing instruments include i) Bond (bond with warrants, convertible bond, plain bond), ii) Medium Term Note, and iii) Equity (ordinary shares, preference shares, warrants). Loan financing instruments include syndicate loans.
Source: Thomson Financial SDC database.

Table 16 List of Top 20 Lead Managers
(in millions of dollars and percentages)

Lead Manager	Amount	Parent Company
Merrill Lynch International Ltd	8741	US
Lehman Brothers	6050	US
JP Morgan Securities Ltd	3819	US
Morgan Stanley Dean Witter & Co	3606	US
Daiwa Securities Co Ltd	3414	Japan
Goldman Sachs (Asia)	2485	US
Salomon Brothers Inc	2464	US
SBC Warburg	2392	UK
Warburg Dillon Read	2382	UK
CS First Boston Limited	2344	US
Nomura Securities Co Ltd	2300	Japan
JP Morgan & Co Inc	1965	US
Merrill Lynch & Co Inc	1941	US
Deutsche Morgan Grenfell	1739	Germany
Morgan Stanley International Ltd	1728	US
Goldman Sachs International	1649	US
Baring Brothers & Co Ltd	1543	UK
UBS Securities Inc	1515	Swiss
Credit Suisse First Boston Inc	1500	Swiss
Jardine Fleming	1325	UK

Country	Amount	No.	%
US	36792	11	61.11
UK	7641	4	22.22
Swiss	3015	2	11.11
Other Europe	1739	1	5.56
West Total	49186	18	90.00
Japan	5714	2	10.00
Singapore	0	0	0.00
Hong Kong	0	0	0.00
Other Asia	0	0	0.00
Asia Total	5714	2	10.00
Total	54900	20	100.00

Note:
The table presents the list of top 20 lead managers ranked by the issue proceeds financed in six Asian countries during the period of 1991-2001. The financial instruments used include (i) Bond (bond with warrants, convertible bond, plain bond); (ii) Medium Term Note; and (iii) Equity (ordinary shares, preference shares, warrants).
Source: Thomson Financial SDC database.

Table 17 List of Top 20 Lead Managers Before and After the East Asian Currency Crisis
(in millions of dollars and percentages)

	1991-1997		
Country	Amount	No.	%
US	23780	10	50
UK	7733	5	25
Swiss	1515	1	5
Other Europe	1739	1	5
West Total	34767	17	85
Japan	5164	2	10
Singapore	0	0	0
Hong Kong	0	0	0
Other Asia	1186	1	5
Asia Total	6351	3	15
Total	41118	20	100

	1998-2001		
Country	Amount	No.	
US	16026	12	60
UK	2086	3	15
Swiss	2322	2	10
Other Europe	500	1	5
West Total	20934	18	90
Japan	550	1	5
Singapore	0	0	0
Hong Kong	0	0	0
Other Asia	704	1	5
Asia Total	1254	2	10
Total	22188	20	100

Note:
The table presents the list of top 20 lead managers before and after the Asian currency crisis. Lead managers are ranked by the issue proceeds financed in six Asian countries during the each period of 1991-1997 and 1998 2001, respectively. The financial instruments used include: (i) Bond (bond with warrants, convertible bond, plain bond); (ii) Medium Term Note; and (iii) Equity (ordinary shares, preference shares, warrants).
Source: Thomson Financial SDC database.

Table 18 Non Performing Loans of Crisis-Affected Countries
(in percentages of total loans)

	1997	1998	1999				2000			
	Dec.	Dec.	Mar.	Jun.	Sep.	Dec.	Mar.	Jun.	Sep.	Latest
Indonesia[a]	-	-	-	-	-	64.0	62.4	63.5	61.7	58.8 (Nov)
Excl. IBRA	7.2	48.6	58.7	39	38.9	32.9	32.1	30	26.9	23.9 (Nov)
Korea[b]	8.0	16.1	17.0	16.4	15.9	15.8	17.9	18.9	17.9	
Excl. KAMCO/KDIC	5.9	10.4	11.4	11.3	10.1	10.9	10.9	13.6	12.3	
Malaysia[c]	6.0	22.6	22.7	23.4	23.6	23.6	23.3	23.2	-	
Excl. Danaharta	-	18.9	18.2	18.1	17.8	16.7	16.7	16.2	16.1	15.3 (Dec)
Philippines[d]	4.7	10.4	13.2	13.1	13.4	12.5	14.4	14.6	15.3	15.1 (Dec)
Thailand[e]	-	45.0	47.0	47.4	44.7	41.5	39.8	34.8	30.6	26.5 (Dec)
Excl. AMCs	-	45	47	47.4	44.7	38.9	37.2	32	22.6	17.7 (Dec)

Notes:
[a] The first line uses the "stringent" definition of an NPL; the second line excludes transfer to IBRA.
[b] NPL figures use the BLC.
[c] Figures include commercial banks, finance companies, merchant banks, and Danaharta.
[d] Figures are for commercial banks.
[e] Commercial banks. First line includes commercial banks, finance companies, and the estimated amount of NPLs transferred to wholly-owned private AMCs.

Source: World Bank (2001).

11

Comment on Yung Chul Park and Kee Hong Bea

Heiner Flassbeck

Professor Parks' chapter raises a number of new issues challenging the conventional wisdom of an old debate, the optimum currency area (OCA) or common currency area (CCA) theory. Financial integration has indeed, up to now, not been considered as one of the classical criteria for OCA's or CCA's. Although favouring a regional currency arrangement in Asia, Professor Park asks whether the development of the financial markets and the dominance of foreign companies in financial relations, i.e. the globalisation of the Asian financial markets, is not driving the region into the wrong direction. In other words, will financial globalisation render regional cooperation in the end much more difficult?

Park presents striking evidence showing that foreigners run important parts of the financial business in Asia thereby intensifying the links with the western world instead of strengthening the collaboration in the region itself. However, Professor Park only briefly mentions the crucial question of causality: Are agents from the western world driving Asia's finance because they are dominant or competitive *per se*, or are they dominant because Asia has never tried to expand its regional ties and to stimulate an inward orientation by a political decision to cooperate and to financially integrate?

At a certain point Park seems to suggest that any decision in this direction would be useless as the dominance of western suppliers of financial services would *a priori* prevent closer collaboration in Asia. This, obviously, means stressing the old "owners problem" which, in most cases in economics, does not lead anywhere. Would rather efficient western financial companies not be able and willing to assist national governments in Asia in an attempt to create a regional currency arrangement?

Moreover, Professor Park stresses that there are only a few of these companies (two rating agencies, five investment banks etc.) on a global scale, reinforcing his argument about monopolistic power of western firms. This argument too, in my opinion, is not very convincing. There are a lot of small numbers on this economic planet beyond financial services which would not lead us to argue in favour of dismantling the regional concentration of the small number of suppliers of certain goods. Roughly, there are only ten producers of globally sold cars, three of sophisticated computer chips, two of machinery for printing etc. His argument, seen from the trade perspective, amounts to asking: Does the dominance of western suppliers of cars, railways and airplanes prevent Asian policymakers from cooperating in terms of transnational traffic routes? Additionally, every good German "Mittelständler" (medium-sized company) tries to be the global leader in his specific niche on the world market. The United States have very few companies being world leader in manufacturing and engineering, I do not mind if they have some world leaders in financial consulting.

There is another small number which will become more and more important in the globalised economy: three currencies. It may well be that a number of decades from now we end up with three currencies instead of the 50 to 100 which are still around. I think, Professor Park, in trying to make the case for regional cooperation in Asia would have been more convincing if he would have asked why countries are desperately searching a solution to their currency problem instead of putting the emphasis on a new criterion in the OCA/CCA debate. The whole debate about semi-fixed exchange rates or soft pegs, in my opinion, is flawed as the OCA/CCA theory is based on the assumption that there is always a viable alternative to pegging the rate, namely to float the rate. But if, in reality, this alternative is not attractive at all for developing countries, the OCA theory is useless and soft pegs are unavoidable as long as the world as a whole is not an optimum currency area.

Exchange rate volatility, gyrations and misalignments seem to have far more serious consequences for developing countries with small and open economies, and with a relatively large stock of external debt denominated in reserve currencies, than for big closed economies like the US, EU and Japan. However, the mainstream economic thinking blames the soft pegs in Asia and elsewhere to have provoked the shocks leading to frequent crisis. Their advise, in case that a common currency area with centralised institutions is not available, is to choose between free floating on the one hand and locking into a reserve currency through a currency board, dollarisation, or a hard peg, on the other hand. But these "corner solutions" may mean to be stuck between the famous rock and a hard place.

The political reason underpinning the widespread fascination about the corners is easy to understand: they seem to offer unilateral monetary solutions in the multilateral framework of a globalised economy. They seem to allow for a world of total market integration without any kind of "cooperation and coordination" at the level of governments and to exclude discretion of governments concerning the external price level. In addition, whereas global solutions in the trade area are about the retreat of governments, global or multilateral solutions in the field of money and currencies are about government interventions.

The corner solution idea is inconsistent, even in theory, if it is applied to a single country in a world of many different solutions including the two corners. If flexible exchange rates would work in a transparent manner and would bring about smooth adjustment, as expected by their advocates, the whole globalised world would have to go for this solution to make it work efficiently. With some countries adopting the idea and others not, the relations between countries would be easily distorted as it would be extremely difficult to equilibrate the competitive positions of countries with and without flexible exchange rates at hand. As the price level as a whole cannot be as flexible as the price level of tradable goods in countries with flexible rates, the countries with fixed rates can be easily pushed out of their markets by means of a depreciation of the currencies of the flex-rate advocates.[1] Argentina and Brazil are a sad proof of this

[1] In a recent article Dilip K. Das from the Asian Development Bank argues that fixed rates "are difficult to sustain in a world of increasing capital mobility" as they may come under speculative attack. But, at the same time, he admits that a country with "significant policy autonomy" under flexible rates may "have trouble gaining credibility in international financial markets" (p. 19). Obviously, the same effects may apply in both systems. A fixed rate may not be credible and policy with flexible

point. The spiralling depreciation of many countries in Latin America after the collapse of the Argentine currency board is proving the inconsistency of the "free float" corner even more impressively.

Developing countries fear free floating as they expect excessive and unmanageable volatility. That is why many developing countries and transition economies have used a nominal anchor in order to bring down inflation and to avoid being a punching ball for international speculation. But the soft pegs like free floating often resulted in erratic capital flows and overshooting of exchange rates. In general, while many countries dis-inflated successfully, orderly exits from such regimes proved to be a main stumbling block. For an individual developing country with low and stable inflation, an intermediate regime targeting real effective exchange rate supported by strict controls on inflows and outflows may provide a temporary alternative. But most developing countries are already committed to close integration into the global financial system and, under pressure from the G-7 and international institutions, opened their markets more or less irreversibly.

Since global arrangements for a stable soft peg system are not forthcoming, regional mechanisms provide the only realistic solution. The EU experience since the collapse of the Bretton Woods system holds useful lessons in this respect. While it is a successful example of anchoring and a soft peg, culminating in the hard peg of monetary union, it is crucially different from unilateral dollarisation and currency boards. There have been mutual responsibilities by a reserve currency and collective mechanisms and institutions designed for this purpose, including implicit or explicit lender-of-last-resort facilities and orderly exit strategies. However, even these arrangements have not been without problems in a world of free capital movements. They required monetary convergence preventing inflation differentials. They also required a certain degree of real convergence, i.e. of overall growth and macroeconomic performance.

Moreover, even if convergence is guaranteed, regional mechanisms are not easy to replicate among developing countries

---

rates may not be credible. Speculation may test a commitment to defend a rate or lead to overshooting and thereby harm the economic policy objectives of governments. These kind of arguments lead to nowhere if the interaction of prices, wages, interest rates and exchange rates are not explicitly analysed. Dilip K. Das, "Asian Crisis: Distilling Critical Lessons", UNCTAD Discussion Papers No. 152, December, 2000.

alone. While intra-regional trade within developing country groupings such as ASEAN or Mercosur is growing rapidly, the trade of such regions with the rest of the world, notably with industrial countries, is much more important than that of the EU. Thus, the scope for them to collectively float vis-à-vis the rest of the world is more limited than for the EU. While appropriate regional arrangements among developing countries may increase the stability of the regional pattern of exchange rates, they do not eliminate the question of what regime to adopt vis-à-vis reserve currencies, but raise it at the regional level.

A better arrangement would be to involve major reserve currency countries in such regional arrangements, as in the EU which included emerging markets (Portugal, Greece, Spain and Ireland) alongside Germany, with mutual responsibilities and appropriate institutions. This could be realised in East Asia at this very moment only if Japan decided to play a dominant role. The United States are not interested in monetary union or regional monetary arrangements with others, and it would be difficult to extend the EU arrangements to Africa and the Middle East. Hence, a global system of a small number of regional monetary arrangements built around major reserve currencies, together with close cooperation among them as global stability is still far away.

The European Case

Seen from a European perspective, Professor Parks "benefits" of a common currency, focusing on capital mobility in face of little wage and price flexibility, have not been very prominent for the European decision to unify in terms of monetary policy. He stresses easy access to cheap capital as a substitute for real adjustment of wages. In my opinion it is just the other way around: the adjustment of nominal wages and prices to external (oil price hikes) and internal shocks (loss of competitiveness vis-à-vis other members of the system) is much more ambitious and strict under a well-designed system of fixed rates and the need to refinance current account deficits much more limited than under floating.[2]

---

[2] See H. Flassbeck, "The Exchange Rate: Economic Policy Tool or Market Price?", UNCTAD Discussion Paper No. 157, November, 2001.

The main arguments for a soft peg European style have different roots. First of all, multilaterally secured soft pegs representing the transitional stage to the corner of a unified currency, as implemented in Europe in the last 30 years, have to be treated quite differently from the unilaterally introduced soft pegs in Asia and South America. In the former case monetary policy is dedicated to the domestic goal of reducing the inflation rate to the level compatible with the convergence needed to reach low inflation and a stable external value of money. The temporarily fixed exchange rate underpins this target by putting pressure on the domestic price setting through the import price channel. One-way-bets, however, on the interest rate of the converging high-inflation economy should be excluded by orderly depreciation restoring competitiveness and normalising the returns on financial assets time and again.

Paradoxically, Europe never adhered to the corner solution thesis although it has reached now the corner of fully fixed exchange rates. But the countries involved did not jump from one corner to the other. Europe took a long and winding adjustment path to finally reach the corner. Nevertheless, the search for a solution for the region as a whole incorporated many advantages. All the countries sacrificed part of their economic policy power, attributing the leading role to Germany as the anchor of the system. But, at the same time, the group as a whole gained autonomy vis-à-vis the power of markets and the influence of multilateral international organisations like the IMF. The German central bank *de facto* acted as lender of last resort for the system, although this role has never been explicitly assigned to her.

But there have been storms and shocks in Europe nevertheless. An anchoring country in which the overall inflation performance is quite similar to the one in the anchor country, is in an easy position from the beginning. Austria in its relation to Germany is a good example. The general inflationary performance in normal times is one thing, but the real test for a successfully anchoring country comes when the anchor reacts to different kinds of shocks.

The most famous and most clear-cut example of an unsustainable peg was the attempt of Italy and the United Kingdom to fix their currencies vis-à-vis the D-Mark already in 1988, i.e. at a very early stage on the way to the monetary union which at that time appeared at the horizon. After the stock market crash in autumn 1987 the central banks in the United States and in Europe had trimmed their interest rates to historical lows despite the fact that the effects of the crash on the real economy were rather limited. Thus, the monetary stimulation at a rather late stage of the recovery gave new momentum to the world economy and world investment. The growth performances of the countries under consideration after the shock were more or less identical. All the countries reached growth rates of 4 percent or more with the United Kingdom being the best performer at the end of the 1980s and Germany outpacing the others at the beginning of the 1990s following the unification boom.

The inflation performance was quite different, however. Whereas the traditional low-inflation countries including the United States remained below an inflation rate of 4 percent, Italy and the UK moved up to 8 percent or more. Even more pronounced were the differences in the growth rates of unit labour costs. Germany, Austria and France experienced a very slow and moderate reaction of wages to falling unemployment and rising growth, the rise in labour costs remained subdued and below the rise in prices. In Italy and the UK, however, growth rates of unit labour costs jumped from 4 to close to 10 percent, outpacing the others and price inflation. Thus, compared with the anchor country the two newcomers in the European Monetary System (EMS), Italy and the UK, lost ground in the direct external competition with Germany, Austria and France. With fixed nominal exchange rates, the real exchange rate (in terms of unit labour costs) of Italy vis-à-vis Germany appreciated from 1987 to 1991 by 23 percent, and the real exchange rate of the UK by 28 percent. The loss of competitive power in these two countries was reflected in a huge swing in the current account from surplus to deficit whereas the surpluses in the stable countries mushroomed.

If the UK and Italy wanted to avoid a deflationary spiral a depreciation of their currencies and the decision to quit the EMS was the only way out. It is easy to understand why the decision of France not to give in to the pressure coming from the "markets" in 1992 was justified. France as well as Austria were able to preserve their competitive position in the aftermath of the positive demand shock. France had been under pressure from the markets because the overall economic situation at that time was rather gloomy compared to Germany or Austria so that a depreciation would have been an easy way out of the recession. But the decision of the French government – with the assistance of most other members of the EMS – to stick to the "unwritten" rules of the game, namely to use depreciation only in case of an external disequilibrium, proved to be right. The other way around, the pressure of the markets in the case of France, was fully unjustified whereas in the case of the UK and Italy it was justified.

This case of a currency crisis in Europe highlights the role which controls and interventions in the market for short-term capital can play and, at the same time, which role they cannot play. To stop capital from fleeing the British pound and the French franc in 1992 would have been justified as a massive and uncontrolled flight was by no means justified in either case. A thorough analysis of the authorities in both countries would have shown what the evidence proves, namely there was a limited need to adjust the pound and no need at all to adjust the franc. There was no reason for panic or any fear of a total collapse of the EMS and controls could have helped to avoid a big and unjustified unrest on the market. But with or without controls the British and the Italian problem had to be solved.

The most important policy lesson to be learned from this event in Europe concerns the short-term macroeconomic steering of the system. A better "early warning system" inside the EMS could have prevented the systemic crisis. If the authorities of the EMS, as well as the national authorities of all the countries involved, would have realised at a much earlier stage that the situation of the lira and the pound was becoming unsustainable, they could have reacted much earlier and could have depreciated the currencies of the two high-inflation countries in 1989 or 1990 already, thereby avoiding the worst troubles of the crisis and avoiding that a country like France became victim of the contagion effects of a general speculation against currencies with fixed exchange rates.

Another fundamental objection has been raised against a simple regional arrangement with a hegemonial currency as anchor. External and internal stability of the price level is just a tool to better accomplish the relevant targets of economic policy, namely more employment and higher growth rates in real income. An anchoring country gives away the tools to achieve these targets too. Thus, its overall economic policy success depends on the anchor country's success. The anchor country's policy, however, may be perfect under the circumstances prevailing in this country, but it does not imply that it is a perfect policy for the whole group formed by the anchor country and its surrounding satellites.

This was one of the main problems in Europe in the last two decades. Germany's monetary policy may have been an adequate policy for Germany. But the German central bank, the Deutsche Bundesbank, was forced by law just to take into account the economic environment in Germany to underpin its decisions – although the D-mark was part of an exchange rate system, the EMS. Germany adopted an economic policy approach which was directed mainly towards gaining additional market shares in the world market by reducing the domestic cost level and the tax burden. For Europe as a whole or the countries now forming the European Monetary Union (EMU) this policy approach, obviously, was not adequate. Europe's openness is only a third of the German one (10 percent) and to move the overall European economy by stimulating exports means to wag the dog by the tail. Hence, the full fledged change to a consistent monetary system for Europe as a whole was unavoidable in the last analysis. With the EMU created in 1999 the European Union has made this final step. As a consequence, this step was not just the result of the attempt of the French government not to be dominated politically by Germany into infinity, as many have argued. From an economic point of view, it was a fully justified step too, given the fact that Germany's monetary policy for systemic reasons could not concur with the European needs.

For very small, extremely open economies, forming just satellites of the anchor country, the anchor approach can be adopted for a very long time if, by and large, the anchor country's economic policy follows reasonable principles and takes the existence of the satellites with benign neglect. But for any larger group and for countries of equal size or economic power, the anchor approach can only be a transitional stage on the way to a monetary union. A consistent monetary policy is only possible for the group as a whole and thus can only be perceived by a united central bank. The transitional phase, however, can last very long. From the first steps to the last it took Europe 30 years.

The Global Solution

The idea of a globalised market is to preserve on a multilateral basis a level playing field to all parties involved. Multilateral trade rules shall apply to every party in the same manner. Deviations from these rules are object of multilateral negotiations. The monetary system cannot be excluded from the definition of the level playing field. Hence, the main idea behind the foundation of the International Monetary Fund in the 1940s was a sound one and is still valid today. An international institution is needed to avoid competitive depreciations in a world where countries have to struggle with unilateral solutions to the currency problem.

Whenever a worldwide crisis began to brew, upward or downward fluctuations in the real exchange rate – that is, changes in the competitive positions of entire national economies or untenable constellations of interest rates – played a pivotal role. In principle, only a new global monetary system can remedy this situation. It must guarantee that the relative competitiveness of national economies remains unchanged, and that enterprises can operate in healthy competition on a level playing field. Strong fluctuations of exchange rates which go beyond the balancing of inflation differentials cause similar distortions in the allocation of resources and investment decisions as unexpected fluctuations of the internal value of a currency or tariffs and quotas on trade. In a new world monetary order exchange rates must be firm enough to permit rational economic decision-making; but, at the same time, they need to be flexible enough to maintain the competitiveness of all nations. This can only be achieved by intense cooperation between the leading industrialised nations and the developing world.

Among countries or groups of countries which have jointly sworn off inflation as an instrument of economic policy, there is no need for exchange rate fluctuations. This is currently true, for example, of the United States, Japan, and Europe. The inflation rates and the growth rates in per-unit labour costs have been very low on both sides of the Atlantic and Japan for some years now. Nevertheless, huge changes in the real exchange rates between the big blocs occurred. The temporary weakness of the euro and the unjustified strength of the yen against the dollar and the quick reversal of these movements can only be viewed as a fundamental mis-evaluation on the part of the market. Such a misalignment does not only distort trade between the big blocs, but, at the same time, trade within the developing world and trade of developing countries with the "G-3". The Asian crisis in part has to be attributed to such a huge misalignment. Thus, the ideas brought forward to stabilise the real value of the G-3 currencies cannot be left aside in the interest of developing as well as industrialised countries. A global approach to tackle the problem, like it had been the case in the system of Bretton Woods, obviously offers the superior solution.

But if the globalised world is not able to cope with the global challenge the cooperation of regions with close trade ties is clearly better than any national corner solution or cutting all trade ties. Asia, for example, despite strong trade relations with the United States, has some potential to follow Europe on the road to monetary union and thereby to create a tripolar global monetary system in the long run. The trade ties in Asia are rather close. If Japan is included the intra-Asian exports before the crisis amounted to nearly 50 percent of overall trade. In Europe intra-trade has a share in overall trade of 65 percent. The trade links with the rest of the world are well balanced, with Europe and the United States being with equal shares the most important trading partners although the overall share of trade with the US is very high in several countries in relation to GDP. But even without Japan and China the intra-Asian exports are as high as a third of overall trade. Intra-trade of the NAFTA countries is much less.

The transforming Eastern European countries are trying to get access to the European Monetary Union as soon as possible. Some of them will be successful in a rather short period of time. The others will form an anchoring system around the EMU and head for full access later. South America is in a much more difficult situation. Some countries have already adopted the US dollar as currency, others have currency boards or informal pegs vis-à-vis the dollar. A Pan-American solution with the USA as anchor seems to be improbable as long as the experiments with different regimes are on their way. But the preconditions to go for a genuine South American approach are not optimal with trade ties not being as close as in Asia and Europe. But there are a few alternatives to monetary cooperation and some may prove to be untenable in due course. Thus, there is hardly an alternative to regional cooperation even under unfavourable circumstances.

Regional cooperation up to a regional monetary union can be an answer to the challenges coming up with globalisation and liberalisation. But even regional monetary systems do not prevent crisis and turmoil on the capital market once and for all. Given the unresolvable conflicts in a world of different nation states in any monetary system that has been tried out after World War II, the Bretton Woods system just as much as the European Monetary System of the 1980s and early 1990s, recurring crisis-like phenomena that forced governments and central banks to intervene have been unavoidable. But destabilising capital movements are less likely to occur, because the markets have been given clear guidelines, and because untenable interest constellations and massive real under- or over-evaluation should be avoided. If there are such guidelines, this system can minimise though not fully avoid surveillance and intervention into the capital account.

Conclusion

Some writers, including implicitly Professor Park ("currency and term mismatches that triggered the crisis", Section 7), are creating *a priori* dilemmas for developing countries by assuming something like the "original sin" of Eichengreen and Hausmann. They argue that maturity mismatches and/or currency mismatches constrain the development of poorer countries as these countries are lacking a deep and stable financial market. Hence, these countries would be unable to integrate financially and need, in one way or the other, capital inflows which are reducing the choice for a currency regime to the corners. This could be a crucial point. ... The Eichengreen-Hausmann thesis hints to an underlying theoretical problem the exchange rate discussion is burdened with. The original sin thesis makes sense if open economies are forced to borrow abroad to meet development and investment needs.

Developing countries may have experienced current account deficits and thus net capital inflows. As current account balances on the macro level are just the aggregation of the accounts on the micro level the same rules of sustainability apply as in the case of deficits of households and companies. But, and this is the crucial difference, a "country" or a region, even a poor region, in general consisting of the same economic entities as any other country *a priori* does not "need" foreign capital.[3] It is only true in a certain theoretical (neoclassical)

---

[3] This fact, which is, according to the above reasoning, the normal outcome has, after the publication of a paper by Horioka and Feldstein (1983), been the basis of many misleading speculations concerning international capital mobility. Feldstein/Horioka argued that the high slope coefficient is evidence for a rather small mobility of capital or restrictions for capital mobility even in the group of industrial countries as otherwise capital should be free to move and "... to seek out the most productive investment opportunities worldwide" (Obstfeld/Rogoff, 1996, p. 162). This is a fundamental misunderstanding. It is just the other way around:

model that countries can suffer from a lack of savings. In different (Keynesian) theoretical models it is a strange idea to believe that poor countries with little savings of private households simply can "draw" on the "existing" savings of industrialised regions to finance their investment without reducing domestic savings – out of profits – at the same time.

In the latter world currency mismatches are not a central issue. Maturity mismatches are of importance only if domestic saving (as non-consumption) determines domestic investment. If it is the other way round, if the level of investment determines the level of saving, the maturity mismatch can be neglected as an economic policy problem too. This is a crucial question and probably the most important one. If the economic world is dominated by the autonomous decision of private agents to choose between spending or saving (consumption today or consumption tomorrow), the maturity mismatch as well as the currency mismatch and, as a consequence, the corner solutions have their merits. One of the arguments the IMF brought forward in transition and in developing countries to defend the anchor approach and/or high interest rates was indeed the "lack of capital" in these countries. According to this orthodox view, an inflow of capital from outside or the mobilisation of domestic savings by high interest rates only could fill the "savings gap" and thus allow for a sufficient amount of investment in fixed capital. But if this is not the relevant theoretical model the whole approach falls apart.

---

the more similar in their structure and the more open the countries under consideration are, the smaller will be the net movements of capital (the balances) between them. Such a finding has no direct implications for gross movements. These can be extremely important and their movement may lead, without the "contradiction" seen by Obstfeld/Rogoff, to "... the remarkable closeness of the interest rates that comparable assets offer despite being located in different industrial countries" (Obstfeld/Rogoff, 1996, p. 162). The "country" is usually no category of importance in the markets nor in economics if we are not dealing with interferences into the market by national governments.

4 At a very early stage of economics as a science, however, this problem was addressed and a preliminary solution was found: The only way to finance additional investment and growth of the overall economy is the artificial creation of additional money. Additional money, so many early writers, including Schumpeter (1912) and von Hayek (1933), would allow increasing investment without negative repercussions from the capital market. This idea found its expression in the phrase of "forced saving" which had occupied many economists in the 1930s.

Saving out of real income, i.e. saving as the deliberate decision not to consume, is pivotal in theoretical models with given (exogenous) real income. If real income is endogenous, i.e. if we are dealing with economic models bound to explain why and how real income is generated or not, the causal nexus of saving and investment is just the other way around. If saving does not create investment but investment creates saving, then the original sin is pointless. In a non-neoclassical, a Keynesian, or better a Schumpeterian, view, the existence of neoclassical savings does not foster the process of development. In this world just the opposite is true. "The decision not to have dinner today ..." (J.M. Keynes) does not stimulate but discourage the creation of capital as demand and profits will fall.[4] In Schumpeter's words, what is needed in these cases is not capital in the sense of realised and unconsumed income but just money to prefinance a process in which capital is created by investment and financed, in the last analysis, by saving which is the result of an unforeseen growth in real income.[5] This is the main reason, in my opinion, for the disastrous results of the IMF's attempt to stimulate the creation of capital in the transforming economies by a policy of austerity including high real interest rates. It is exactly the opposite of the reasonable in a Schumpeterian world.[6]

Hence, I fundamentally disagree with Professor Park's conclusion that "A macroeconomic policy framework focusing on free floating and inflation targeting has not been tested for its effectiveness in sustaining financial stability with robust growth in emerging market

---

5 The importance of money had been clearly recognised at the beginning of this century by J.A. Schumpeter in his "Theory of Economic Development" of 1911 (cf. Schumpeter, 1964). Hayek (1933) joined his view that only abundant money will allow high growth rates and a quick development of nations. For Schumpeter it is explicitly a potentially inflationary policy which spurs economic development. Monetary policy has to "prefinance" the process of development without knowing with certainty that the additional money will be used for real growth. This explains why catching-up processes are usually endangered by inflationary acceleration. The whole process is potentially inflationary without becoming inflationary in the least analysis. While a lot of studies deal with the microeconomics of Schumpeter's theory, the even more important macroeconomics are neglected.

6 As money saving in the economy as a whole is necessarily zero, the notion of "saving" which is needed to "finance" investment is not useful at all. Investment is highly correlated with the dynamics of the overall economy. The overall economy, however, is stimulated and not depressed by a fall in the savings rate of private households.

economies." Obviously, neither floating nor inflation targeting are new ideas. If it would be so simple to find a solution, the test would have been made successfully a lot of times somewhere in the world in the last three decades. But, as far as I see, there is not one developing or developed country with free floating which, additionally, is surrounded by other free floaters without producing enormous friction. The few examples of (more or less dirty) successful floating all happened in the niches left by some sort of fix-rate system (like the UK or Switzerland in relation to the European monetary systems) or in countries attached to one big trading partner like Canada to the United States.

12

Asian Cooperation and the End of Pax Americana

Eisuke Sakakibara

It has been said by many, particularly in the United States, that the world will never be the same again after September 11, 2001. Nevertheless, it is hard to believe that one incident, however grave, could so suddenly and drastically affect the entire world. Indeed, September 11 has changed our perception of the world, but the process seems to have originated earlier – in the latter half of the 1990s.

This change in perception is particularly noticeable in the United States. To the Americans, the terrorist attacks on the World Trade Center and the Pentagon brought home powerfully that they, too, are vulnerable to a direct foreign attack and that the far-flung web of forward bastions the United States maintains around the globe is no longer sufficient for its defense. The Americans, in other words, recognise that they are in the same boat as the rest of the world.

With regard to the global governance system, there are some irreversible aspects of this ongoing change. First, the age of international economics, or the age of global capitalism, seems to be moving toward the age of international politics. In other words, we are witnessing the beginning of the end of "Pax Americana", or global capitalism under American hegemony. True, the United States is still a dominant power, both militarily and economically, but it is apparent that the international governance system that was led by the United States, the G-7, and international organisations, such as the IMF and the World Bank, has started to change.

Just as in 1914 or 1915 World War I signalled the end of Pax Britannica, the new global war against terrorism seems to be the symbolic event that historians may one day designate as the beginning of the end of Pax Americana. However, in my view we have been witnessing the beginning of the end of Pax Americana since the mid-1990s. The United States is gradually losing its position as the hub of the world. This has consequences for other regions of the world, including Asia, and may act as another stimulus for the promotion of regional cooperation.

In this chapter, I will discuss what type of regional cooperation is feasible in Asia. But before getting into the current state of, and future prospects for, regional cooperation in Asia, I would like to share with you my long-term perspective on the Asian economy. I wish to do this not only because I am proud of Asia's history, but also because I think it is quite important to understand the legacy of Asia in building a new regional cooperative scheme.

1 Asia as the Centre of the World

As you may know, between the 8th and 18th centuries, Asia was the centre of the world economy and of world trade. According to Angus Maddison, even as late as 1820, that is some decades after the industrial revolution started in Europe, China and India together accounted for as much as 46 percent of world GDP and 55 percent of the world's population.[1]

Except for the last 150 years when the West and later Japan were dominant, Asian countries, especially China, India and the Islamic empires, were the centre of the world economy. I am not saying this out of arrogance as an Asian, but am emphasising this historical fact to remind you that the infrastructure for global trading and investment was created in Asia a long time ago.

Hard and soft infrastructure for global trading and investment has been present in Asia for centuries. Hard infrastructure has existed in the form of well-organised ports, sea lanes, roads, and various kinds of river transportation, while the equally important soft infrastructure has been there in the form of entrepreneurship, commercial

[1] Angus Maddison, *The World Economy: A Millennial Perspective*, OECD Development Centre, Paris, 2001.

minds, and networks of Chinese and Indians living overseas (i.e. diasporas). Even during the period of colonisation, the British and others used the existing infrastructure quite skilfully to engage in global trading. So, historically Asia has been the hub of globalism.

We have already begun to see a shift in economic power to countries like China and India. China's economy has been growing at almost 10 percent a year since the late 1970s. India is expected to register a 4.4 percent growth rate in 2002, surpassing the expected ASEAN growth rate of around 3 percent. China, India, and a few other Asian countries combined account for more than half of the world's population and generate a significant portion of world savings. It will not be long before production in these countries increases commensurate with the size of their populations and savings. From a long-term perspective, these developments point to a reorientation of the world economy from West to East.

China should not be overestimated in the area of technology, but in manufacturing China will no doubt emerge as a major force and will fundamentally change the international division of labour both in Asia and in the rest of the world. China will become a key player in the Asian economy as well as in the world economy. The Chinese have been sleeping for the last 200 years, but they have now awakened and have the capacity and the entrepreneurship to again become the centre of the world.

Since World War II, particularly in the 1970s and 1980s, Asian countries have used very well their existing hard and soft infrastructure to establish Asia as a global economic entity. If you look at the export-import structure and direct investment patterns in Asian countries, you will notice that they are quite global. This is not unnatural. In addition to a dramatic increase in intra-regional trade and investment over the last few decades, investment from and trade with the United States and Europe have risen significantly. Asia has become virtually a global manufacturing site for the world.

2 Asian Cooperation and the Role of China

There are some regional organisations in Asia (for example, ASEAN) whose formation was politically motivated. ASEAN was formed in the 1960s, at the time of the Vietnam war, as a political coalition against communism. Eventually, the ASEAN organisation came to promote two types of cooperation – political and economic. Although an ASEAN Free Trade Area (AFTA) has been established, in general the integration process has been very slow. ASEAN remains essentially a political forum for discussions among heads of state under the principles of the "ASEAN way", which is characterised as voluntary, non-binding, and consensual.

There is another regional forum, APEC, which comprises the United States and other Pacific-rim countries, including Australia and New Zealand. This is not a genuine regional organisation either. APEC's major function has been to promote global deregulation, the GATT and the WTO, an activity wherein it has played a significant role. But the enthusiasm for APEC has subsided since the Clinton Administration lost interest in the organisation.

Until two years ago, China, Korea, and Japan were the only major countries in the world that were not involved in any regional cooperative scheme. We were excluded from Asian regionalism because we functioned as its hub.

Why have intra-regional trade and investment increased in Asia despite the global nature of Asian countries? Basically this was triggered by Japan's investment in East and South Asian countries in the late 1980s, followed by similar moves of the so-called Asian Tigers (i.e. Korea, Taiwan, Hong Kong, and Singapore). This phenomenon was called the "Flying Geese Formation" with Japan at the forefront followed by the Four Tigers and then by the ASEAN countries. It established a fairly exquisite division of labour in manufacturing in the Asian region.

This Flying Geese Formation existed up until quite recently and has resulted in an increase in intra-regional trade, which naturally followed the direct investment. Intra-regional trade was preceded by the direct investment of, first, Japanese corporations and, then, the multinationals of the United States, Europe, Korea, Taiwan, and others. This investment was the major stimulus for a dramatic increase in intra-regional trade over the course of the last few decades. And regional integration will progress as Taiwan, Japan, Singapore, Hong Kong, and others invest in China and in other Asian countries. However, the global nature of Asia's trade and investment will not change, but will continue as before.

Except for Japan, most of the East Asian and South Asian countries have an export-to-GDP ratio of more than 20 percent. Countries like Singapore and Malaysia have an even higher ratio of over 100 percent. Asian countries are very open and global, and because of that, there has not been much interest in regional cooperation in Asia until recently. Globalisation has benefited Asia. Asia has probably been the major beneficiary of global deregulation and liberalisation that took place in the 1960s, 1970s and 1980s. That was most likely the major cause of what has been called the "Asian miracle".

As I stated before, the global nature of trade and investment in Asia will not change – even though there has been an increase in intra-regional trade and investment. China will continue to attract investment both from Europe and the United States, because these major global players need to have factories in China. About a month ago, I was told by the CEO of Thyssen, the German Steel Company, that they have developed the technology for a high-speed train that can run 500 km per hour – double the speed of the Eurostar and the Japanese Bled train. The original intention was to connect Munich and Cologne by this high-speed train, but for some reason the company was unable to do that. So they reached an agreement with the Chinese government to construct a network for the train between Shanghai and other major cities. The operation was to start January 1, 2003, and by 2008, the year the Olympics is to be held in Beijing, the high-speed train, which runs at half the speed of an airplane, would connect Shanghai and Beijing.

China has been very savvy in importing technology which cannot be used in Europe, so China is not only a country of labour-intensive industries but also one with a variety of high-tech industries that drive a number of regional industrial clusters in the country.

A major change that has been witnessed over the last four or five years is, as I already mentioned, the emergence of China as a global manufacturing centre. The Flying Geese Formation is now being quickly realigned – with China in the lead. A number of industrial clusters are being created in China, e.g. in Shanghai, Hong Kong, Beijing, and Dalian. Furthermore, those industrial clusters have started to interact with the rest of Asia resulting in increased contact between Asia and various regions within China.

Most major Taiwanese companies have now established a foothold in mainland China. Singapore has gone into China as well. And many Japanese corporations are now relocating their production sites to various parts of China.

Recently, I was told by the CEO of a very well-known Japanese company, "Until now, Sakakibara, we have been very successful in China, but all those goods produced in China were for export while we have continued to produce goods for consumption in Japan in our Japanese factory. However, the quality of the goods produced in China is the same as that in Japan, but the cost is about one-third in China." Naturally I asked him why he continues to produce goods for Japanese consumers in Japan, to which he replied, "It is a social obligation for the corporation to maintain employment in Japan."

His company is very famous for its lifetime employment system and is profoundly concerned for its employees' security and the quality of their employment. But even he has had to change his mind and confessed to me that from now he must move his Japanese factories to China.

This is the major structural change that is now taking place in Asia, including Japan, and it will eventually reach Europe as well. It is very likely that China will fundamentally change the division of labour in manufacturing in Asia and the world. As I said, the Chinese have been sleeping for the last 200 years, but they have now awakened and have the capacity and the entrepreneurship to again become the centre of the world.

It is important to understand the key concept for China, which is competition. There is strong competition taking place everywhere in China. Japan and Germany are more socialistic than China. There exists a higher degree of entrepreneurship and competition in China than in these two countries. China is a very energetic country.

Of course, the Chinese have many problems; e.g. non-performing asset problems and SOE problems. At the time of the Cultural Revolution China was a communist country without any competition. It has transformed that structure within a matter of 10 to 15 years and, in the process, has created huge problems in some areas. The non-performing asset problem is much larger than that of Japan. However, China is undergoing major structural changes.

3 Lessons of the Asian Crisis

After the East Asian crisis of 1997-98, Asian countries strongly perceived the vulnerability of their region, which does not have any viable regional cooperative scheme. They recognised that there is no global lender of last resort, that international organisations like the

IMF and the World Bank were not of much use in preventing or addressing the crisis, and that the United States did not infuse much in the way of resources into Asian countries when the crisis broke. The United States provided resources to Brazil and Mexico, of course, but never to Korea or Indonesia.

The United States has its own national and regional interests, and that is understandable. But we in Asia did not realise this fact before the East Asian crisis erupted. I am not critical of the United States, because the United States is not a lender of last resort. The United States is a nation-state which has its own national interest. So the East Asian crisis brought to Asian people the awareness that the so-called hub-and-spoke relationship does not have a genuine hub. The hub country is a nation-state which has its own interests – national and regional.

The East Asian crisis of 1997-98 has also given rise to the recognition of imperfections or the lack of governance in globalised markets. The Asian miracle, to a significant degree a result of the open and global nature of this region, suddenly turned into the Asian crisis. Not only global institutions, like the IMF and the World Bank, but also regional organisations, like ASEAN and APEC, were unable to play a useful role in stopping the contagion of the crisis.

Also, initial prescriptions by the IMF were misguided and might have actually aggravated the crisis rather than arresting it. It is not only the policy recommendations made during the crisis, but also those made before the crisis, that need to be re-examined. The strong pressure to deregulate, particularly in international finance, without comparable strengthening of financial supervision, exposed many countries in the region to a degree of risk unmanageable by national governments. International organisations could not substitute for national governments in managing these new market risks. What is necessary is not the substitution of market for government but rather the redefinition of the role of government in view of the rapidly changing international environment. In his book, *Rethinking the East Asian Miracle*, Joseph Stiglitz correctly points out what needs to be done in the future.

> "Just as before they were misled by the chimera of deregulation – they should have asked instead what is the *right* regulatory structure for their current situation – so too in the future, they will have to resist accepting without question the current mantras of

> the global marketplace of ideas. There will have to be *strengthened* regulation of securities markets and an improved overall legal environment, especially in areas such as corporate governance and bankruptcy. The legal structures will have to comport with international standards, yet be adapted to their own special situations; wholesale borrowing will not work."[2]

Policy efforts must be largely national. However, the question here in relation to regional cooperation is whether genuine regional institutions, similar to the EU, would help national governments in Asia to accelerate their efforts in the right direction. Or should we leave these matters to global international organisations, such as the IMF and the WTO.

I endorse the establishment of a genuine regional organisation in Asia, or at least in East Asia, on several grounds. First, existing global institutions are strongly biased toward market fundamentalism or the neoclassical paradigm, and their past records in international capital and finance are very poor. The establishment of a genuine regional organisation could provide a countervailing force and would contribute to reforming international institutions. Indeed, international institutions are necessary, but healthy competition among global and regional institutions would help improve their performance.

Second, international organisations, politically dominated by Western countries and staffed largely by Western economists, often lack sufficient knowledge of regional values, culture, and history and tend to impose their own views on, or try to "Westernise", the country in question. Indeed, international standards need to be adhered to, but standards should reflect existing diversities of culture and institutions. Regional organisations can supplement global ones effectively in such areas.

Third, as in the case of the EU, necessary structural reforms, such as those mentioned by Stiglitz, can be more smoothly and willingly implemented if such reforms are deemed essential for regional integration. There has been increasing resistance to externally

---

[2] Joseph Stiglitz, "From Miracle to Crisis to Recovery: Lessons from Four Decades of East Asian Experience," In: Joseph Stiglitz and Shahid Yusuf (eds.), *Rethinking the East Asian Miracle*, Oxford University Press, New York, 2001, p. 523.

imposed reforms. Regional cooperation or integration (even slow integration) is a more effective way to internalise reforms.

Fourth, the lack of global governance, including a global lender of last resort and international financial regulation, is not expected to be remedied in the near future. However, rather than relying solely on national governance, there seems to be a role for regional governance, even though in a region like Asia where there is enormous diversity, regional governance is more difficult than in Europe, for example. However, more flexible and softer cooperation could be developed.

Fifth, regional integration has been proceeding quickly in Europe and a little more slowly in the Americas, although there also it is rapidly accelerating. Is it politically feasible or desirable for Asia to be as open and global as in the past? Might not Asia be victimised by these two predatory empires in the future, as it was in the 19th and 20th centuries? This is a rather defensive posture, but it has been a major driving force recently for regional cooperation in Asia.

4 Financial Cooperation in Asia

In Asia, there is a strong case to be made for expediting financial cooperation by way of foreign exchange cooperation. This may seem strange, because usually financial cooperation comes at the end of the regional integration effort – as the process in Europe illustrates. But in the case of Asia, the creation of a common currency, or some kind of currency union, is the type of regional cooperation that should be pursued. Because as regional interaction in trade and foreign investment accelerates, Japan, Korea, and China will become not only complementary but also competitive in their imports.

At this moment, Korea and Japan are competing in steel and ship building. Depending upon the movements of the dollar-yen rate or the won-yen rate, industries in both these countries have at times been hit very hard. In this case, stabilising the won-yen rate would alleviate the situation. This could also apply to the emerging steel market in China. Korea, China, and Japan will be the major players in the global steel market, along with Brazil and a few other countries. This supports the case for stabilising intra-regional exchange rates.

Of course, it is difficult to immediately create an Asian currency union, but regional coordination of monetary intervention policy, at least, is possible now. As a matter of fact, Yung Chul Park informed me recently that when Japan aggressively intervened in the market during the last two weeks of June 2002, the Japanese government had consulted with both the Korean and Chinese governments concerning the intervention. It is probable that the Koreans and the Chinese imposed some restrictions on the mode of the intervention. To my knowledge, this is the first time the Japanese authorities had consulted the Korean and Chinese authorities concerning an intervention.

Having been deeply involved in the foreign currency market myself, I have never believed in the concept of "free floating", because every floating currency is managed to some extent. The degree of management differs depending upon the country, but the floating rate is always managed. In attempting to coordinate the management of floating rate currencies, the major difficulty at this point is with China's currency which still has a *de facto* fixed rate. But as China gradually deregulates foreign exchange controls and starts to move to a managed float, cooperation between China, Japan, and Korea could develop. China most likely does not need technical assistance because the Bank of China is well known for its delivery operations in the foreign markets, which indicates its familiarity with the technology. Thus, coordination among the three countries would be most beneficial in the area of foreign exchange.

Initial moves have already taken place. A target of 10-15 years from now could be set for the formation of a currency union among the three countries. At this point it is important to start by exchanging information. In my time, when we intervened in the yen-dollar market, the only financial authority we informed was the US Federal Reserve because it was an intervention vis-à-vis the dollar. Likewise, when the intervention involved the yen and the euro, we informed only the European Central Bank. Never did we contact Korean or Chinese authorities. However, officials are beginning to take that step now.

We have discussed in this conference the issue of formulating an exit policy for the currency board system and have agreed that this could be very difficult. Hong Kong has a currency board system, and China seems to cooperate with Hong Kong in that system. So, some kind of exit policy is necessary both for China and Hong Kong. A regional cooperative effort could facilitate the exit from a currency board.

The currency board system in Hong Kong is based on the US dollar. For a cooperative scheme among China, Japan, and Korea we should target the formation of some kind of Asian Monetary System, similar to the EMS, within 10 to 15 years. I agree with Charles Wyplosz that creating a common basket of currencies is not desirable. Instead, we should move directly to a currency union or to pragmatic cooperation among the authorities in coordinating our exchange rates. We could start there and later target the formation of a currency union, but not a common basket.

I don't know why so many Japanese economists like the common currency basket. It does not make sense because the yen would be included in the basket with the dollar and the euro; however, the yen has to be coordinated with the won and the yuan. We need to jointly float our currencies vis-à-vis the US dollar and the euro, thus, the Japanese yen must be on the side of the Asian currencies, not on the dollar/euro side.

One other thing that has been pointed out in our discussions relative to regional cooperation is that it is necessary to have the political will to form a regional cooperative scheme, particularly if a common currency is the goal. Not a great deal has been accomplished yet in this area, but some gradual progress has been made.

China and Japan together are the key to developing a common political will in Asia. The role of China and Japan in East Asia's integration process is synonymous with that of France and Germany in Europe's integration process. Korea could be a very effective mediator in the cultivation of a common will between China and Japan. In a broader context, the cultivation of a common will involving a wider group of Asian countries would necessitate the inclusion of Japan as a counter-balancing power vis-à-vis China. This is because most Asian countries fear being absorbed by China based on experiences of 150 years ago. That is another historical legacy.

The formulation of a common policy among China, Japan, and Korea would be the key to regional cooperation in the monetary and foreign exchange area in this region. Another key issue concerns the type of institution that is appropriate for the region – which countries should be its members and what issues should it address? A survey of existing regional institutions in East Asia seems to indicate that ASEAN+3 (ASEAN countries plus China, Korea and Japan) may be the appropriate one for development into a genuine regional organisation.

ASEAN+3 could be extended to include Australia and New Zealand. The complementary nature of these two economies with those of Japan, Korea, and China could make cooperation and integration more rewarding than if only ASEAN+3 countries were involved.

In terms of coverage, regional interest is quite strong in the area of international finance, as evidenced by the Chiang Mai Initiative, in addition to trade. It is my view that cooperation, and ultimately integration, should proceed simultaneously rather than sequentially in trade, FDI, and international finance, which differs from the process that took place in Europe.

China and the ASEAN countries agreed in late 2001 to form an free trade area within ten years, allowing for some preferential treatment for less developed ASEAN countries. Korea and Japan could join that arrangement making it an ASEAN+3 free trade area. Given the diverse nature of the participating countries, the free trade area could, and should, include some exceptions and preferential treatment at least in the initial stage. A pragmatic rather than purist approach is required here. The formulation of parallel and reciprocal FDI agreements should proceed simultaneously with trade liberalisation.

In the area of international finance, there are two major items on the agenda for the Asian region. First, coordination of foreign exchange policies to stabilise the relationship among currencies of the region seems long overdue. If the won-yen rate, yuan-yen rate and baht-yen rate, for example, move within a relatively narrow range, coordinating the foreign exchange policies of Korea, China, Thailand, and Japan could contribute to the stability of these economies. Eventually, cooperation should progress to the formation of an Asian currency unit (ACU) with a flexible snake around the central value, similar to the ECU and the snake – that is, the joint floating of Asian currencies vis-à-vis the US dollar and euro with a relatively wide band around the central rate. Although the creation of a common currency à la the euro may not be feasible in the short run, a soft and flexible form of currency union with an ACU should be possible and beneficial. It would enhance and accelerate integration through trade and FDI.

Speculative attacks are a realistic possibility, but with a wide and flexible band Asian countries should be able to fend off such speculation using the huge foreign reserves at their disposal, as long as effective coordination of macro policies accompanies joint foreign exchange interventions.

The need to jointly defend an ACU with a wide band logically leads to the extension of the Chiang Mai Initiative into an Asian Monetary Fund (AMF), which would pool a portion of the foreign reserves of participating countries and conduct macroeconomic surveillance. Participating countries can conduct joint intervention and coordination of macro policies with the AMF as the Secretariat. Articles of the AMF can provide the modality and modus operandi of coordination and intervention.

We could designate a different name for the AMF, but I would propose to have some kind of a G-7-like regular meeting among ASEAN+3 countries. We need some type of forum to coordinate the exchange rate policies and macro policies and should have regular meetings three or four times a year. The Asian Monetary Fund should perform in a manner similar to that of the G-7 and provide a similar kind of surveillance of the countries involved.

Let me emphasise that the concrete proposal I have outlined is just one possibility, and the process of forming a genuine regional organisation should be gradual and pragmatic. As in the case of China's national policy, structural reform needs to proceed simultaneously with opening or liberalisation. The moves need to be gradual and simultaneous on all fronts.

5 Conclusions

In concluding, let me reiterate that in the medium- to long-term the spotlight of the world economy seems to be shifting from West to East, and Asian countries need to build appropriate institutional infrastructure to pave the way for this change. Establishment of regional mechanisms consistent with existing global institutions seems to be the best strategy, at least for the immediate future.

Given the global nature and historical legacy of the countries in this region, it would be advisable for regional cooperation to focus on foreign exchange and monetary policies. The eventual target in 10 to 15 years is the creation of a common currency. Immediate steps to be taken are the initiation of some form of effective coordination of foreign exchange policies among Korea, Japan, and China and other advanced Asian countries and the development of some type of new forum for an Asian G-7, including the creation of a Secretariat. The Secretariat could be small and named something other than "Asian Monetary Fund", if that is preferred.

At the height of the crisis in East Asia, I proposed the formation of an Asian Monetary Fund (AMF). There was considerable enthusiastic support for the idea among Asian countries, but I made a strategic mistake. I had to draft the proposal in haste and, as a result, did not consult the Chinese as would have been sensible. I probably hurt their pride and that was a major mistake on my part. Another problem was that the United States did not favour the idea. When I talked about the idea with Kunio Saito, then head of the IMF's regional office for Asia and the Pacific, he initially agreed with me but was later swayed by some lobby causing him to reject the "Asian Monetary Fund" name.

However, even after the AMF idea was abandoned, primarily because of opposition from the United States for their own good reasons, there remains in Asia an interest in regional financial cooperation. What is more crucial than anything else, is the formation of a commonwealth among China, Korea, and Japan.

13

Comment on Eisuke Sakakibara

Amar Bhattacharya

Professor Sakakibara's discussion of regional cooperation follows quite nicely on the discussion on Eastern Europe, where deep integration is taken for granted. It has already happened in trade, and now the micro and macro alignment in finance is quite far advanced. The only remaining issue is whether the terminal monetary integration will happen in 2006 or 2008.

This shows you how far at least in one region things have gone. In Latin America, we did not discuss integration but the Free Trade Arrangement for the Americas (FTAA). There is a political commitment to launch that by 2005, although it is not clear whether it would lead to a single currency type arrangement. There are also questions about the way the FTAA will relate to sub-regional arrangements such as Mercosur.

East Asia stands out for its relative lack of regional institutions, which is, as Professor Sakakibara points out, is abnormal given the scale of Asia. He cites some numbers to make this point, but it is even more striking if you run the clock a little bit fast forward. If you take a long view, by 2020 China will be fast approaching the US as the largest economy of the world. South East Asia as a whole will also exceed the size of many G-7 countries if it resumes growth at 5 or 6 percent annually.

The other thing Professor Sakakibara points out is that Asia is very open, that its share of world exports is already about 27 percent and that this number will increase, especially with China entering the WTO. In terms of the international financial system, as Professor Park points out, East Asia has more than 1.1 trillion of foreign exchange reserves, much of which is intermediated elsewhere.

All this is impressive, and raises the question of why East Asia has not seen a more rapid pace of regional integration and does not occupy a more prominent place in the multilateral order. As Professor Sakakibara said, it has to do with politics, and with the issue of governance of the global system. I will focus more on the economic side, raising four different issues.

My first point is on trade. It is not just that East Asia is benefiting from global market places, as Professor Sakakibara mentioned, but it is that East Asia stands to gain the most from a multilateral approach to trade – more than any other region in the world. Our calculations at the World Bank, for example, show that if there were full-scale multilateral trade liberalisation, the increment to income for East Asia would be 2 percent, a huge amount compared to 1.2 percent for other developing countries and compared to 0.5 percent for the rich countries. East Asia's approach to the trade agenda has to be therefore quite different given its large stake in the global trading system.

My second point, to put the trade picture in perspective, is that the world today in terms of trade barriers is very different than when Europe was contemplating its trade integration or even when Mexico and the US were contemplating their trade integration. Against that background, there is a lot of discussion in East Asia about regional trade arrangements. There is a whole variety of regional proposals – there is ASEAN+3, there is ASEAN+3 + New Zealand + Australia, there is APEC Preferential Free Trade Area, there is APEC MFN-based liberalisation – and the important point about all these arrangements is that the benefit is the greater the larger the number and more diverse the membership is.

Using just the example that Professor Sakakibara mentions in his chapter, ASEAN+3 as a basis for trade liberalisation would give global gains on the order of 11 billion dollars. For APEC the increase approaches something like 48 billion dollars in terms of global welfare.

Again, the important point is that East Asia benefits much more from multilateral trade liberalisation than it does from sub-regional or bilateral arrangements. Does this mean that there is no role then for regional action? No, there is a role, but the actions are much more in the area of trade facilitation, in the area of harmonisation and in the area of investment policy. This is one of the objectives of the non-discriminatory free trade arrangements that some countries have been pursuing on a bilateral basis in the region.

My third point is on finance. As Professor Park mentioned, capital markets are global, which has implications for the nature and scope for regional action. Certainly the formation of a currency union can be a powerful catalyst for trade and financial integration. But it works also as a political driver of integration, in the sense of getting finance at the micro and the macro level right. However, as Professor Sakakibara said, the building of a currency union will inevitably take time in East Asia, so there are things you can do in the short run such as improving coordination in terms of exchange rate regimes.

The second aspect of financial integration where there is potential for regional action has to do with financial stability, where Professor Sakakibara has proposed better regional arrangements to deal with contagion risks. There are some difficult issues here. One is covariance risk. Inevitably the risks will be greater within the region, and it is not clear that regional arrangements will necessarily be the best approach for risk pooling. Another difficult issue that arises is the need to make a determination on the balance between financing and adjustment and how to "bail-in" the private sector. These judgments and agreements will be most effective if all actors are involved, globally and regionally. The fundamental point therefore is, that while you could think of a regional financial stability arrangement as a complementary to international mechanisms, as indeed the Chiang Mai Initiative has been conceived as, it is very difficult to think of it as an alternative, which is implicit in the chapter of Professor Sakakibara and which seems to be implicit in his presentation.

So I would argue that if you have global financial markets, then you have to have global arrangements – obviously reinforced through regional mechanisms.

The fourth point Professor Sakakibara did not mention, and where I think there is scope for regional cooperation, is regional infrastructure. Professor Park mentioned that there is a big risk that Asia will be over-run by foreign financial institutions. The answer he provided is not to keep foreign institutions out, but to develop the market infrastructure, to develop the standards and to develop the human capital so that you are able to compete. Indeed, I would argue that is the key, rather than to be concerned about ownership and keep the foreigners out.

Professor Sakakibara is right that there are weaknesses in the global governance system, but it would be a mistake to withdraw to a regional system. If anything, Asia is now well equipped to play a large role and it should seek a larger role in global governance. The entry of China into the WTO shifted the balance of trade in favour of Asia. Given the changing role of Asia in trade and finance, it is entirely appropriate that Asia is seeking a greater role in international financial institutions and, indeed, in global financial governance.

So the agenda on enhancing regional cooperation in a globalising world rests on three pillars. First, Asia should seek a greater role in the global financial governance system, just as it strengthens regional arrangements. Second, I would argue very strongly that Asia has a disproportionate interest in a multilateral system of trade. There is a big risk that there could be a spaghetti bowl of confusion if Asia goes for multiple regional trade arrangements and multiple bilateral free trade arrangements, which are potentially inconsistent and can detract from the attention and span of policymakers. Third, in the financial arena, while there is considerable scope to pursue regional initiatives, such as in developing bond markets, these should be seen as complementary to strengthening the international financial architecture if we are to address the concerns on crisis prevention and resolution in globally integrated capital markets.

14

Comment on Eisuke Sakakibara

Barbara Stallings

From his post in the Japanese Finance Ministry, Eisuke Sakakibara was a major player in global economic policy making in the 1990s, so his views on this topic area are of particular interest. In his paper for this volume, those views are expressed through personal reflections on Asia's historical place in the world economy, projections about the future shape of the international political economy, and policy proposals with emphasis on financial cooperation in the Asian region. Given the subject matter of the volume, the third aspect is most relevant, so my comments will centre of that part of the paper. Their main aim is to locate Professor Sakakibara's ideas in the more general discussion of Asian economic cooperation and to identify some questions that need further clarification.

The Status Quo Ante

Sakakibara's discussion of recent developments in Asia dates from the Plaza Accords of 1985, which led to a surge of Japanese investment in other Asian countries. He refers to this process by the commonly used phrase "Flying Geese Formation', whereby Japan was alleged to transfer its technological prowess to its less developed neighbours in a staged process. Although used with great frequency in the literature, this concept is nonetheless controversial since (a) it takes for granted the role of Japan as "lead goose" and (b) assumes that the other "geese" are all adopting the same features.[1] Both assumptions will become relevant in analysing the proposals for increased financial integration below. Another characteristic of the flying geese model is that this form of regional integration, which centred on foreign direct investment and trade, was governed by market mechanisms rather than inter-state treaties. Indeed, Asian integration schemes in general have been less institutionalised than their western counterparts in Europe or the developing world. This tradition would be scrapped in the proposals that we will examine below.

Reasons for Change

Asian growth rates in the post-war period were spectacular, exceeding those of other regions by a substantial amount. Exactly what role the Flying Geese Formation played in the success of Asia's development may be debated, but other regions increasingly looked to East Asia for an example of a national development model, including the regional integration component.[2] All of this came to an abrupt halt in 1997-98, as a financial crisis hit the region. Among the side effects of the crisis was a reconsideration of the nature of regional integration; Sakakibara's discussion of reasons for change derives to a large extent from experiences during the crisis. These centre on the policy conditionality accompanying loans by the International Monetary Fund (IMF) to Korea, Thailand, and Indonesia as well as the failure of the United States to take an active role in dealing with the Asian crisis in contrast to similar situations in Latin America. Beyond the crisis, however, geopolitical changes were also taking place as Japanese economic power declined, while that of China rose rapidly. The decade-long recession in Japan has reduced the resources the country can invest abroad, while China's dramatic growth has raised its profile in economic as well as political and military terms. The resulting disequilibria with respect to the Flying Wild Geese scheme clearly require some kind of restructuring.

---

[1] For a critique, see Mitchell Bernard and John Ravenhill, "Beyond Product Cycles and Flying Geese: Regionalization, Hierarchy, and the Industrialization of East Asia", In: *World Politics*, Vol. 47, January, 1995. pp. 171-209.

[2] See, for example, Michael Mortimore, "Flying Geese or Sitting Ducks? Transnationals and Industry in Developing Countries", In: *CEPAL Review 51*, December, 1993, pp. 15-34.

The Actors

The processes already mentioned imply a necessary shift in the cast of characters in the regional drama – and in their relative importance. Taking the mid-1980s as a starting point, a study of the literature reveals almost total concentration on Japan, on the one hand, and the "four tigers" (Korea, Taiwan, Hong Kong, and Singapore), on the other. By the late 1980s and early 1990s, South-East Asia was beginning to attract attention, but in an essentially passive role as a recipient of investment from Japan and the four tigers. China (and Indochina) were still on the sidelines. A dramatic indication of the failure to take China into account is Sakakibara's admission that he did not even consult China before announcing his proposal for an Asian Monetary Fund (AMF) in 1997. Now, however, he appears to be moving in the opposite direction and according China a (the?) central place in his new proposals. When he says that "the Flying Geese Formation is now being quickly realigned – with China in the lead", it is not clear if he means that China will replace Japan as the lead goose or if China is simply taking the lead in forcing change more generally. In either case, China has joined Japan as the dominant actors in the new scheme that he proposes although, as will be discussed below, the relationship is far from harmonious. The other key player is South Korea, to which Sakakibara assigns the awkward role as "mediator in the cultivation of a common will between China and Japan".

The Proposals

The discussion thus far has provided background for this section on the proposals *per se* for a new regional integration system in East Asia. Sakakibara's paper is confined to a presentation of his own views. As mentioned earlier, these are the views of an informed and influential policymaker, but they do not exist in a vacuum. It is thus useful to consider his proposals in light of the extensive literature that has emerged on this topic since Malaysian prime minister Mohamad Mahathir proposed the East Asian Economic Caucus in the early 1990s. Obviously not all of it can be discussed in these brief comments, but some other proposals can be compared with those of Professor Sakakibara.

Sakakibara's main message is that East Asian countries need to move forward rapidly in the area of financial integration, not waiting for trade integration to develop further. Specifically, he says, "it is my view that cooperation, and ultimately integration, should proceed simultaneously rather than sequentially in trade, FDI, and international finance, which differs from the process that took place in Europe". In order to achieve this goal, he proposes two main tasks. First is coordination of foreign exchange policy, leading to the formation of an Asian currency unit (ACU) that would float within a flexible band, similar to the ECU and the snake. The need to defend the value of the ACU leads to the second task, which is the creation of an institution to pool the region's huge foreign exchange reserves. As the reincarnation of his earlier proposal for an Asian Monetary Fund, the new institution would be based on the so-called Chiang Mai Initiative of 2000. The Chiang Mai Initiative, with its ASEAN+3 (Japan, China, and Korea) membership, is an agreement to provide bilateral swaps in the event of a member needing access to foreign exchange. The new institution would meet regularly to coordinate policies and conduct surveillance of each other's economies.

How does this set of proposals relate to others that have been put forward, both in Asia and elsewhere in the world? Two differences merit consideration. First, the Sakakibara proposals are more optimistic, but less clear, than most others. A recent paper by two influential economists from the United States (Fred Bergsten, director of the Institute for International Economics) and Korea (Yung Chul Park, professor at Korea University and former government official) strongly supports greater financial integration in Asia but is more doubtful about chances for success.[3] In particular, they are concerned about the "looming economic rivalry" between Japan and China (p.78), to which Professor Sakakibara pays little attention. Furthermore, they place much more stress than does Sakakibara on the need for a regional surveillance mechanism among member countries to monitor policies that might have negative ramifications for the region as a whole and to avoid moral hazard in lending. A related paper, published by Bergsten's institute, "conditionally" supports the Chiang Mai Initiative, expressing

[3] C. Fred Bergsten and Yung Chul Park, *Toward Creating a Regional Monetary Arrangement in East Asia*, Research Paper No. 50, Asian Development Bank Institute, Tokyo, 2002.

approval about the fact that it is much more modest than the AMF proposal.[4] The author also emphasises the necessity to get support from, and to cooperate with, the IMF. The relationship with the IMF was a major stumbling block for the AMF, over the issue of whether a new regional institution would be a substitute or complement. Unfortunately, Sakakibara does not spell out his position on this issue, although he implies that he now favours a regional financial institution that would complement the IMF. His rather oblique comment in the concluding section of the paper is: "Establishment of regional mechanisms consistent with existing global institutions seems to be the best strategy, at least for the immediate future."

A second difference between Sakakibara's proposal and others in the literature is their relative scope. Sakakibara focuses exclusively on government-to-government relations, while others usefully add in proposals for private sector development and the strengthening of existing financial institutions. One such proposal is that of Thai prime minister, Thaksin Shinawatra, to establish an Asian Bond Fund. Regional governments would contribute a small percentage of their international reserves to a fund dedicated to purchasing bonds of member countries and thus strengthening national bond markets – a concern of most Asian governments after the financial crisis.[5] This proposal was put into effect in June 2003. While small in scale, some see it as an initial step that could become more important in the future. A second proposal is the one by Yung Chul Park in this volume, which focuses on the need to develop locally based private sector institutions in financial services, such as commercial banks, investment banks, insurance, derivatives, and merger and acquisition firms. Currently, Park argues, such institutions are heavily dominated by foreign firms, which leaves the region vulnerable to the whims of outsiders. These proposals dealing with private sector institutions could, of course, be combined with an inter-governmental institution as proposed by Sakakibara.

---

[4] C. Randall Henning, *East Asian Financial Cooperation*, Institute for International Economics, Washington D.C., 2002.

[5] See discussion by Ramkishen Rajan, "A Bond Fund for Asia", In: *Far Eastern Economic Review*, March 20, 2003, p. 43.

Implications for Other Regions

Although Professor Sakakibara has no reason to mention it, the debate on East Asian regionalism is resonating beyond the borders of the countries directly involved. This is especially true in Latin America, but also in South Asia and Africa to a lesser extent. Central and Eastern Europe, of course, have already begun the process to join the European Union, so the regionalism debate has been resolved there. In Latin America, regionalism has mainly focused on trade until now. Recently, however, discussion has begun within the sub-regional associations, especially Mercosur, about macroeconomic coordination and even a common currency. Likewise, more emphasis has been accorded to regional financial institutions, several of which already exist in Latin America. The two most important are the Andean Development Fund (CAF), which lends money for investment projects to members of the Andean regional group, and the Latin American Reserve Fund (FLAR), which provides balance-of-payments support to member countries.[6] Both are fairly small-scale operations, but there have been proposals to expand their scope. In this context, Latin America has been an interested observer of the Asian debates about financial integration, but it might also be useful for East Asia to study the successes and shortcomings of CAF and FLAR. Such dialogue has already begun. An important example is the Interregional Meeting on Financing for Development, organised by the Regional Commissions of the United Nations as a preparatory forum for the Monterrey Conference in March 2002, which gave major consideration to regional financial institutions.[7] Continued interchange would be useful for all.

---

[6] For a description of these institutions, see Daniel Titelman, *Multilateral Banking and Development Financing in a Context of Financial Volatility*, Financiamiento del Desarrollo Series No. 121, Section V, 2002.

[7] See "Summary of Conclusions", Interregional Meeting on Financing for Development, Mexico City, Section II.5, January 2002.

Barbara Stallings

15

Floor Discussion of "Asia: A New Agenda of Financial Reform and Regional Cooperation"

The Park Paper

Age Bakker of the central bank of the Netherlands, wondered what problem Yung Chul Park was addressing in his paper. "The paper has lots of statistics, but I lack a definition of the problem," he said. "What exactly is the problem for Asia? Is the problem that exchange rate movements vis-à-vis the dollar are not the same? Is the problem that exchange rate movements hamper regional trade integration? Is the problem that you are not able to define your own monetary policy? It is not clear to me what the starting point is of the discussion."

Bakker added that in Europe, monetary integration was motivated by the fact that trade integration was indeed hampered by intra-regional exchange rate fluctuations. But in the case of Asia, regional trade integration seemed to be moving very well. So if Professor Park saw the challenge as one of regional financial integration, Bakker was afraid he was choosing the wrong road. "Regional financial integration is not going to help Asia, because financial integration, by definition, is a global phenomenon. Capital is fungible, it can flow anywhere, and in Europe we have never opted for first having European financial integration and then opening up to the outside world, because according to our analysis, that is an impossible route. There will always be escape routes."

A second point raised by Bakker was the purpose of the Chiang

Mai Initiative and whether the envisaged reserve funds would be large enough. "With regard to the reserve funds, the European experience shows that you need to have a very clear purpose before it will do anything tangible. An Asian Monetary Fund is not going to impress the financial markets if it is unclear what it is trying to achieve. If it is trying to achieve stabilisation of Asian currencies vis-à-vis the dollar, then you will need tremendous funds. But if its purpose is to help regional countries that will be hit by contagion and by financial crisis, then you first need to define what sort of exchange rate relations you would like to have among yourselves. There, the European experience shows that a starting point would be to agree politically that your bilateral exchange rates are a matter of mutual interest. Now, for that you don't need statistics. What you need is political willingness. You might even need a hub, for instance Japan."

Eisuke Sakakibara, former vice minister of Finance of Japan, suggested that Yung Chul Park's view reflected a nationalistic and xenophobic backlash against foreign investment banks all over Asia. "We had this backlash in Japan as well," he said. "Several American investment banks received harsh penalties for minor violations of the law. But basically this is a reflection of the sense of insecurity and the sense of vulnerability of the Asian countries. I am not surprised by the statistics that Yung Chul has given us. This hub-and-spoke relationship has existed between Asia and the United States for decades. Look at the national security arrangement between the US and Japan, this is also a hub-and-spoke arrangement. It is the nature of the Asian economies, being dependent on the US. This strong relationship between the US interest rates and money supply and our domestic interest rates and money supply is not surprising. Even after floating, we continue to manage our exchange rates vis-à-vis the dollar. There is no market between the Korean won and the Japanese yen, there is only a yen/dollar market and a won/dollar market, and we have managed those floats through intervention vis-à-vis the dollar. However, it is important to realise that after the East Asian crisis in 1997, Asia has become aware of its heavy dependence on the US and that it may give rise to increasing vulnerability of the countries in the region because it is an inherently unstable relationship. This is why the fever for regional cooperation has intensified after 1997. After the crisis people came to recognise this very heavy dependence on all fronts on the US."

Sakakibara told of an experience on an Advisory Board which was chaired by Henry Kissinger. "When I started to talk about ASEAN+3 and regional economic cooperation among China, Korea and Japan, Kissinger jumped and said: 'Sakakibara, are you choosing China over the US? Then we have to rearrange all of the things we have agreed on in our security relationship with you and the rest of Asia'. That's the very typical American perception, a hub-and-spoke relationship in all fronts with Asian countries. My perception is that time has come to gradually change that relationship vis-à-vis the US. Maybe it is still too early to create a won/yen market, but we can at least coordinate our intervention efforts or our management of the floating rate vis-à-vis the dollar between Korea and Japan."

Marek Dabrowski, a former vice minister of Finance of Poland, said that Park and Sakakibara were not talking about an exclusive Asian problem. "All financial transactions are, in fact, going through a very small number of global financial centres. It is the same in Eastern Europe and in Europe in general, where most of the transactions are going through London and New York. This is the natural organisation of financial markets. For technical reasons, this market is much more centralised than the markets of goods or services. We must live with it."

Dabrowski stressed that, if Asians were thinking about building a new regional currency, one of the key questions was whether it could sustain competition with currencies like the dollar and the euro. Another key question was, in his view, that "in order to build any kind of regional currency you must have a minimal political commitment and some supranational political institution. If you take the political decision to build a monetary union, this helps to eliminate asymmetric shocks, synchronise business cycles and promote trade and capital flows inside the future common currency area. Political readiness to run common monetary policies is very important. I don't know of any historical experience where a monetary union could be sustained without political commitment."

Zdeněk Drábek, of the WTO, also wondered what problem Park was discussing in his paper. "The one interesting answer that I was trying to give to myself," he said, "is that there must be a big difference between integrating trade as opposed to integrating financial institutions. I am very encouraged to see that the Asians are integrating on the trade level. At the same time, I am not surprised at all that the financial integration is not taking place as you would like to think. But I would like to pursue the question further and go beyond the variance analysis. If you ask, what really are the impediments to the fact that the syndicated loans are not run by Japanese banks or Thai banks, you will find interesting answers. Maybe it is the fact that there are five investment banks that dominate the capital markets, or the fact that there are three major world currencies. Those are the major issues, but at the same time I ask myself if it really matters. Ten years ago we were all worried that we were going to be taken up by Japanese banks. How quickly things can change. So I would not worry so much about the fact that regional financial integration has not proceeded as fast as you would have wished."

Rogério Studart, of ECLAC, thought that the problem of financial globalisation was not so much a question of ownership of capital, nor the oligopolistic characteristic of it, but the clash of institutional settings. "Every country has developed a certain type of financial institution that was functional to the process of development. For many years in East Asia, the banks were machines for financing investment and trade. In the 1990s, this institutional setting lost a little bit of its functionality with financial deregulation when the existing institutions began failing for competitive reasons or for other reasons. This led to a situation where the institutional setting that was once functional, began to disintegrate. What I see in the 1990s in East Asia is that the problem was no so much financial integration but the fact that financial deregulation destroyed some of the institutional settings that had been created within the financial system to finance investment and trade and nothing was put there to replace them."

Stephany Griffith-Jones, of the Institute of Development Studies, thought that she understood very well what problem Yung Chul Park was trying to solve through Asian monetary cooperation, namely the serious problem of the vulnerability of developing countries to large international capital flows. "But what I don't really understand," she said, "is why the Asians just don't go ahead with monetary cooperation, because as Yung Chul has pointed out so clearly in previous Fondad meetings, the reserves that are available in the Asian countries are very large, more than 1000 billions dollars."

Griffith-Jones also wondered why the Asians should worry about security arrangements with the United States. "If the Americans had said the same things to the Europeans, as Kissinger has said to Sakakibara, I don't think the Europeans would have worried so much about it."

Charles Wyplosz followed up on Sakakibara's comment that Park's paper was about nationalism and pointed to the importance of political movements. "I suspect that in Argentina after the crisis there might also be a rise of nationalism," he said.

"Anybody who knows what nationalism is, would not say that," Yung Chul Park retorted. "You are turning my paper into a paper about nationalism..."

"That is not what I am saying," Wyplosz replied, "I am saying that nationalism is playing a role and that this is something we should be concerned about because we are talking about multilateralism and financial integration. For us, as economists, financial integration makes a lot of sense, it is about efficiency and so on, but if the people down in the street see it as foreign interference, then the whole thing would collapse. We already went through the opening up and closing down of the international financial system once (in the first half of 20th century), under deep political pressure, and that's why I became scared by Eisuke Sakakibara's interpretation. I see that Yung Chul doesn't like this interpretation, but he should not complain to me but to Eisuke."

Wouter Raab, of the Dutch Ministry of Finance, did not like the term nationalism and moved the discussion in another direction. "Part of the answer to Yung Chul Park's question of why liberalisation of financial markets has not automatically led to integration of financial markets, is that you need an awful lot of regulation and an awful lot of harmonisation before that takes place. Financial integration does not follow automatically by opening up, you need to do a lot of hard work. This is even more so than in the case of trade, because even when there are numerous non-trade barriers, you can still ship goods from one country to the other. But in the financial sector, to give you an example from the Netherlands, you are not allowed to offer any financial products to, for instance, Germany. There are still a lot of barriers that have to be broken down."

In his reply to the comments, Yung Chul Park expressed amazement that so many people suggested that the problem he addressed in his paper was unclear. "I am trying to write a scientific paper. It has nothing to do with politics, with nationalism or anything else. That is the last thing I have in mind. If you read some of the recent papers by Andrew Rose and his associates, the empirical evidence is clear that the formation of a currency union among a number of countries leads to a substantial increases in trade, and that it is a welfare gaining activity. There is no doubt about it. Second, the formation of a currency union is not a stumbling block, but a building block for global integration. My point is that in East Asia, 13countries have been working together to establish a regional financial arrangement with the long-term objective of creating its own currency, and this objective has nothing to do with nationalism or anything else. If you look at the trade side, you see that the 13countries are clearly moving toward a currency union. Within 5 or 10 years the 13 countries will be able to agree on monetary integration if you only look at the trade side, and there will be a lot of gains to be made by fixing their exchange rates or creating their own currency."

Park mentioned some of these gains by recalling the "crazy fact" that the 13 countries of East Asia are running a financial surplus and are financing deficits of the rest of the world, including the US, while none of these Asian countries, except Japan, has been able to borrow from international financial markets in their own currencies. "If you create your own currency and currency union, then securities denominated in regional currencies will automatically spring up. And if these countries can establish regional financial markets, then regional financial markets may be able to finance more of investment in East Asia."

Park concluded: "As for the definition of the problem, I have many definitional problems, but let us not forget that economics is a definitional problem to begin with. I don't understand how what I am saying can be interpreted as nationalistic. I am not against financial globalisation, I am saying that we can have financial globalisation and, at the same time, regional financial integration. These two can go together. In Europe, you have Europe-based financial markets and Europe-based financial integration and that is not inconsistent with globalisation."

The Sakakibara Paper

In the discussion on Sakakibara's paper, Yung Chul Park returned to the criticism of Europeans to Asia's efforts at regional financial cooperation. "Why is the formation of a regional arrangement in East Asia receiving such a hostile reception from Europeans, who worked for many years to come to where they are now?" wondered Park. "I would think that the European Union would be supporting an East Asian regional arrangement more than any other country or grouping of the world. But that is not the case. And why is Europe so anxious to expand its territory (to the east) and its influence at the same time?"

Following up on Sakakibara's paper, Park addressed the question of whether the Chiang Mai Initiative or the bilateral swap arrangements were going to be a substitute or a complement to global arrangements from institutions like the IMF. "It should obviously be a substitute," he said. "After the East Asian crisis, most of the crises are going to be current account crises and what you need in such crises is immediate, large amounts of liquidity without any conditions. You can worry about conditionality later. In the case of Korea, it took 10 days to agree to the IMF conditionality. But if there are any symptoms of a currency crisis, you need an immediate supply of a large amount of liquidity and this can only be provided at the regional level. Even though East Asia is not one of the richest regions in terms of living standards, it is one of the richest regions in terms of savings with more than 1 trillion dollars in reserves. Isn't it a crime that we are lending these dollars to the US? We could lend it for better purposes, we could lend it to Africa, to Latin America maybe even to Central Europe."

José Antonio Ocampo, of ECLAC, stressed that regional institutions should not only be complementary but also competitive to global institutions. "There are three arguments for competition. The first one is what I have called the federalist argument – a heterogeneous community will not always want to have an all powerful central power. This is why Europe would never have allowed the crisis of the EMS to be managed by the International Monetary Fund. The second argument has to do with the problem of control over the global institutions. Global institutions are not democratic. Since there are specific interests behind the world institutions, it is good to have competition. A third argument relates to small players. Small players always like competition, that is the traditional neo-classical argument. So why not have competition in the supply of financial safety nets? If a small country like Honduras goes into a crisis, it is better off with three or four alternative institutions supplying it with financial support rather than one."

Charles Wyplosz supported José Antonio Ocampo's plea for

competition by regional institutions, and gave an additional argument. "The IMF, like any institution, is bound to make mistakes in its analysis, but when the IMF makes mistakes, it doesn't pay the price and the costs can be huge for the countries that have to go through their conditions. A good reason for competition by regional institutions is that it would increase the competition for ideas. So when the IMF says: 'We think Korea should do this' or 'Argentina should do that', a competing Fund could say: 'No, this is wrong', and a healthy debate will be triggered. However, in a crisis situation you can't discuss too long."

Roy Culpeper, of the North-South Institute, thought that both Eisuke Sakakibara and Yung Chul Park (as well as José Antonio Ocampo and Stephany Griffith-Jones) had clearly demonstrated the weaknesses of the global financial system as well as the rationale for regional solutions. "I see the strengthening of regional cooperation as a strategy for trying to remedy what the global architecture has been unable to do. Since 1997, we have seen discussions about collective actions clauses, about debt standstills, and recently there was a glimmer of hope with the debt work-out arrangements that Anne Krueger put on the table in the IMF. But all of these proposals have been on hold and this has contributed to a sense of frustration both in Latin America as well as in Asia. Let's be honest about it: it is global real-politik that determines how global institutions work. And if regions of the world want a financial architecture that really does look after their interests, they have to look to a regional solution."

Culpeper went back to the question of what one really gains with financial and capital market liberalisation and said that the answer was not yet clear. "Amar Bhattacharya gave some numbers for the gains of trade liberalisation, but even on the cause of the relationship between trade openness and economic growth, the jury is still out. But the jury is certainly out on issues of financial sector liberalisation. All of the evidence and analyses that I have seen suggest that the gains from financial sector liberalisation and capital account opening are very questionable, perhaps even negative.

I am reminded of some work that Martin Feldstein and Charles Horioka did over a decade ago, which pointed to high correlations between domestic savings and investment. They were actually talking about how little the world capital market was integrated and this is reinforced in large part by the work of people like Dani Rodrik who argued that, if you are concerned about growth and development and poverty reduction, basically what you have to do is increase your savings rate and your domestic investment. That is what it is all about."

Heiner Flassbeck, of UNCTAD, thought that Roy Culpeper stated it too simply. "I agree that there are a lot of disputable assumptions in the theory that opening everything would be the best for the world, but to go to the other extreme and say, 'Don't care about capital markets and just promote your savings and investment', is too simple because what will happen is that countries will not stop trading but will start having trade wars and the like. You will have shocks of huge dimensions coming from devaluation, which is the best instrument you have to promote exports, and from subsidies and other instruments you have to promote exports such as lowering taxes. We need solutions for some problems, we have to try to find common rules for certain kinds of interventions by governments in the market. Saying that you can just rely on your national powers and abilities, is going a step too far."

In his reply, Eisuke Sakakibara stressed that one of the major motivations for the creation of an institution like the Asian Monetary Fund is that the globalising financial market is inheritably unstable without a global lender of last resort and without a global regulator. "In Asia," he said, "the idea is: If we are accumulating 1 trillion dollars of reserves, why not pool the reserves regionally and create a regional lender of last resort? Let's pool half of it and come up with a joint strategy in terms of crisis management and stabilisation of exchange rates."

Sakakibara warned that if financial markets are fully liberalised without having a lender of last resort and global regulator, the world is left with a completely unstable financial system. "The crises will hit us over and over again as globalisation proceeds. If the IMF could play the function of a lender of last resort to some extent, it would be a different story, but it has proven that it cannot do that nor does it have the political mandate to do that. We have gone through all kinds of discussions on the international financial architecture, I myself have been involved in the discussions and I respect the efforts that have been made, but not much has ever come from it.

We need competition to reform international financial institutions. I am not against financial integration or financial liberalisation. You should let the market proceed, provided that we have some public mechanism of lender of last resort and regulation, provided that competition policy is imposed in those institutions, and provided that conflicts of interest of accounting firms, rating agencies and so on be pointed out and that these firms are regularly inspected. Let the public institutions develop either globally or regionally to stabilise inherently unstable global financial institutions.

What we try to promote in Asia is horizontal networking. Japan has no intention of becoming a hub in Asia, we can't, we don't have the capacity nor the attitude to be a hub in Asia – if anything China could be hub. One of my favourite jokes these days is that within 10 to 20 years, Japan may become the 51st state of the US or the far East province of China. What we need is networking and horizontal cooperation, not hierarchy.

The time for G-7 is over. Europe has now been integrated into one unity. There is no reason to have Italians, French and Germans separately in the G-7, you should have one European country. Other fora are needed that include Europe, the US, China and India along with Japan and Russia.

We need a completely different type of organisation, we need an international negotiating forum. I have participated in G-7 processes for about a decade but the effectiveness of G-7 has declined throughout this period. The effectiveness of – and I'm sorry to say this – the IMF and the World Bank has also declined throughout this decade. So some other international financial and development infrastructure is now required."

Part IV

The Role for Market Participants and Financial Authorities

16

Promoting Financial Stability: The Role of Central Banks

Age Bakker

Promoting financial stability is not just another mission of central banks. Indeed, while central banks have had increasing success in safeguarding monetary stability, their concerns about financial stability have risen together with the growing systemic dimensions of financial crises.

I will discuss the nexus between two main central bank missions, price stability and financial stability. Targeting both stability goals at the same time can be challenging to policymakers. I will focus my remarks on the role central banks have to play in this respect, the policy instruments available to them and the new challenges that the increasingly systemic dimensions of crises pose.

The Nexus Between Price Stability and Financial Stability

Mr. Greenspan has defined price stability as inflationary expectations that do not significantly influence economic behaviour. Some concepts of price stability are more precise, like the definition of the European Central Bank, that stipulates price stability as an annual rise of the consumer price index of less than 2 percent in the medium term. A host of emerging countries have also adopted a well-defined policy objective by switching to an inflation targeting strategy (like Brazil, Chile, Czech Republic, Indonesia, Israel, Mexico, the Philippines and South-Korea).

In a broad sense, financial stability may be considered as a situation in which the financial sector is able to mobilise savings and allocate funds efficiently and to absorb shocks without major damage to the real economy or other parts of the financial system. Financial stability can be distinguished in the concepts of micro stability, which involves the health of individual financial institutions, and macro stability, which focuses on the health of the financial system as a whole, including the interrelationship between financial institutions, payment and settlement systems and financial markets. The costs of financial instability can be high, especially in emerging markets, where financial buffers to absorb shocks are much smaller.

So how do these objectives of price stability and financial stability fit together? Traditionally, it has been assumed that price stability contributes to financial stability and vice versa. However, the issue is more complex. Indeed, the 1990s taught us that price stability is necessary, but not sufficient to safeguard financial stability. The 1997/98 financial crisis in Asia is illustrative here. In the run-up to the Asian crisis, large imbalances were built up in the real estate and other asset markets, although inflation was relatively low.

The Role of Central Banks

Can central banks deliver both stable prices and financial stability simultaneously? In my view, there are three ways in which the central bank should be involved in financial stability. These include the identification of vulnerabilities in the financial system (by monitoring risks), the analysis of the transmission of shocks in the financial system (analysing transmission channels, financial market behaviour) and the implementation of policies to make the financial system shock resistant. Such policies will include public disclosure rules, transparency standards, supervisory rules and the like. Let me briefly mention the main other instruments central banks have available to foster the separate objective of financial stability.

The central bank by its nature is involved in policies to mitigate the negative impact in the unhoped-for event of a financial crisis. Besides the use of the interest rate, financial stability can be supported in a number of other ways. One of these, of course, is the lender of last resort instrument. Traditionally, this instrument is available to support individual institutions. Besides, liquidity injections may be given to the financial system in general. This function has become more important, because of the increasingly systemic dimensions of financial tensions.

The organisation of a deposit insurance system is important to safeguard confidence in the financial system. By (partially) guaranteeing bank accounts, the risk of bank runs is reduced. Oversight of payment and settlement systems is also a key element in the financial stability policy of central banks. Mutual credit and liquidity risks have been reduced significantly by the implementation of real time gross payment systems, like Target in the euro area.

The aftermath of 11 September provides a recent example of the use of central bank instruments in relationship to the maintenance of financial stability. The Eurosystem provided no less than 110 billion to support the liquidity of banks. Moreover, the Fed and the ECB cut interest rates with 50 basis points. This was a display of complementary interaction between monetary and financial stability instruments as well as good international cooperation between financial stability authorities. This could avoid a systemic crisis.

Challenges

Although central banks are not always responsible for supervision, they are often involved in designing or advising on the regulation. Safeguarding financial stability requires a changing focus of supervision. Traditionally, prudential supervision is designed to work bottom-up, focusing on individual financial institutions. However, to serve the stability of the financial system, supervision should also have a top-down point of view. Such a design focuses supervision on systemic risks of failing institutions and the macroeconomic costs of these outcomes.

In emerging markets in particular, supervision issues rapidly take on systemic dimensions since a few financial institutions are dominant. In such a situation, it may be advisable to concentrate the guardianship of both financial stability and price stability within one institution, the central bank. Such a model has another advantage, since it combines financial expertise that might be sparsely available in emerging markets.

Central banks are continuously being challenged to deliver both price stability and financial stability. The increasingly systemic dimensions of financial activities pose new challenges for financial stability authorities. With the ongoing process of financial deepening and increasing cross-border financial synchronicity, systemic aspects are raising the stakes. Fortunately, central banks have an extensive toolkit at their disposal. Indeed, the swift reaction after the 11September 2001 events shows that policymakers are up to the job.

17

The Lack of Stable Capital Flows to Developing Countries

Stephany Griffith-Jones

I want to make two short caveats before I start. First, the title of this session is "Fostering Global Financial Stability", and I think we should change it into "Fostering Global Financial Stability and Growth", because we need to think about how the global financial system can provide both important public goods. It is often forgotten in the discussion that the ultimate aim is growth and employment and so on, although of course such aim is embedded in Article 1 of the IMF.

The second caveat is that it was surprising that so much of the discussion has been at the national and regional level, important as these are, because the traditional Fondad focus has always been on the global level, and there has been a lot of pioneering discussions in Fondad meetings. Rather than being a criticism, I would urge Fondad to continue in this tradition.

We have had a very interesting discussion, certainly at the regional and the national level, and before I go to the international dimensions, I just want to make a point about Argentina. We have not really learned lessons. In the current Argentina crisis there is much in common with what happened in the early 1980s: short-term foreign exchange liabilities, fixed exchange rates, and so on. So we have to ask the question, all of us, at the national and international level, public and private: how can we learn from experience and how can we transmit this experience, so that we do not have another crisis again in ten years which looks exactly the same.

Going to the issue of the pursuit of international financial stability, there are two aims. The first is the pursuit of financial stability *per se*, that is, the agenda of crisis prevention and management. The second is the provision of sufficient capital flows, both private and public, to different categories of developing countries to help sustain growth.

The Pursuit of Financial Stability

On financial stability, we concluded that progress has been insufficient, asymmetrical and also that there have been important reversals. I want to talk a bit more about the reversals. One of the reasons – I don't know if it is the main one, but certainly it is a very important reason – why the Argentinean crisis was so deep and has continued for so long, is that there has been a reversal in international financial governance. The Argentinean crisis happened to occur at a time when the developed countries, and particularly the US, became unwilling to continue large IMF lending packages to manage crises and, at the same time, there was no framework for orderly debt workout in place. Argentina was just very unlucky; it had a lot of its own problems, but it happened to fall in a 'lacuna', or institutional vacuum. Yung Chul Park was complaining that it took Korea ten days to sign an agreement with the IMF; six months after the start of the Argentinean crisis, there is still no agreement.

Argentina's difficulty in obtaining IMF lending has to do with an overstating of the problem of moral hazard. Moral hazard is a problem, but I don't think that financial markets' exuberance is only due to the fact that the IMF lends. Because we have had lots of crises, starting for example here in the Netherlands with the tulip crisis in the 17th century, when there was no IMF and the markets were still very exuberant with boom-bust patterns and so on. So we should not overstate the problem of moral hazard.

Two points on why the IMF has been so slow. There is a parallel with East Asia. The IMF has demanded a number of structural reforms from the Argentinean economy. Many of them are probably necessary. But it is not a good moment to do structural reforms in the middle of a crisis. You first have to deal with the crisis and then you do the structural reforms because they take a lot of time and are particularly difficult to do in a crisis. This is a point that we discussed during the Asian crisis. The IMF itself recognises this mistake in some documents it has produced, but it is not applying the lessons. The second point, which was also recognised in this nice evaluation the IMF did on East Asia, is that you have to be careful how much fiscal adjustment you require in times of crisis. Because when there is a dramatic fall of GDP, this leads of course to great difficulties in tax collection and getting enough fiscal revenues. Therefore, if you are too demanding, you deepen a recession.

On other issues of progress in international financial reform, I just want to make the point that a number of people – particularly colleagues from Asia – have talked about the lack of a global financial regulator. There has been a quite brave step in the creation of the Financial Stability Forum and other attempts, but they are weak and they don't represent developing countries. Yet this attempt to improve global financial regulation is important because, however one might want to criticise the IMF and other institutions for being insufficiently democratic, one of the deepest flaws in democracy – also something I learned in a Fondad meeting – is the lack of accountability of markets. There is no democratic accountability, and the only, very technocratic, way of doing it is through regulation.

The Provision of Sufficient Capital Flows

I want to talk about a second area of concern. We used to complain about the fact that we have too much volatile capital flows, and some are still talking about it. But the key problem that most developing countries at the moment are facing – not Eastern Europe – is the lack of sufficient capital flows. And having criticised the IMF, I will now use their data on capital flows to developing countries because they are the best ones we have. If you look at the build-up during the 1990s of net capital flows to emerging markets, you see that they peak in 1995-96 at more than 200 billion dollars, then they fall sharply, and they have stagnated for the last five years at around 60 billion. This is a dramatic fall and I think the next crisis may be the result of insufficient flows. We have to start adapting the discussion and the understanding of policies to this new reality.

A first question to ask is: Is this just a cyclical thing? Is this the memory of the recent crisis, the slowdown of the US economy, and so on? Is it just a cyclical reversal that will go away with time? Or are there important structural elements? I think there are important structural elements, which I will go through quickly.

One is the fact that banks have crossed the borders and prefer to lend in local currency, and therefore lend less in foreign exchange. Another, and worrying, structural element is that one of the few regulatory changes that have been pursued is the revision of the Basel Capital Accord. That revision may actually institutionalise the unwillingness of banks to lend to developing countries because it is going to use banks' own risk models to determine the level of capital requirements. And by using the banks' own models, it will make high risks more costly. As developing countries are perceived as high risk, they will have to pay more. Second, it will make lending even more pro-cyclical. In equity and bond markets there is a problem that, to the extent that these flows are increasingly going to the private sector, people in the market are saying, that there are not enough suitable borrowers or companies to invest in because they have either been privatised or they have been sold to foreign investors, and in some small or low-income countries there are just not a lot of large companies. These days it is very hard to find fund managers specialising in emerging markets or particularly in low-income countries like Sub-Saharan Africa. There seems to be a greater recourse to global fund managers investing a little bit of their money in emerging markets, which makes it – as a recent IMF report pointed out – more unstable because investors move very easily. When they see problems in emerging markets they pull out their one or two percent which they have in those markets very quickly and put it back in US or European paper. You don't buy to hold, these people say, it is more the case that you buy and sell all the time. The intention is increasingly short-term, except for FDI, which is the only good and important part of the story.

So the question is whether the presence of foreign companies, banks and other investors brings the developing countries the foreign exchange they need. If the capital flows do not come then the whole point of making efforts to attract private flows through liberalising the capital account and privatisation would be quite futile because you would only get the expertise – which is important – but you would not get the complementary foreign exchange. Therefore, a new challenge for the international community is to design measures – both in the receiving countries and in the source countries – on how to encourage sufficient stable flows to developing countries.

How can we mix public and private guarantees, possible subsidies, tax incentives and so on, both globally and regionally, to try and encourage sufficient flows to developing countries?

18

Private Sector Views on Financial Stability

Frans van Loon

Let me give you some views from the private sector. First, I will share a thought from my institution and myself and then I would like to relay the main points that we have collectively agreed on in a large group of banks, the Institute of International Finance, with regard to private sector involvement in financial stability (and growth).

My first general point is that ING, as a large financial institution involved with the whole range of finance and a large number of individual clients, with lots of contacts, and with thousands if not hundreds of thousands of clients all over the world, is very aware of the deep unease so broadly felt about the development process, about globalisation, and specifically about the role of finance in globalisation. The concern is there, we do not deny it, and it is a real concern that is related to the dominant role that finance has played in globalisation as the most globalised of all the economic sectors.

With the benefit of hindsight, we see that the attention of the last ten years or so has been heavily focused on the cross-border elements of the internationalisation of the financial system. That is where we, the financial sector, have put our people, where we have put our assets, where we bought companies, and where we put our thinking power. It has been placed in promoting cross-border flows in the securities area, in corporate financing, in the bond area, in the equity markets, in the financing of trade. This was all wonderful business, and it was extremely profitable and exciting – for a while.

But the situation has changed and, looking back, I think we have focused too much on cross-border flows. It has been overdone in the sense that we neglected to put enough focus on the primary necessity of strengthening domestic financial markets, domestic systems, and domestic institutions – for it own sake, and also as a necessary basis on which to base stable international flows.

We in the financial sector now see the necessity to focus on domestic financial systems in the broadest sense much more clearly than before: payment systems, transfer mechanisms of every type, institutional savings. At ING, we emphasise this broad sense, being an institution that is an integrated financial services institution, not a bank; we want to cover the whole range of financial instruments. This new view is rather deeply felt and it translates into clear changes in strategy of our institution and quite a number of other institutions, but it also leads to a diversion within the group of financial sector institutions.

Within the Institute of International Finance I see a divergence between the few strong big international players in cross-border flows, certainly in the capital market area – the investment banks in New York, who are usually very dominant in the international discussion – and us, the more integrated financial services organisations, located mainly in Europe. We have a broader range of interests and are not so much focused just on the international bond issues and the intermediation of international flows, we have a broader range. There is also a divergence because of the increasingly strong role of the holders of the assets, the bondholders: pension funds, insurance funds, and all of the various mutual funds. They are generally taking a much more independent view, independent especially from the investment banks.

What have we decided collectively within the Institute of International Finance? Even though the IIF is a group that ranges from the big Wall Street investment houses to the integrated financial service companies, the emerging markets banks and everybody else, we still reach pretty good consensus on the main lines. Interestingly, the first big point we all agree on is the necessity of domestic financial sector development. This is accepted by everybody as the main emphasis, because weak financial systems have been at the centre of broader economic crises in emerging markets too frequently.

The second point we agree on is that of technical arrangements to reduce risks, which includes three areas for action. The first area is the need to improve investor relations. It has been often emphasised by the private sector that there is a need to have a continuous exchange of views and information between the official sector and the whole range of private sector institutions, about government debt, the public finances, etc., so that the holders of bonds, the short-term, the long-term, the medium-term investors, all of the people in the private sector involved with putting up cross-border positions in a certain country, have access to the authority in a structured and organised way. That has generally been lacking in the past, now it is quickly improving. For instance, Mexico is doing a great job in this as are many other countries. It is a big point for us to emphasise the need for those investor relationships. Of course the same story goes for the transparency of macroeconomic and financial data and the dissemination of these data – which is a second area. A lot of progress has been made here, but it still remains a key point, closely related to the first.

The third area is the old idea of contingent credit lines to prevent financial crises. Unfortunately, it has not really worked very well. Countries considered it a sign of potential problems and weakness. There have been certain misgivings about contingent credit lines, both within the IMF and the private sector, but we think they again deserve attention as do public-private cooperation schemes. There are ways that risks can be shared that should not be forgotten.

Finally, I come to the third and key point of an orderly sovereign debt restructuring process. We see three lines of action.

First, strong emphasis should be placed on the consultative element. The lack of consultation with the IMF has always been a complaint of the private sector, partly as a result of the secrecy element of IMF consultation with member countries. This is already changing; there is a private sector contact group. It needs to be expanded, institutionalised and broadened because the range of financial products present in cross-border exposure is wide, much wider than in the 1980s. We need to work on a strong consultative process between the private financial sector and essentially the IMF.

The second line of action is the contractual element, which really means working on the collective action clauses. Much work has already been done, and most of us want this to happen; the large European and American borrowers need to get on board, we have to push that practical steps are advanced to include collective action clauses in bond and loans contracts.

The third line of action is a legal element, where we need to put some teeth into fighting those creditors who are against conforming to the majority. We need a targeted legal strategy to address vulture funds and limit disruptive litigation stemming from holdout creditors.

19

Fostering Financial Stability: The Role for Ministries of Finance

Wouter Raab

I will identify four types of intervention that ministries of Finance can use to foster global financial stability: (i) participation in international financial institutions, through which the international financial system is managed; (ii) keeping their own house in order by pursuing sound and credible fiscal policies; (iii) fostering trade liberalisation and improving market access; (iv) adequate financial market regulation and (particularly in Europe) financial market integration.

The Netherlands being a small and very open and internationally-minded economy, the Dutch Finance Ministry sees its role primarily through the active participation in the multilateral fora and institutions that are dealing with financial stability, such as the IMF, the World Bank, the Financial Stability Forum and the Financial Action Task Force on Money-Laundering. We believe in a strong rules-based international system, where there is equal treatment and in which every country has a voice. Only such a system can take decisions that are effective, legitimate and that will find the widest possible support in the international community. For us, the IMF, with its almost universal membership is the central institution for global financial stability. The G-7 can never substitute for that, because of the inherent limitations to the G-7 concept.

Global financial stability is high on the agenda on the IMF, notably through the work on crisis prevention and on crisis management. Making countries' financial systems stronger and more resilient and promoting transparency by disseminating more financial data is the aim of the many standards and codes the adherence to which the IMF is monitoring, notably in the so-called Report on the Observance on Standards and Codes (ROSC). In addition, the IMF's Financial Sector Assessment Programme (FSAP) reviews the strengths and weaknesses of a country's financial sector. Although the participation in these exercises do make a heavy demand on the often limited resources of emerging market economies, the benefits are also clear: reform of a financial sector so that international standards are fully or almost met, will improve a country's creditworthiness in the international capital markets.

In the field of crisis management, efforts in the IMF have focussed on the wider introduction of so-called Collective Action Clauses in bond contracts and the design of a Sovereign Debt Restructuring Mechanism (SDRM), through which sovereign debt restructurings can take place in a more orderly manner than has been the case so far. Particularly, the work on Collective Action Clauses has been relatively successful, given its much wider use recently. While it has been difficult to find agreement on the SDRM among the IMF member states, the discussion has led to a better understanding of the crucial role of transparency and of early and continuous communication between debtors and creditors, particularly in times of stress, when a debtor country has (or is perceived to have) difficulties in repaying its creditors. In this context, proposals for Codes of (Good) Conduct have been made by the Institute of International Finance and the Banque de France.

A second element of how ministries of Finance can contribute to global financial stability is to keep or put their own house in order. Sound fiscal policies are key to this. Developed countries in particular should commit themselves to sustainable fiscal positions. Credible medium- and long-term fiscal strategies and their implementation will lead to lower long-term interest rates. As most public budgets in developed countries will be burdened by rising costs because of the ageing of their populations, most countries still have some work to do. Failure to put public finances on a sustainable footing will not only lead to higher interest rates, but also to a situation where international savings will be used to finance public deficits in the developed world, rather than financing investment in developing countries. In Europe, the Stability and Growth Pact provides for a well-defined process of multilateral surveillance and peer pressure with the explicit aim of ensuring both medium and long-term sustainability of public finances.

A third element is the advocacy role of ministries of Finance, in particular regarding trade liberalisation and access to trade for developing countries. Greater access to trade would make developing countries less susceptible to shocks in private capital and reversals in ODA flows and so could lead to greater stability. Most ministries of Finance do not have a direct responsibility for trade issues, but, given their central role in economic policy-making, both nationally as well as internationally, they have an important role to play in focusing the international community in taking actions to move forward with trade liberalisation. In particular, the reduction of agricultural subsidies in developed countries needs to be addressed, since they burden the budgets of developed countries as well as prevent developing countries from exploiting their comparative advantages.

Last, but certainly not least, ministries of Finance are responsible for the regulation of their national financial markets and for providing the institutional structure for supervision of domestic financial markets and institutions. In the aftermath of the past stock-market bubble and in the post-Enron world, the need for adequate regulation of financial markets, supervision and for strengthened accounting standards and improved corporate governance is almost self-evident.

In Europe, there is a strong drive to financial markets integration to arrive at a fully integrated single European financial market. In 1999, EU ministers of Finance adopted the Financial Services Action Plan (FSAP). It has three main strategic objectives:

1. to establish a common legal framework for integrated securities and derivatives markets; financial integrity is a cornerstone of this objective;
2. to establish open and secure retail markets;
3. to have state-of-the-art prudential rules and supervision.

A deeper and more liquid EU-wide capital market will be able to provide participants from inside or outside Europe with more tailor-made financial instruments, will facilitate access to credits at lower costs, and will be able to absorb shocks better.

Appendix

List of Participants in the Conference on "Financial Stability and Development in Emerging Economies: Steps Forward for Bankers and Financial Authorities", held at De Nederlandsche Bank in Amsterdam on 3-4 June 2002.

Mr. Age Akkerman	Economist, Forum on Debt and Development, The Hague
Mr. Mark Allen	Deputy Director, Policy Development and Review Department, International Monetary Fund, Washington D.C.
Mr. Age Bakker	Deputy Director, De Nederlandsche Bank, Amsterdam
Mr. Amar Bhattacharya	Senior Adviser, Poverty Reduction and Economic Management Network, The World Bank, Washington D.C.
Mr. Onno de Beaufort Wijnholds	Executive Director, International Monetary Fund, Washington D.C.
Mr. Hein Bogaard	Financial Sector Specialist, Department for Sustainable Economic Development, Ministry of Foreign Affairs, The Hague
Mr. Henk Brouwer	Executive Director, De Nederlandsche Bank, Amsterdam
Mr. Ariel Buira	Senior Member, Department of Economics and St. Antony's College, Oxford
Mr. Roy Culpeper	President, The North-South Institute, Ottawa

Mr. Marek Dabrowski	Director, Center for Social and Economic Research (CASE), Warsaw
Mr. Zdeněk Drábek	Senior Adviser, Economic Research and Analysis, World Trade Organization, Geneva
Mr. José María Fanelli	Senior Research Fellow, Center for the Study of State and Society (CEDES), Buenos Aires
Mr. Heiner Flassbeck	Senior Economist, Division on Globalization and Development Strategies, UNCTAD, Geneva
Ms. Stephany Griffith-Jones	Professorial Fellow, Institute of Development Studies, Brighton, Sussex
Mr. Aerdt Houben	Deputy Departmental Director, Monetary and Economic Policy Department, De Nederlandsche Bank, Amsterdam
Mr. Brian Kahn	Deputy Chief Economist and Head of the Monetary Policy Research Unit, South African Reserve Bank, Pretoria
Mr. Frans van Loon	Managing Director, Global Head, Governments and International Organisations, ING Group, Amsterdam
Mr. José Antonio Ocampo	Executive Secretary, Economic Commission for Latin America and the Caribbean (ECLAC), Santiago de Chile
Mr. Yung Chul Park	Professor of Economics, Korea University, Seoul
Mr. Wouter Raab	Director, Foreign Financial Relations, Ministry of Finance, The Hague

Mr. Eisuke Sakakibara	Professor of Economics, Global Security Research Center, Tokyo
Ms. Barbara Stallings	Director, Economic Development Division, ECLAC, Santiago / Visiting Professor, Watson Institute for International Studies, Brown University, Providence
Mr. Jürgen Stark	Vice-President, Deutsche Bundesbank, Frankfurt
Mr. Rogério Studart	Economic Affairs Officer, Economic Development Division, ECLAC, Santiago de Chile
Mr. György Szapáry	Deputy President, National Bank of Hungary, Budapest
Mr. Jan Joost Teunissen	Director, Forum on Debt and Development, The Hague
Mr. Mark Teunissen	Economist, Monetary and Economic Policy Department, De Nederlandsche Bank, Amsterdam
Mr. Nout Wellink	President, De Nederlandsche Bank, Amsterdam
Ms. Ngaire Woods	Fellow in Politics and International Relations, University College, Oxford University, Oxford
Mr. Charles Wyplosz	Professor of Economics, Graduate Institute of International Studies, Geneva

Other Publications by Fondad

Jan Joost Teunissen and Age Akkerman (eds.), **The Crisis That Was Not Prevented: Lessons for Argentina, the IMF, and Globalisation**, January 2003.
ISBN: 90-74208-20-7, 164 pages.
The financial crisis in Argentina has led to an avalanche of studies explaining its origins and suggesting remedies. In a broad and in-depth approach, this book gives a unique overview of the current thinking about the lessons of the Argentine crisis. The book provides a wealth of facts, arguments and policy suggestions, that go beyond the specific case of Argentina. Contributors to the book include Mark Allen (IMF), Onno de Beaufort Wijnholds (IMF), José María Fanelli (University of Buenos Aires), Ricardo Ffrench-Davis (ECLAC), Bernardo Lischinsky, José Antonio Ocampo (ECLAC), Dani Rodrik (Harvard University), and Rogério Studart (ECLAC).

Jan Joost Teunissen (ed.), **A Regional Approach to Financial Crisis Prevention: Lessons from Europe and Initiatives in Asia, Latin American and Africa**, November 2002.
ISBN: 90-74208-19-3, 216 pages.
Can regional financial arrangements help prevent financial crises in emerging and developing economies? Should these countries follow Western Europe's example by fixing the exchange rates to each other rather than to the dollar, the yen or the euro? Should the IMF and the World Bank become more supportive to regional monetary arrangements? Such are the questions discussed in this book. In light of the recurring financial crises of the last eight years – Mexico (1994), East Asia (1997), Russia (1998), Argentina (2001) – these questions are highly relevant for policymakers as well as the public at large. The book presents the views of prominent international experts and officials from different regions of the world. Contributors to the book include Amar Bhattacharya (World Bank), Oldřich Dědek (Czech National Bank), Zdeněk Drábek (WTO), Stephany Griffith-Jones (IDS), Daniel Heymann (ECLAC), Paul Jenkins (Department of Finance of Canada), Brian Kahn (Reserve Bank of South Africa), Heiner Flassbeck (UNCTAD), Leslie Lipschitz (IMF), José Antonio Ocampo (ECLAC), Yung Chul Park (Korea University), János Vincze (National Bank of Hungary), William White (BIS), and Charles Wyplosz (Graduate Institute of International Studies).

Jan Joost Teunissen (ed.), **New Challenges of Crisis Prevention: Addressing Economic Imbalances in the North and Boom-Bust Cycles in the South**, December 2001.
ISBN: 90-74208-18-5, 224 pages.
Over the past few years a standard agenda of crisis prevention measures has been developed to which most policymakers and analysts adhere. Opinions differ,

however, when it comes to the specific policy that each country, given its particular circumstances, should choose from the variety of options available. This book reflects on today's policy discussions about the standard agenda of crisis prevention, but most of all, it deals with two themes that ought to have been – but were not – included in the agenda. The first concerns the possibilities for major industrial countries to address global economic imbalances, and the second is how developing countries could apply anti-cyclical policies to counter boom-bust cycles. Contributors to the book include Amar Bhattacharya (World Bank), Zdeněk Drábek (WTO), José María Fanelli (CEDES), Stephany Griffith-Jones (IDS), Brian Kahn (Reserve Bank of South Africa), Jan Kregel (UNCTAD), Carlos Massad (Central Bank of Chile), José Antonio Ocampo (ECLAC), Yung Chul Park (Korea University), Liliana Rojas-Suárez (IIE and formerly with Deutsche Bank), Chi-Young Song (Kookmin University), and John Williamson (IIE).

Jan Joost Teunissen (ed.), **Reforming the International Financial System: Crisis Prevention and Response**, December 2000.
ISBN: 90-74208-17-7, 232 pages.
The international community is seized at the moment with the topic of reforming the international monetary system in the context of a debate over the costs and benefits of globalisation and market-oriented policies. This four part book brings together Northern and Southern perspectives in a groundbreaking analysis of this pressing issue. It discusses a broad agenda of reform, looks at a new framework for private sector involvement in crisis prevention and crisis management, deals with the recent initiatives to improve the regulation and supervision of private capital flows, and focuses on proposals to make the IMF more effective, transparent and accountable. Contributors to the book include Yilmaz Akyüz (UNCTAD), Amar Bhattacharya (World Bank), Jack Boorman and Mark Allen (IMF), Howard Brown (Canadian Department of Finance), Ariel Buira (formerly with the Central Bank of Mexico), Stephany Griffith-Jones (IDS and Commonwealth Secretariat), Louis Kasekende (Bank of Uganda), Guillermo Le Fort (Central Bank of Chile), Aziz Ali Mohammed (G-24), José Antonio Ocampo (ECLAC), Yung Chul Park (Korea University), Wouter Raab (Dutch Ministry of Finance), Maria Ramos (South African Department of Finance), Yunjong Wang (KIEP) and William White (BIS).

Jan Joost Teunissen (ed.), The **Management of Global Financial Markets**, April 2000.
ISBN: 90-74208-16-9, 261 pages.
During the 1990s, a number of serious financial crises have affected economies, businesses and, most importantly, the living conditions of millions of people, particularly in the developing regions. Crisis prevention has therefore become a priority issue for policymakers and analysts around the world. This book first focuses on new strategies for dealing with the inherent instability of financial markets. It then looks at the ways in which financial markets work and the implications for more effective supervision. The third part of the book deals with the Asian, Latin American and Central European responses to the instability of financial markets. And in the fourth part, there is a discussion of gaps in the international institutional framework. The prominent international experts who

have contributed to this book include Age Bakker (Dutch Central Bank), Jack Boorman (IMF), Stephany Griffith-Jones (IDS), Jan Kregel (UNCTAD), Martin Mayer (Brookings Institution), György Szapáry (National Bank of Hungary), William White (BIS) and John Williamson. The book discusses a variety of key policy issues that range from the prevention of excessive surges of capital inflows to the lack of global economic governance.

Nils Bhinda, Jonathan Leape, Matthew Martin, Stephany Griffith-Jones *et al.*, **Private Capital Flows to Africa: Perception and Reality**, November 1999.
ISBN: 90-74208-15-0, 176 pages.
When the research underlying this book began, it was generally believed that private flows to Africa were insignificant. Yet senior African government officials from 14 African countries, and especially South Africa, Tanzania, Uganda, Zambia and Zimbabwe, were telling a different story. They knew that a surge of flows to emerging markets, and the liberalisation of their economies, were prompting unprecedented inflows of private capital. This book presents the facts on the scale and composition of private capital flows to Africa and the difficulties in monitoring them, looks at what motivates people to invest, focuses on the macroeconomic impact and policy implications of capital flows, and identifies measures which will help African governments to attract more development-oriented private flows. This first systematic analysis of the recent African experience with private capital flows, provides a rich source of new ideas for rapid policy responses by national and international policymakers.

Jan Joost Teunissen (ed.), **Regulatory and Supervisory Challenges in a New Era of Global Finance**, December 1998.
ISBN: 90-74208-14-2, 280 pages.
The recent financial crisis in Asia has once again alerted the international community to the fragility of the global financial system and the serious consequences of enormous, rapid private capital flows. In this book, experts from around the world discuss the implications of financial crises in developing and transition countries. Yung Chul Park (Korea Institute of Finance) presents an up-to-date account of the effects of and remedies for financial crisis in Asia and elsewhere. Charles Wyplosz (Graduate Institute of International Studies) reviews the lessons learnt, and not yet learnt. Jack Boorman (IMF) reflects on the causes and consequences of the Asian crisis and suggests how the IMF, other creditors and the private sector should be involved in dealing with future crises. Ariel Buira (formerly with the Central Bank of Mexico) suggests an alternative approach to dealing with financial crises by e.g. the timely provision of sufficient IMF support. Susan Phillips (US Fed) dwells on sound international supervision. William White (BIS) discusses the role of the Bank for International Settlements in promoting financial stability, Amaret Sila-On (Financial Sector Restructuring Authority, Thailand) and György Szapáry (National Bank of Hungary) discuss specific financial issues in each of their countries. Christian Larraín (Chile) deals extensively with the challenges of banking supervision in developing economies.

Jan Joost Teunissen (ed.), **The Policy Challenges of Global Financial Integration**, June 1998.
ISBN: 90-74208-13-4, 126 pages.
One of the main features of the globalising economy is the surge of cross-border capital flows around the world in the form of portfolio as well as foreign direct investment. In this book, H. Johannes Witteveen (former Managing Director of the IMF), Stephany Griffith-Jones (IDS), Zdeněk Drábek (WTO) and Percy Mistry (Oxford International) give their views on the current policy challenges facing the international financial community. Witteveen presents a broad, long-term perspective on globalisation; Griffith-Jones looks at the regulatory challenges of surges in capital flows for source countries; Drábek presents an advocacy paper for the envisaged and much-debated Multilateral Agreement on Investment; and Mistry gives an original and well-informed account of the challenges to national and international financial institutions posed by emerging markets.

Jan Joost Teunissen (ed.), **Regional Integration and Multilateral Cooperation in the Global Economy**, June 1998.
ISBN: 90-74208-12-6, 241 pages.
This book concludes a multi-volume series which explores how regional integration and multilateral cooperation can be promoted in a mutually reinforcing manner. It includes papers presented at a two-day conference in which scholars and policymakers from various national and international organisations examined the role of regional integration and multilateral cooperation in a globalising economy. Contributors to the volume are Ernest Aryeety, Robert Devlin, Mohamed A. El-Erian, Ricardo Ffrench-Davis, Björn Hettne, András Inotai, Mats Karlsson, Hans Peter Lankes, Charles P. Oman, Arvind Panagariya, Miria Pigato, Jan P. Pronk, Piritta Sorsa and Rosalind H. Thomas. In addition, the volume includes summaries of the floor discussions at the conference.

Jan Joost Teunissen (ed.), **Regionalism and the Global Economy: The Case of Central and Eastern Europe**, June 1997.
ISBN: 90-74208-11-8, 254 pages.
New opportunities for regional integration were presented to the countries of Central and Eastern Europe when they embarked on their transition to democratic market economies at the end of the 1980s. While the ultimate goal is that these countries become members of the EU, they are also engaged in sub-regional integration efforts, as the free trade agreements among the Baltics as well as among the Central European countries demonstrate. This volume includes contributions from Zdeněk Drábek, Miroslav Hrnčiř, András Inotai, Piritta Sorsa, Mark Allen, Franz-Lothar Altmann, Mats Karlsson, Ricardo Lago, Friedemann Müller, Joan Pearce, Roberto Rocha, Inna Šteinbuka, and Per Magnus Wijkman. It presents an encompassing analysis of Central and Eastern European economic integration and the prospects for EU enlargement.

Jan Joost Teunissen (ed.), **Regionalism and the Global Economy: The Case of Africa**, November 1996.
ISBN: 90-74208-10-X, 312 pages.
This book explores why most cooperation and integration arrangements in Africa have failed, and how regional integration could be made more successful. Outstanding economists from African as well as international institutions, such as the World Bank, the African Development Bank and the International Monetary Fund, provide an in-depth analysis of Africa's past and future prospects for economic integration. It includes contributions from Ernest Aryeetey, Peter Robinson, William Lyakurwa, Percy Mistry, Sam Assante, Alieu Jeng, Louis Kasekende, Mohsin Khan, Gavin Maasdorp, Sindiso Ngwenya, Gene Tidrick, and Samuel Wangwe. The book is enriched by a vivid account of a two-day conference in which the research was discussed in a creative and frank manner. Questions addressed include: What form of regional cooperation would be most relevant in different parts of the continent? How can policies of national governments and international financial institutions be improved in design as well as implementation?

Percy S. Mistry, **Regional Integration Arrangements in Economic Development: Panacea or Pitfall?**, October 1996.
ISBN: 90-74208-08-8, 98 pages.
This study is written by one of the stimulating forces in Fondad's research project on regionalism and multilateralism, Indian economist and investment banker Percy S. Mistry. Mistry reviews issues arising from experience with arrangements for regional economic cooperation and integration in developing and developed regions of the world. Given the plethora and complexity of the issues involved – ranging from trade, finance and monetary matters to institutional, social and political affairs – the author has chosen a broad approach. However, at various points Mistry also presents some of his more detailed insights and policy suggestions.

Percy S. Mistry, **Resolving Africa's Multilateral Debt Problem: A Response to the IMF and the World Bank**, September 1996.
ISBN: 90-74208-09-6, 70 pages.
Since 1993, public concern about the problem of the growing multilateral debt overhang of poor countries has increased. While the IMF and the World Bank have proposed a special debt initiative for the heavily-indebted poor countries, Percy Mistry argues that a different approach is needed. He suggests compelling arguments for a new strategy to resolve the multilateral debt problem of poor countries in Africa (and elsewhere) and spells out a set of alternative principles and measures on which a new strategy should be based.

Jan Joost Teunissen (ed.), **Can Currency Crises Be Prevented or Better Managed? Lessons from Mexico**, June 1996.
ISBN 90-74208-07-X, 115 pages.
Private capital flows are playing a growing and crucial role in industrial as well as developing countries. They may promote economic development or suddenly

disrupt economic order and create serious crises. Mexico's currency crisis of December 1994 is a recent example. Discussing both the origins of and the remedies for Mexico-style crises, this book provides profound insights into a problem which is of concern to policymakers and the public at large in many countries of the world. The book reports on an in-depth discussion of both short-term and long-term proposals by a group of highly experienced researchers and central bankers. It includes papers by Ariel Buira, Peter Kenen, Stephany Griffith-Jones, and a joint paper by Barry Eichengreen and Charles Wyplosz. Buira reviews the main hypotheses that have been advanced to explain the Mexican crisis. Kenen addresses the more general issue of how the disruption to national economies that results from fluctuations in cross-border flows can be minimised. Griffith-Jones considers the new features of recent and possible future currency crises. Wyplosz and Eichengreen draw out some lessons from exchange rate crises that have occurred over the last thirty years in a large number of industrial countries.

Jan Joost Teunissen (ed.), **Regionalism and the Global Economy: The Case of Latin America and the Caribbean**, November 1995.
ISBN: 90-74208-06-1, 163 pages.
Many books and articles have appeared on the topic of regional integration in Latin America and the Caribbean, yet the debate is far from concluded. There is not only a lack of consensus but also a lack of factual information on important aspects. By focusing primarily on financial issues and by reporting extensively on a two-day discussion between experienced researchers and policymakers, this book both provides new information and shape new opinions. Percy Mistry presents a thought-provoking and broad view of the problem; Stephany Griffith-Jones explores the little-researched financial aspects of Latin American integration; Ricardo Ffrench-Davis focuses on the crucial role of intra-regional trade; Roberto Bouzas looks at the policy dilemmas and prospects posed by NAFTA.

Percy S. Mistry, **Multilateral Development Banks: An Assessment of their Financial Structures, Policies and Practices**, February 1995.
ISBN: 90-74208-05-3, 308 pages.
As development agencies, multilateral development banks (MDBs) have received the greatest attention for their lending policies, for their technical assistance and advisory functions and, more recently, for their policy reform and adjustment prescriptions. Since the 1980s, they have become important instruments of economic and political governance over the developing world instead of being simply international financial intermediaries. However, very little is known publicly about their *financial* policies and operations. This book attempts to render understandable to those who are not financial experts, the main financial policies and practices of the MDBs as well as the implications and consequences of those policies and practices.

Percy S. Mistry, **Multilateral Debt: An Emerging Crisis?**, February 1994.
ISBN: 90-74208-04-5, 76 pages.
This study is the first in-depth analysis of a problem which is of growing concern to world financial policymakers. While most attention has been focused on the

attempts to alleviate the burdens of both commercial and official bilateral debt of the countries affected, a new problem has emerged: the pyramiding of multilateral debt.

Jan Joost Teunissen (ed.), **The Pursuit of Reform: Global Finance and the Developing Countries**, November 1993.
ISBN: 90-74208-03-7, 196 pages.
Against the background of the daily reports on the dynamic developments taking place in the world economy, a group of eminent scholars and policymakers was invited to discuss the functioning of the international monetary and financial system – with particular reference to the developing world and Eastern Europe. The book includes four papers presented by Richard N. Cooper, Stephany Griffith-Jones, Peter B. Kenen, and John Williamson; other contributors include Ariel Buira, Mohamed A. El-Erian, Vitor Gaspar, Gerald K. Helleiner, Wim Kok, Richard Portes, Jan P. Pronk, Kumiharu Shigehara and Niels Thygesen.

Jan Joost Teunissen (ed.), **Fragile Finance: Rethinking the International Monetary System**, November 1992.
ISBN: 90-74208-02-9, 132 pages.
This book seeks to revive the policy debate on the functioning of the world financial system. It includes three thought-provoking papers presented by well-known experts, Stephany Griffith-Jones, Arjun Sengupta and John Williamson at an international workshop in The Hague and reports on the ensuing lively and in-depth debate by a group of eminent officials, private bankers, researchers and politicians, including Age Bakker, Jack Boorman, Ricardo Ffrench-Davis, Mats Karlsson, John Langmore and Delphin Rwegasira.

Percy S. Mistry, **African Debt Revisited: Procrastination or Progress?**, November 1991.
ISBN: 90-74208-01-0, 84 pages.
African Debt Revisited is an authoritative and compelling study on Africa's problems with bilateral, multilateral and private creditors. It suggests to policymakers, bankers and legislators what they could do to resolve Africa's debt problem.

Visit **www.fondad.org** for more information.

You can fax or email your order to:

Fondad
Noordeinde 107a
2514 GE The Hague
The Netherlands
Tel. 31 70 365 3820
Fax 31 70 346 3939
Email: info@fondad.org

Order Form

Number of copies, title and price (euros)

( ) Financial Stability and Growth in Emerging Economies: The Role of the Financial Sector (€ 24.50)
( ) The Crisis That Was Not Prevented: Lessons for Argentina, the IMF, and Globalisation (€ 15.00)
( ) A Regional Approach to Financial Crisis Prevention: Europe's Lessons and Prospects in the Developing World (€ 23.00)
( ) New Challenges of Crisis Prevention: Addressing Economic Imbalances in the North and Boom-Bust Cycles in the South (€ 23.00)
( ) Reforming the International Financial System: Crisis Prevention and Response (€ 23.00)
( ) The Management of Global Financial Markets (€ 21.55)
( ) Private Capital Flows to Africa: Perception and Reality (€ 18.15)
( ) Regulatory and Supervisory Challenges in a New Era of Global Finance (€ 21.55)
( ) The Policy Challenges of Global Financial Integration (€ 13.61)
( ) Regional Integration and Multilateral Cooperation in the Global Economy (€ 20.42)
( ) Regionalism and the Global Economy: The Case of Central and Eastern Europe (€ 20.42)
( ) Regionalism and the Global Economy: The Case of Africa (€ 21.55)
( ) Regional Integration Arrangements in Economic Development: Panacea or Pitfall? (€ 11.35)
( ) Resolving Africa's Multilateral Debt Problem: A Response to the IMF and the World Bank (€ 11.35)
( ) Can Currency Crises Be Prevented or Better Managed? Lessons from Mexico (€ 11.35)
( ) Regionalism and the Global Economy: The Case of Latin America and the Caribbean (€ 17.02)
( ) Multilateral Development Banks: An Assessment of their Financial Structures, Policies and Practices (€ 21.55)
( ) Multilateral Debt: An Emerging Crisis? (€ 6.81)
( ) The Pursuit of Reform: Global Finance and the Developing Countries (€ 11.35)
( ) Fragile Finance: Rethinking the International Monetary System (€ 6.81)
( ) African Debt Revisited: Procrastination or Progress? (€ 4.54)

Name ....

Address ....

City .... Postal Code ....

Country ....

Payment Options

☐ Please send an invoice.
☐ Please debit my credit card for the corresponding amount in euros.

( ) Mastercard ( ) Visa ( ) JCB Card ( ) Diner's Club ( ) American Express

Name of Cardholder ....

Card number .... Expiry date ....

VCC (3 last digits, back side of the card) .... Signature